For the Common Good

A HISTORY OF WOMEN'S ROLES in LA CROSSE COUNTY, 1920–1980

for Sue
— an inspiration
for me and the
community

with love and
admiration,
Margaret

MARGARET LARSON

League of Women Voters of La Crosse County

and

League of Women Voters Education Fund

League of Women Voters Education Fund
P.O. Box 363
La Crosse, Wisconsin 54602-0363

Library of Congress Catalog Card Number: 96-77789

ISBN 0-9653841-0-1

Cover photo
Josephine Fletcher, superintendent, frequently read to young residents of the
La Crosse Home for Children before bedtime, 1940.

Family and Children's Center

Contents

Preface and

Acknowledgments

This book truly represents a cooperative effort. A gift for the community to celebrate La Crosse County women in all their roles was the brainchild of Rachel Gundersen and Jean Marck, co-chairs of the 75th Anniversary Committee of the League of Women Voters of La Crosse County. Together with the other members of the committee, Anita Evans, Shirley Haas, Marian Ramlow, Ellen Rosborough, Pat Roslansky, and Signe Schroeder, they chose this project as a lasting way to recognize the dual seventy-fifth anniversaries of the Nineteenth Amendment to the U.S. Constitution, which gave women the right to vote, and of the formation of the League of Women Voters. The board of directors and general membership of the League of Women Voters of La Crosse County gave their whole-hearted support.

People from throughout the county have shared their memories and photographs, conducted research and interviews, and transformed files of material into rough drafts. Gloria Bailey Jackson gave the research effort a head start when she loaned her files on prominent women of early La Crosse. Students of La Crosse County public high schools dug into local history. Community groups responded to questionnaires about their histories and accomplishments. The names of researchers and synthesizers have been incorporated into the footnotes connected with their contributions to the content of the book.

Anita Evans, Margaret Fish, Roberta Gelatt, Patricia Muller, and Marian Ramlow comprised the Editorial Advisory Board. Each one critiqued the content and style from her own unique perspective. In addition, Roberta's assistance with the writing had a calming effect on the rough drafts. Erin Richardson, Lisa Reinhardt, and Andrea Gelatt were invaluable assistants in ferreting out and verifying information. Heidi Sjostrom and Margaret Odegard offered encouragement and sage advice. The staffs of the La Crosse Public Library Archives, led by Anita Doering, and of the Special Collections Department of the University of Wisconsin-La Crosse Murphy Library, guided by Edwin Hill and Linda Sondreal, provided a wealth of material and invaluable assistance.

A large share of information for this book came from oral history interviews. When one relies on oral history, one operates with the knowledge that individuals have their own version of the truth. Whenever possible, the facts have been verified. Sometimes there was no information to support or refute. However, it is important that their voices be given credence.

In virtually all cases, the information collected has been abbreviated in order to include as many stories as possible. Further information about any person, activity or aspect may be found by referring to the footnotes which appear at the end of the book. Some resource materials remain in private collections. However, many references can be found in the Archives and Local History Area of the La Crosse Public Library and in the Special Collections Department of Murphy Library on the University of Wisconsin-La Crosse campus.

Although this book could not possibly mention every La Crosse County woman, it honors all women and gives recognition and expresses appreciation for all they have done. The stories that have been retrieved and recorded are intended to give the reader an idea of the broad scope of responsibility and involvement of La Crosse County women from approximately 1920, when women got the right to vote, to the early 1980s, when the most recent campaign for an equal rights amendment to the U.S. Constitution failed. The stories that illustrate women's activities in the home, in the workplace, and in the community are meant to evoke memories of others.

Gloria Steinem has said that the chief characteristic of women's history is that it is lost and rediscovered, then lost again, thus forcing each generation to rediscover all of that history by itself. The League of Women Voters of La Crosse County offers this book as a gift to future generations.

❖ ❖ ❖

For the Common Good was prepared by the League of Women Voters of La Crosse County, published by the League of Women Voters Education Fund, and made possible by many financial contributors.

Those who chose to honor special people in their lives by providing significant financial support include:

Sabina Bosshard in memory of her mother, Rylla Bosshard

Mary Gundersen Bugge and Cameron Baldwin Gundersen in memory of their mother, Mary Baldwin Gundersen

The Burgess nieces and nephews in memory of their aunt, Frances Burgess

Gail K. Cleary in honor of her mother, Lillian Hope Staats Kumm

Loraine Dahl in memory of her mother, Mrs. Cora Anson

Ellen McGarty Flynn and Father Bernard McGarty in memory of their mother, Mary McGarty

Jean L. Foss and Norene A. Smith in honor of Shirley J. Haas

Barbara Schieche Frank in honor of her mother, Irene Meyer Schieche

C. D. Gelatt in honor of a great teacher, Miss Anna M. Mashek

Roberta Kaplan Gelatt in memory of her mother, Lillian Kaplan

Sarah Gelatt Gephart in honor of her mother, Jane Leicht Kaiser

Carol W. Gundersen in honor of her daughters, Andrea Gundersen and Lisa Gundersen, and her daughter-in-law, Ellen Ott

Rachel Gutzke Gundersen in memory of her mother, Doris Ott Gutzke

Sigurd and Avery Gundersen in memory of Eleanor Head Gundersen

Jane L. Kaiser in memory of her mother, Hazel Brown Leicht

La Crosse Catholic Women's League to honor their Deceased and Living Members

La Crosse Rotary Foundation in honor of women in Rotary everywhere

Jean Theige Marck in memory of her mother, Minnie Mathison Theige

Forbes Olberg in memory of his aunt, Ethel Olberg Tausche

Marian Schlabach Ramlow in memory of Eleanor Hugus Schlabach

D. B. and Marjorie Reinhart in honor of the Franciscan Sisters of Perpetual Adoration

St. Francis Auxiliary in honor of St. Francis Auxiliary Charter Members

Hans and Susan, Kurt and Jodi, Martha, and Harry Schroeder in honor of their mother and wife, Signe Gundersen Schroeder

Signe Gundersen Schroeder in memory of her mother, Carroll McCarty Gundersen

Arthur Soell to honor his wife, Maxine Soell

Richard and Kathryn Tausche in memory of Ethel Olberg Tausche

Norma Gillette Vinger in memory of her mother, Jean Martin Gillette, and her grandmother, Lillian Gerst Martin

Roger and Jack Whiting in memory of their mother, Florence Whiting

Elaine B. Yerly in memory of her husband, Everett Yerly

The League of Women Voters of La Crosse County also met the challenge grant which the *La Crosse Community Foundation* offered in support of this historical record for the La Crosse area.

A Note about Names

In order to give women proper recognition, an attempt was made to identify them as accurately as possible. Searches through organization records, newspaper articles, telephone books, city directories and cemetery lists were partially successful. Whenever additional information was found, it has been included in parentheses with the woman's name.

The usage of names may differ from one woman to the next. What may appear to be inconsistency was an attempt to reflect the practice of the times in which each woman lived. The way in which society has identified women, particularly married women, has changed during the time span covered by this book. While a single woman was identified by her own first and last names, a married woman was referred to by her husband's name. For example, when Alice Green taught at La Crosse Central High School in the early 1900s, she was known as Miss Alice Green. However, when she married Frank Hixon in 1921, she became known as Mrs. Frank Hixon. The practice of not using a woman's first name, in effect, made her invisible. In some cases it could result in misidentification. For example, Alice Green was the second of two Mrs. Frank Hixons. The first, Minnie Louise Scott, died in 1909.

It was not until the 1970s that the way in which women were identified in membership lists, newspaper stories and the telephone book began to change. For years, organizations listed a married member by her husband's name. Thus, when Alice Hixon served as the first president of the League of Women Voters of La Crosse, in 1924, her name appeared on the membership roll as Mrs. Frank Hixon. In the 1970s, women's groups modified the listing to include the woman's first name, usually in parentheses, e.g., Mrs. Frank (Alice) Hixon. The next step gave prominence to the woman's given name, e.g., Alice (Mrs. Frank) Hixon. In most groups, the reference to the husband's name eventually was eliminated.

Over the course of that decade, the *La Crosse Tribune* made the transition from Mrs. Frank Hixon and Mrs. Alice Hixon (with the second reference as Mrs. Hixon) to Alice Hixon (second reference, Hixon with no Mrs.). There was a complication, however, if a married woman had kept her own name rather than taken the surname of her husband. In that case, the newspaper's first reference was "Alice Green," and the second reference was "Green, who prefers the designation Ms." The *Tribune* eventually dropped that last phrase.

In 1975, members of the local chapters of the National Organization for Women and the National Women's Political Caucus joined a successful statewide effort to convince the Public Service Commission that telephone books should include the first name of a married woman with her husband's at no additional cost. The La Crosse telephone directory complied with the 1976 PSC ruling in its 1978 edition.

These changes gave women a visibility they previously did not have.

Local medical and educational institutions also went through a series of name changes. When a hospital, college, university or vocational school is mentioned, this book uses the name appropriate for the time in which the reference is made.

Introduction

Six months before the seventy-two year long struggle for woman's suffrage ended in success in 1920, the National American Woman Suffrage Association launched an independent organization "to increase the effectiveness of women's votes in furthering better government."[1] The women who had the tenacity to campaign for decades also understood the time had come to prepare women to exercise their new right of citizenship. Thus the League of Women Voters and the Nineteenth Amendment to the U.S. Constitution share the same birth year.

Four years later Mrs. Frank (Alice) Hixon invited several women to discuss the possibility of forming a League chapter in La Crosse. Mrs. Harry Thomas of Sheboygan, representing the League of Women Voters of Wisconsin, met with the interested women on August 22, 1924. The group acted quickly and officially chartered the League of Women Voters of La Crosse three days later. Mrs. Hixon was president; Mrs. A. J. (Ella) Roberge, first vice-president; Mrs. O. J. (Emma) Oyen, recording secretary; Mrs. H. (Lottie Beckett) Spence, corresponding secretary; and Miss Mabel Young, treasurer. Mrs. Andrew (Charlotte B.) Lees headed a committee of ten to get out the vote. The next month, committee members began contacting women to encourage them to register to vote for the fall election. League membership flourished. In 1926, there were one hundred fifty-nine members from La Crosse, West Salem, and Bangor. Probably the first money-raising project was a rest room at the Interstate Fair in 1925. League members distributed information and provided first aid and a checking service for ten cents an item. Other projects of the time were get-out-the-vote campaigns, citizenship classes, candidate meetings, and interviews with and letters to legislators.

The La Crosse League of Women Voters, which organized to promote voter awareness and participation in government, always has been active in studying issues and lobbying at the local, state, and national levels. Before taking a position on an issue, League members were required to study it thoroughly. As a result, they were instrumental in the change of policy to chlorinate and fluoridate La Crosse drinking water. They also campaigned for marital property reform which called for the state of Wisconsin to look upon marriage as an economic partnership to which the non-income-producing spouse also added value. One of the results of the change in the law was that a widow no longer was required to prove that she had been an equal partner with her husband in their economic livelihood. Prior to the change, the onerous death and inheritance taxes could cause the widow to lose the business or farm she and her husband had operated together. League members also have influenced national public policy ranging from the environment, health and education to defense and international relations. They were active in promoting the United Nations in its early years.

Carroll Gundersen said of her many years with the League of Women Voters, "I really feel that I've taken the equivalent of a Ph. D. in political science in my years of League work."[2] She joined the La Crosse League in 1939 and served as its president from 1943 to 1947. She was president of the LWV of Wisconsin (1952-54) and served the LWV-US as board member (1954) and second vice president (1958). From 1969 to 1972, she chaired the League's 50th Anniversary Committee and the national fund drive that raised eleven million dollars. She was the first chair of the League of Women Voters Education Fund.

In between her presidencies, Carroll observed the early days of the United Nations. In 1947, she was part of a delegation that spent one week at Lake Success, New York, the first home of the United Nations. Two years later she was chosen as one of two Wisconsin women to visit and study sessions at the United Nations. She was a speaker in demand when she returned to La Crosse. In order to respond to all the requests, she organized a group of ten League members who studied and then presented the work of the United Nations to more than 150 groups throughout the city and area. When the League panel made its U. N. Day presentation three times on March 22, 1949, approximately 1,000 people attended.

Recognizing that there always were women distinguishing themselves in the home, in the workplace, and in the community, the League of Women Voters of La Crosse County offers this book as a record of women's influence in the life and history of the county. The book includes a few examples of women's roles from the time of the first white settlers in this area, in the 1840s, to the early 1900s. The vast majority of stories illustrate women's activities and accomplishments from 1920 until 1980. Because this book is meant to be a seed for future historical research and writing as well as a companion to existing recorded history, it concludes with a "snapshot" which reflects the visibility of women in La Crosse County after 1980.

In the Home

An aim for every homemaker

To have the home
    economically sound
    mechanically convenient
    physically healthful
    morally wholesome
    mentally stimulating
    spiritually inspiring
    socially responsible and
    founded upon mutual love and respect.[1]

Urban and rural women throughout La Crosse County have subscribed to this description of homemaking in varying degrees. In the early days of the U.S. republic, long before white settlers populated this area, a woman's role was prescribed as the moral force which guided the family and, indirectly, the nation.[2] Despite the productive work women did at home and in the marketplace during the gradual process of industrialization of the nineteenth century, the belief that women, by nature, were suited to the private sphere of home and family held sway.[3]

By the time the twentieth century arrived, women in La Crosse County, as elsewhere, were the primary housekeepers and family caregivers while men were the primary breadwinners. Homemakers managed the family resources by performing, without pay, nearly all the household labor. They arranged their schedules each hour, each day, and according to the season in order to accomplish what needed to be done. They grew, preserved, and prepared food. They sewed and altered clothing for their children and themselves, mended ready-made clothing worn by the men, and spent an entire day each week laundering the family garments and household linens. They fought the accumulation of soot from the wood or coal burning stoves and furnaces and nursed the sick or infirm with the aid of homemade remedies and, sometimes, the advice of doctors. They nurtured, disciplined and socialized their children: sending them to school, taking them to church, and expecting them to tend to household chores such as carrying in firewood, feeding the animals, drying dishes, and snapping beans. Homemakers arranged for their children to take lessons in piano and dance. When their work was done, and if time and energy permitted, they joined together with other women from church or a civic or cultural club to seek ways to improve themselves, their families, and their communities.

Caregiving

Before daycare centers and nursery schools became a standard part of our community, most women took care of their own children twenty-four hours a day. The daily tasks of child care — bathing, feeding, clothing the children, taking them for walks, toilet training, instilling manners, and putting them to bed — formed the core of women's daily lives. Women often cared for elderly relatives as well. In addition, many opened their homes to neighbors and others in need.

Whether a woman did the household chores, shopped at the market, or gathered with friends, it was common to have her children with her. Although "those years were a blur," Priscilla Anderson Dvorak's memory of her early years as a mother in La Crosse is coupled with daily afternoon walks with her children in town in the late 1940s and early 1950s. "I would have a tiny baby in the buggy, sometimes a bigger baby sitting in the buggy, and one hanging on to me or the buggy, just toddling along," the mother of five recalled.[1]

Local housewives looked forward to outings which gave them the opportunity to talk with other adults while they watched their children play. Della Berg and Lorraine Fiet, both of Bangor, took their young children berry and nut picking in the 1950s.[2] Mary Lou Ryan took her children to the park as well as ice skating and swimming. "We did things that used up energy and were free," said the mother of six children born in the 1950s and 1960s.[3]

Even a social evening out usually included children. Mary Lou Ryan and her older sister accompanied their parents to parties in the homes of friends. "They couldn't afford a babysitter in the 1930s so my sister and I went along. When bedtime came, we were nestled among the guests' coats piled on the beds," she remembered.[4] In the 1950s, going out to eat was a rare event, but drive-in movies provided an inexpensive family outing. Parents loaded the car with a grocery bag filled with home-popped popcorn, pillows, and children, dressed in pajamas, for a late night of movies.[5]

Women's forays into the community met with uneven success. In the mid 1930s, Mildred Nelson, who was interested in joining her church's Ladies' Aid Society, brought her toddler to her first meeting. Part way through the gathering, little Marilyn discovered the refreshment table. Unobserved, she climbed onto it and devoured the angel food cake meant to refresh the ladies at the end of their discussion. Mildred was so embarrassed by what her daughter had done that she never returned.[6]

Mary Lou Ryan discovered that events advertised for women were not necessarily free of children. Shortly after moving to La Crosse in 1968, she sent her six children off to school and prepared to attend what she thought would be a fun, relaxing afternoon of arts and crafts with the Campus Dames, the organization for wives of Wisconsin State University faculty. When she walked into the room, she saw "wall to wall babies."[7] Instead of returning to the arts and crafts group, she decided to spend her time with the League of Women Voters which provided baby-sitting and thus a child-free time for members to study current issues such as education, foreign policy, and equal rights.

In the 1950s, a group of Bangor women worked out a successful plan for getting away from their husbands and children one evening a month. When the men left for their Rod and Gun Club meeting, the women tucked the children into bed, gave instructions to an older child or sitter, and traveled to a designated home. It was a once-a-month holiday. The women did not conduct business, play cards, or dress up. They did order pizza so they could eat without having to cook. When asked if children ever came along, Della Berg, a sweet, soft-spoken woman, raised her voice ever so slightly. "Oh, never," she insisted.[8]

Through the years, women contrived various ways to share child rearing and its routine. Some families counted on live-in help or extended family to ease the burden of housework and childrearing. During the 1930s, a country girl who wanted to leave the farm and settle into town and a divorced woman who needed a place for herself and her child met their own needs by doing domestic work in the Otto and Eleanor Schlabach household. Eleanor was the oldest of several siblings who had grown up near Wheeling, West Virginia, in a big farm house that required an enormous amount of housework. As a result, when she and her husband established their home in La Crosse, she was interested in having a smaller family but still hired domestic help to lighten her load. These domestic workers blended into the Schlabach household. In return for her services, each woman received a little money and a place to live before taking the next step in her life. For the country girl, that step was nursing school; for the divorced woman, it was remarriage.[9]

Sometimes maiden aunts served as the extra caregiver, seamstress, or laborer for the larger family. Children in extended families were used to having more than one or two adults watching over them, giving them direction, putting them to work, teaching, and caring for them. While Eleanor Roellig Meinert worked at the Tausche Hardware Company, her oldest sister,

Olga Roellig, took care of Eleanor's young sons. Olga was born in 1870. She never married, but she helped raise her seven younger brothers and sisters including the twins, Eleanor and Lenore, who were born in 1893. While Eleanor's husband was fighting in the trenches during World War I, she and their twin sons lived with her parents and Olga. When Eleanor's husband returned, they set up housekeeping across and down the alley from the Roelligs. The close-knit, extended family was always there to give support and help to one another.[10]

One unmarried Onalaska native who formed her own small family through adoption eventually found a childcare arrangement that worked to everyone's benefit. At a time when female teachers were not allowed to be married, Flora Brooks devoted her life to teaching and to raising her adopted son, Billy. After earning her two-year certificate from La Crosse Normal School (now the University of Wisconsin-La Crosse) in 1923, she found a teaching position in the Wisconsin lumber town of Rib Lake. Early one September morning in 1937, word came that there was a baby boy to adopt. Still wearing her housecoat and slippers, Flora ran from her apartment above a grocery store to the hospital to see him. One look at the brown-eyed infant was all it took. "He's mine, he's mine. Don't you let anybody else see him," she pronounced.[11] In a flurry of activity, she taught school all day, hired a woman to take care of her new son during teaching hours, went shopping for baby clothes and supplies, and directed an attorney to start adoption proceedings. The home inspection visit occurred at Christmas time. When the state worker saw the Christmas tree heaped with gifts from every faculty member and numerous friends, she commented, "This baby must be loved."

The following year Flora was thrilled to return to teach in her hometown, Onalaska. Because her mother had died the previous year, Flora had no family to help care for Billy. In order to continue teaching, she took him to the homes of various babysitters. Eventually a young woman named Laura Woods came to Flora's attention. Laura was looking for a place to live in town so she could attend Onalaska High School. In exchange for room and board, Laura did housework and watched Billy, who was attending school during the same time as Laura. The arrangement worked so well that the family of two evolved into a "family" of three.

A more modern alternative — a babysitting co-operative — gave women a place to leave their children while they attended meetings and classes or kept appointments. One such neighborhood arrangement offered sixteen La Crosse women child-free time in the 1970s. "For ten years or so, we exchanged children and points," recalled Joyce Arthur.[12] She used this bartering system while serving as president of the League of Women Voters of La Crosse County in 1972 and 1973 and as a member of the La Crosse County Board of Supervisors from 1976 to 1984. Sometimes her children accompanied her to these meetings. However, when she needed to be free of distraction, Joyce left them with another member of the co-operative. Each time one member took care of the children of others, she earned points. Each time she left her child(ren) with someone else, she paid points.

An illness in the family drastically altered a woman's daily routine of caring for children and the household. In mid-November 1930, Geneva and James Feak's daughter developed scarlet fever. The contagious disease turned the household upside down. Just a few months earlier, the Feaks and their two children had moved from La Crosse to rural Bangor where they shared a farmhouse with James' parents and two children of James' sister. When ten-year-old Della caught scarlet fever, she and her mother were confined to the parlor and a connecting bedroom. A "No Admittance" sign was posted on the house to indicate that no one could leave or enter. Heavy paper covered the doorway to the sick rooms as another precaution to prevent the spread of the contagious disease. Within a few weeks, however, Della's cousin, Corrine, and brother, Robert, also joined the sick ward. For three months, Geneva nursed her young patients, giving sponge baths, taking temperatures, and reading to them in rooms which were kept dark for fear the light might damage their eyesight. She washed out underwear with water she heated in a tea kettle on a heating stove in the parlor. Her mother-in-law did the rest of the housework and kept track of the other little cousin, Gene, who suffered from asthma. The elder Mrs. Feak also cooked all the meals and passed food through a window into the rooms in which the ill children were confined, nursed her dying husband, and welcomed the doctor on his daily visits. The men of the family could not risk exposure to scarlet fever because that might contaminate the milk. Instead, they stayed at the next farm, returning only to milk the cows, to carry firewood to the house for cooking and heating, and to open the pipes which filled the stove's reservoir with water. They were not allowed inside until the children regained their health.[13]

As women advanced through the stages of their lives, caregiving was a constant, but the focus of their care changed from their own young children to aging parents and to grandchildren. During the Depression, Thelma Orr Zumach Stokes not only raised her own four children but also watched over several neighborhood children whose mother had died. Thelma's daughter, Marion, recalled that the Zumach household consisted of their family of six, two grandparents, and "the strays — people, not cats and dogs — my mother was always taking in."[14] They all lived in a four-bedroom house in La Crescent, Minnesota, with an outhouse in the back. Thelma fed the children, her husband, and his parents from her garden which produced "beans by the bushel." She canned vegetables, beef, and chicken. In 1939 and 1940, her mother-in-law and father-in-law suffered disabling strokes less than a year apart. During the few months that each was

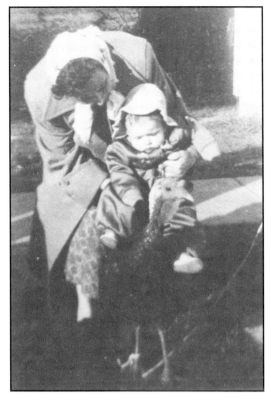

"Ginger, Old Tom and the Old Granny"
Thelma Zumach balanced her one-year-old granddaughter, Ginger Hopkins, on a turkey tied out by the garage of her home in La Crescent, 1951.
Ginger Hopkins Jentz

bedridden before dying, Thelma fed, bathed, and comforted them. Thelma's children were grown when her husband, William, died unexpectedly in December 1949. A few months later, her first grandchild was born to their daughter, Marion. In a mutually-beneficial arrangement, Thelma, who was living alone, took on full-time care of her granddaughter during the week while Marion and her husband worked in La Crosse. Every Sunday for three years, Thelma's daughter and son-in-law brought first one and then two young daughters to spend the week at their grandmother's home.

When Lee and Josie (Twite) Broadhead married in 1932, they began a life together which included nearly sixty years of farming in Breidel Coulee along Highway 14 and raising at least twenty foster children in addition to their own three.

Beverly Broadhead Ranis

Prior to the wide availability of formal social services,[15] women filled the gap by providing a helping hand or unofficial social services. If there was a family in need, someone in the neighborhood or the community did something about it. Neighbors kept track of one another, knew what would be helpful and what would be accepted without injuring someone's pride. That might mean gathering clothing, preparing an extra meal, risking one's own health in order to nurse the sick, or serving as an unofficial foster parent.

Josie and Lee Broadhead raised at least twenty children in addition to their own three. Their large home was always open to friends and to children needing foster care. Beverly Broadhead Ranis said of her mother, "She was a homemaker, but not in the sense that Monday was washday and Tuesday was for ironing. It was more important to her to do for others. She had a zest to make things better for people. Her attitude was 'wherever you are, whatever you are doing, there are no limits to what you can do.'"[16]

When the Broadheads married in 1932, they purchased a dairy farm from Lee's father. During the nearly sixty years they worked the farm, Josie cooked many huge meals for seasonal work crews of fifteen or more and for her extra-large family. She baked all the bread and pies first on a Kalamazoo wood burning stove and then on an electric stove she won in a raffle from the local rural electrification association. Her pressure cooker got a summer-long workout while she put up garden surplus, meat, and 150 to 200 gallons of tomato juice. As a farmwife, she kept the books and ran the errands to get feed for animals and parts for machinery.

Visitors to the Broadhead place in Breidel Coulee along Highway 14 never left empty-handed. Josie plied them with pumpkins, squash, potatoes, whatever was ripe at the moment. As a little girl, Sue Strehl looked forward to crossing the road with her father to buy non-homogenized fresh whole milk for fifty cents a gallon from the Broadhead's bulk tank. There was always a chance that it was Josie's baking day. As the small girl brought the money into the house, she sniffed the air for the possibility of a warm, glazed doughnut.[17]

Josie loved to write. In her written reflections and recollections, she described her own mother sitting down after the day's work was done, resting her feet in the oven, and writing in her journal.[18] Josie also recorded her thoughts about and experiences with numerous foster children, most of whom were distant relatives. When a family of eight great-nieces and nephews was about to be split up, Josie took them in, set up more beds, and strung clothesline in the basement to which she clipped their pairs of socks.

She incorporated into several of her writings the tribulations of coping with one severely emotionally disturbed youth. In "Terry, an Abused, Troubled Boy,"[19] she described his arrival:

> *One Sunday afternoon ... in 1955, as we were picnicking out in our backyard, a taxi-cab drove in, unloaded two leather suitcases on our gravel driveway, helped a frail, limping youngster (dressed in a tailored, blue serge suit, wearing a gold wrist watch) out, then drove away.*

Josie also wrote about the decision she and Lee made to take Terry into their home while the county sheriff traced the boy's family.

> *I had had a heart attack a few months previous to this boy's invasion into our home and was given 3 months to live. During that period I did a lot of soul searching and praying....I made a vow with God. If He would let me live I would undertake any job, any service, no matter how small, trivial, difficult, or challenging. I knew without a doubt that caring for this boy for the summer was to be my first assignment.*

When they discovered Terry's father was in no condition to raise his son, the Broadheads decided to take responsibility for Terry. Their love and guidance from the time he was eight years old helped him learn to cope with the world. Josie discovered Terry's genius for mechanics when, in desperation, she asked him to repair her typewriter. Because of his erratic behavior, she was not sure she would see her typewriter in one piece again. However, in a few days, he returned it to her in perfect working condition. Terry used his mechanical abilities to obtain work in a radio store and, within a short time, became the manager of that store plus two others. When a fatal car accident ended his life at the age of thirty, Josie wrote, "My first assignment was over, but my vow with God is still on. There is a healing in serving others. It healed my damaged heart."

Resources outside the home became more prevalent throughout the twentieth century: daycare centers and sitters for the young, hospitals and nursing homes for the ill and the elderly, and formalized social services for those with serious problems. More often than not, it was the woman who investigated and selected the best option for her young child, for the elderly parent, for the acquaintance who needed counseling. When women were not directly providing care, they were making arrangements with the people who would provide it in their place. The important task of taking care of others long has been, and likely will remain, primarily the responsibility of women.

Labor Intensive Housekeeping

In the early part of this century, housekeeping required a great deal of manual labor. Sometimes producing just the basics of water and heat required brute strength. If a home did not have indoor plumbing, all water for cooking and cleaning needed to be carried into the house. Afterwards the dirty water had to be carried outside. Before central heating or in those La Crosse homes which were not hooked up to city-supplied steam heat, all fuel — whether wood, coal, or oil — also had to be brought inside. Ruth and Ed Snodgrass began married life in 1941 in a house without a furnace. She recalled filling a five-gallon can with oil from a big tank in the garage and carrying it to the house to fill the stove: "Oh, that was a hard job. I hated that....When it was icy, I remember falling really bad with the five gallons of oil all over."[1]

Into the middle of the twentieth century, a housewife could assemble ingredients for meals without leaving her home. Food that did not come from her garden was obtained from the neighborhood grocery store. The 1940 La Crosse City Directory listed 130 grocery stores, one on almost every block. Because the ice box held small amounts of food for a brief time, the housewife ordered groceries for one day which were delivered into her kitchen.

Icemen, who traveled by horse and wagon and later by truck, delivered ice directly into each home's icebox. "When we wanted ice, we put a sign in the window — 25 pounds or 30 pounds — and then the iceman would come with a truck and deliver ice and put it in there," recalled Ruth Snodgrass.[2] Ice, cut from the river in winter, was stored for months in buildings insulated with straw or sawdust. Betty Lamb Dell Hyde, who lived at 1602 Mississippi Street in La Crosse as a child, recalled the corrugated metal ice storage building in the alley behind her house. "We played hide and seek in that building until we discovered rats as big as dogs inside. We pulled a wagon to the storage building to get our ice because it was cheaper if you hauled it yourself rather than have it delivered," she remembered.[3]

Home delivery of dairy products was common, too. During the 1940s and 1950s, Mary Lou Rudolph recalled, the Borden's milkman delivered to the house where she, her husband, and their seven children lived. "If you bought cottage cheese, it came in aluminum glasses which we collected and used for drinking. When milk delivery stopped, we took the baby buggy or a wagon to the milk station on Sixteenth Street between Adams and Johnson streets in La Crosse. We picked up three or four gallons every couple days."[4]

There was an overriding belief during the early and middle part of the twentieth century that the house had to be in a certain order. Housewives cleaned the house from top to bottom for company — even the dirt under the refrigerator. They ironed sheets and starched and ironed their husbands' shirts. For company and for the family's Sunday dinner, there was an expectation of elaborate meals which were served on the family's best dishes. Utilitarian work stretched the life of socks which were darned, collars on men's shirts which were turned, and sheets which were slit down the center and resewn with the original outer edges joined in the middle. "Housewives identified themselves much more by strict housekeeping standards than they do today. They weren't sentimental about the work. They just did what needed to be done, one job after another. It was a hard-working world," recalled Marian Ramlow and Margaret Fish.[5]

Most women did their own household work. Some middle class families hired help that worked side by side with the housewife to provide an additional pair of hands on a regular basis or for a couple of weeks during spring housecleaning. Domestic work was a common and acceptable occupation for young women who were hired to do cooking, cleaning, sewing, and laundry in exchange for room and board in middle class as well as upper class homes.

Emma Oldenburg came to La Crosse from a large farm family in the early 1900s. She found work as a cook first for the Dr. Edward and Sarah Thompson Evans household and then for the Irene and Joseph M. Hixon family. Emma's younger sister, Florence, described Emma's work conditions, "My sister didn't do other housework, she just cooked. She had a couple weeks vacation in the summer and would go home to the farm to relax.... She received room and board....The other house staff was supervised by Mrs. Hixon. There was a dining room girl who took care of the dining room and the downstairs rooms ... she took care of the dishes and serving.... After my sister got married, she did catering work for wealthy people.... She did lots of baking — Christmas cookies and special cakes."[6]

Housecleaning and
Home Improvement

Daily housecleaning included dusting, washing dishes and, before electricity, cleaning smoke from the glass chimneys of lamps. There was weekly work like scrubbing the kitchen floor and scouring the bathroom, if it was indoors. In the early part of the century, there was extensive seasonal housework. Wood burning stoves for heating and cooking required major cleaning. In the spring, the entire family went to work removing the stove and pipes, cleaning out the wood box, removing spoiled food from the cellar, and cleaning the back yard which had accumulated the winter's dishwater, wash water, ashes, and assorted trash. They also scrubbed the soot from the walls, washed, starched and stretched or ironed the curtains, carried the parlor carpet outside to remove months of dust with the wire rug beater, and aired the mattresses and bedding.[7]

Women welcomed various appliances and machines which made their job a little less arduous. Gas or electric stoves were easier to use and easier to clean. The Bissell carpet sweeper brushed up dirt and lint from rugs. "Non-electric carpet sweepers — always dominated by the Bissell company — had literally swept the nation beginning in the 1880s."[8] Betty Hyde recalled that her mother owned a sweeper in the 1920s and Betty had one when she married in the 1940s. Vacuum cleaners, which did a better job of sucking up dirt, eventually eliminated the infrequent but back-breaking work of carpet beating. The housewife still used a dust mop to clean up around the edges of the rug. Although scatter rugs strategically placed by the sink and stove caught many spills, the kitchen floor was scrubbed, usually on hands and knees, at least once a week. Mary Lou Rudolph did not need a vacuum cleaner because all the floors in her house were covered with linoleum. "I scrubbed the floors on my hands and knees. Later on I learned to use a mop."[9]

Because the home was her domain, the housewife also stripped, painted and reupholstered furniture; patched, painted and papered walls; and made rugs for the floor, curtains for the windows, slipcovers for old chairs, and sheets and pillowcases for the beds. In the early 1950s, when her second daughter was still a baby, Della Berg patched the plaster walls and ceiling of the living room in the older home she and her husband owned in Bangor. "I'd check on the baby, climb up the ladder, apply some patching compound, climb down the ladder, check on the baby, and start all over again," she said.[10] Ruth Snodgrass worked in a factory for more than thirty years and, with her husband, raised eight children. She also made "real pretty bedspreads for all the beds. Sometimes I didn't get home from work till midnight. I would be sewing bedspreads till one or two in the morning, then up at six to go back to work."[11]

Sewing

Prior to World War I, the majority of clothing for women and children and shirts for men was made in the household with purchased fabric or by reusing and altering other garments. Therefore, working as an independent seamstress or dressmaker was a common occupation for women.[12] At the age of seventeen, Anna Johanna Benson, born in Sweden in 1873, put her sewing and design skills to use as a traveling seamstress in La Crosse. She moved from home to home in the area of Fourteenth, Fifteenth, King and Cass streets, also known as Orchard Place. She stayed in each home for several weeks to sew garments for the entire family. Her daughter, Helen Hanson, recalled that "leg-o-mutton sleeves were popular then, with lots of buttons down each sleeve. My mother covered the buttons by hand with fabric to match or complement the sleeve." In 1897, when Anna married Ole Sigvard Hanson, she continued sewing for others from her own home.[13]

As the century progressed, more ready-made clothing became available and was priced within the reach of more families. The choice to purchase clothing or to make it usually was based on the best way to budget the family income. When the Geneva and James Feak family lived in La Crosse during the 1920s, each spring they hired one of their aunts to help sew everything from dresses to men's shirts. The aunt temporarily moved into their home and worked side by side with Geneva "sewing up a storm" until the family's wardrobe was complete. After the Feaks moved to a Bangor area farm in 1930, Geneva did the sewing alone. She was especially skilled at altering an old coat into a "new" winter coat for her daughter, Della. "My mother had a nice touch with this so garments didn't look remodeled," Della remembered. "However, in my freshman year of high school, I wanted to buy a ready-made camel hair coat from the Sears catalogue with the 4-H prize money I had won and saved. My mother was reluctant, perhaps because she already had remade something for me. But my father said I should be allowed to spend my prize money on a new coat if that was what I wanted."[14]

Laundry

Of all the household chores, women described laundry as the most onerous task in the first half of this century. Because laundering required so much work, clean clothing was a sign of a skilled woman.[15] Although most performed the work themselves, women of all degrees of financial means did whatever they could to alleviate the back-breaking task. Some enlisted assistance from other family members; a few sent the soiled items out to a self-employed laundress or to a commercial laundry; a smaller number hired someone who came in once a week to assist them or employed a live-in laundress.

Monday was "wash day." Irene Radcliffe described how her own mother did the household laundry during the 1920s.

> *She carried water into the boiler on the cook stove. It was a wood burning stove but we burned more corn cobs and coal than wood. She heated the water which she added, dipperful by dipperful, to a washtub of cold water. Next she rubbed the clothes with a bar of soap on the washboard. Stubborn dirt needed a second scrubbing. Then she wrung out the garment. White clothing went into the boiler to be boiled with soap. She fished these out with a pronged washstick and put them into a dishpan to rinse. Bluing was added to the last rinse to keep things white. Then she wrung them out by hand. She starched shirts, dresses and table linens just before hanging them up to dry. She cooked the starch on the stove and diluted it to a light, medium or heavy strength. Then she spent the next day ironing. Most everything needed ironing because it was cotton or linen.[16]*

A few techniques offered slight savings in time. Rain water collected in a rain barrel provided soft water. The water reservoir of the stove maintained a limited supply of hot water. Before the advent of granulated soap, a butcher knife kept handy in the laundry area could shave the Fels Naptha bar into small slices so it would dissolve more easily.

There were minor hazards to hanging clothing and bedding out to dry: kids and dogs often managed to get tangled in them, birds flying overhead often soiled them before they were dry, the laundered items froze in the winter, and factory soot blackened them. In March 1944, residents near Green Bay, Redfield, Eighth and Ninth streets petitioned the La Crosse Common Council to take action against the nearby Swift Company plant for

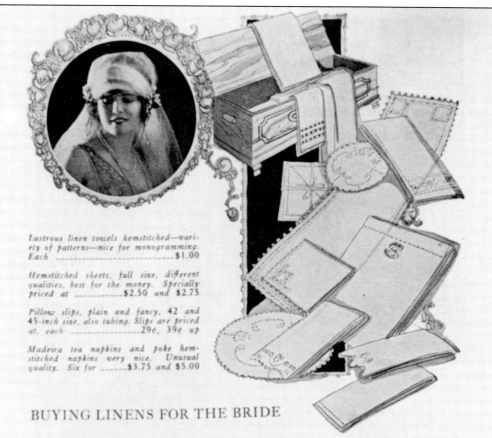

Lustrous linen towels hemstitched—variety of patterns—nice for monogramming. Each _____$1.00

Hemstitched sheets, full size, different qualities, best for the money. Specially priced at _____$2.50 and $2.75

Pillow slips, plain and fancy, 42 and 45-inch size, also tubing. Slips are priced at, each _____29¢, 39¢ up

Madeira tea napkins and poke hemstitched napkins very nice. Unusual quality. Six for _____$3.75 and $5.00

BUYING LINENS FOR THE BRIDE

THEY may have hopes but very few girls have Hope Boxes these days. Instead of putting her money into a fine linen towel or table cloth, the modern girl buys something for immediate use, till suddenly she is confronted by the fact that she and THE MAN won't relish a linen closet as bare as Mother Hubbard's cupboard.

That's one reason why the nicest compliment you can pay a bride is to give her a linen shower. The guests will enjoy selecting fine pieces for her diningroom, the guest chamber or the kitchen. We have a splendid assortment of the nicer decorative linens which make such lovely gifts. Have you seen the "waffle sets"—yellow, blue, green and pink lunch cloths and napkins? Do you know that three-piece doily sets are the thing for buffet as well as vanity dresser? Oblong doily sets are suitable for the refectory style dining table, popular today. Pattern table cloths repeat the motif of the most popular china

designs. Embroidered pillow slips of all sizes, novelty bedspreads, and a splendid display of fine sheets and pillow slips, also "white goods by-the-yard" suitable for domestic purposes are included in our special sales for May.

LINENS NEEDED FOR FIRST YEAR

4 *Table Cloths 2x2½ yards*
1 *Table Cloth, 2x3 yards*
1 *Table Cloth, 2x3½ yards*
1 *Dozen Breakfast Napkins*
2 *Dozen Dinner Napkins*
1 *Dozen Tea Napkins*
1 *Luncheon Set*
1 *Luncheon Set, extra nice*
1 *Table Pad*
4 *Dozen Face Towels*
2 *Dozen Bath Towels*
1 *Dozen Guest Towels*
2 *Dozen Dish Towels*
8 *Pairs Pillow Cases*
8 *Pairs Cotton Sheets*
1 *Pair Fancy Sheets*
3 *Bedspreads and Bolsters*

The *Doerflinger's Store News* of May 1924 advertised a 1920s standard for setting up housekeeping.

La Crosse County Historical Society

creating a "dreadful smoke and soot condition." Housewives complained that the wash they hung out on clotheslines became so covered with soot that it needed to be rewashed.[17]

The first washing machine to replace the washboard was operated manually by pulling a lever in and out to operate the agitator which swished the clothes. It was as repetitive and as boring as churning butter. Wringers later replaced hand wringing. To squeeze out the water, clothing and sheets were forced between hard rubber rollers which were cranked by hand. Prior to the addition of a safety release, many fingers and hands got caught in the rollers. Wash tubs doubled as swimming pools for babies in the pre-plastic age. Mothers hauled the heavy metal tubs up from the cellar and filled them with water to warm in the sun for their children's water play.

Gasoline engines powered a few early washing machines, especially on farms, but electric engines soon replaced them. Mary Lou Ryan recalled that her mother had one of the early electric washing machines before people knew much about electricity and safety. One Monday morning in 1934, when Mary Lou's mother reached up to turn off the machine where it was plugged into a dangling socket, the electrical current grabbed her. She struggled but could not get loose. She screamed and jumped and finally landed on one tiny dry spot of the basement floor before the current released her. Luckily she was wearing rubbers over her shoes for washday. Sixty years later Mary Lou still remembered the bone-crushing hug she received as a four-year-old immediately afterward.

Ruth Snodgrass' first washing machine was second hand. "I got one from my aunt.... It had two tubs that kept rocking back and forth. You could hear it a mile away whenever I plugged it in."[18] Mary Lou Rudolph also had a used washing machine — her mother's old Maytag wringer washer — during the 1940s.

> *I washed laundry real often — every other day when the kids were little. The neighbor man used to joke about all the diapers hanging on the clothesline. 'Mrs. Rudolph must have done a lot of dishes, just look at all those dishtowels,' he'd say. And when I ran out of clothesline space, I'd use the neighbor's lines when she wasn't using them. My mother taught me to iron, and I was a real good ironer. But it really piled up. I spent twelve hours ironing every weekend. My husband worked in an office so he wore white shirts and he liked them lightly starched.... I didn't really mind the ironing. Every once in a while, my mother would come over and do some while I was at work. But wash and wear [fabric which did not require ironing] was a godsend.[19]*

On the way to our present automatic washers and dryers, there were other innovations to help remove drudgery from wash day. The electric iron replaced flatirons, which had to be heated and reheated on top of the stove. The mangle, a machine for pressing fabrics by feeding them through heated rollers, was a relatively quick way to iron sheets. If one became skilled, it was a quick way to press shirts, too.

By the late 1950s many homes had large appliances, powered with electricity or gas, to prepare food or keep it chilled, to wash dishes or clothes, to dry laundry or to suck up dirt. In addition to a stove, refrigerator and washing machine, Jean Wulling had "an electric appliance most women never had" — a soft drink vending machine.[20] Jean plugged the pop machine into her garage which faced the narrow street that ran along the college tennis courts. The city had not yet installed a drinking fountain by the courts so thirsty tennis players were happy and willing to exchange their coins for a cold drink. Each evening Jean refilled the machine and removed and counted the coins. She said, "I loved counting the coins," which were used to fund trophies and other expenses for the competitive tennis club her children belonged to in the 1950s and 1960s.

When a woman's identity was defined by and through her home, the condition of her house and the clothing worn by her family were measures of how well she was doing her job as a housewife. According to Suellen Hoy, author of *Chasing Dirt: The American Pursuit of Cleanliness*, the U.S. culture of cleanliness developed after World War II. Unlike other countries involved in the war, the United States was not faced with the task of rebuilding. The country was undamaged and enjoyed high employment. To boost the sales of soaps and other cleaning agents, the advertising industry promoted cleanliness as an indicator of success and superiority. The American aversion to odors was learned from advertisers who placed the burdens of cleanliness on women.[21] For instance, it was the wife's responsibility to get rid of "ring around the collar" on her husband's shirts rather than his responsibility to wash his neck.

As the century progressed, the intensity of housekeeping diminished. Women in fewer households routinely ironed bed sheets, turned the collars of men's shirts, darned socks, or disrupted the entire house for a week or two of spring cleaning. "Today we don't have homes like our mothers," said Suellen Hoy, who is in her fifties. "We spend time in other ways. Although we still appreciate cleanliness, we don't need to be obsessed with it."[22]

Domestic Science

From the 1920s onward, the introduction of technology into the home coincided with a sharp decline in the number of unmarried girls and women employed as household servants. Electricity, indoor plumbing, washing machines, and small appliances eased the heavy labor of housework. As industry produced more items for home use, housewives needed to educate themselves about the new conveniences so they could make wise choices. Washing machines, for example, constantly improved. Mary Lou Ryan's mother owned a Speed Queen Washer, with a wringer that moved into three locked positions — between the suds and rinse water, between the rinse water and bluing solution, and between bluing and washbasket. Dorothy Van Schoyck of La Crosse owned an Easy Spin Dryer, which included a separate vertical cylinder to spin clothes after they had been washed. These two operations were later merged into the Bendix washer spin-dryer combination.

In the 1920s, professional home economists began helping La Crosse County housewives prepare for the shift in homemaking priorities and products by providing up-to-date information about the details of household management, raising children, health, hygiene, home decorating, nutrition and food preparation, clothing production, and consumer education. There was a trend in the business world, particularly among utility companies, to employ formally-trained home economists in order to expand their business and to calm public fears about using new electrical appliances.[1] In 1926, the local office of the Wisconsin-Minnesota Light and Power Company hired Mary Dvorak Lamb to start its Home Service Department. She demonstrated how to use the new washing machines, stoves, water heaters, and waffle irons sold by the company which eventually became Northern States Power.[2] When people bought a new stove from the Light Company, Mary visited their home to demonstrate the stove's features while preparing a meal for the family. One of Mary's successors, Doris Flick, remembered demonstrating new washing machines after they were delivered and recalled vividly the kinds of loads new owners typically chose to wash first — diapers. "I washed more diapers than any mother," Doris claimed.[3]

La Crosse County
Extension Homemakers

Meanwhile, home economics specialists, headquartered at the University of Wisconsin in Madison, made periodic visits to present lessons on food preparation, clothing production, and household management to the growing number of Homemakers Clubs in La Crosse County.[4] Women in the Town of Campbell, with the assistance of Gladys Stillman of the University of Wisconsin Extension Service and Ellen Teare of the Onalaska Agricultural School, organized the county's first homemakers club in 1920. By 1923, there were ten clubs belonging to the La Crosse County Homemakers Association. When the county association affiliated with the Wisconsin Extension Homemakers in 1936, the county allocated funds to hire its first permanent, full-time extension home economist, Anita Gundlach. As the home demonstration agent, she assisted the local Homemakers Clubs until 1948. Her successors, all professional home economists, were Edith Brevig (1948-63), Nanna Christman (1963-74), Judy Rommel (1975-85), and Mary Meehan-Strub (1985-present).

Believing strongly that education made for strong families and strong citizens, Extension Homemakers Clubs proved to be a reliable and affordable source of information. During the Depression, when families often did not have money to subscribe to a magazine, the nickel-a-month club dues provided a great bargain for the homemaker. Marge Hughes Gollnik joined the Adams Valley Club near Bangor in 1957, but her identity as a homemaker took shape at an early age. "I became a homemaker at three or four," she recalled. "As a child, I attended the all-day meetings with my mother."[5] Because Marge's mother and Aunt Elsie were among the few women who drove, they picked up several women on the way to the home of the hostess. The women opened their meeting in the morning with the Homemakers Creed which is still in use today:

> *We, the homemakers of Wisconsin, believe in the sanctity of*
> *the Home, the cradle of character, blessed by motherly devotion*
> *and guarded by fatherly protection.*
> *We pledge ourselves:*
> *to work for the preservation and improvement of home*
> *and community life;*

to strive for healthier minds and bodies and better living;
to promote the welfare of our boys and girls, the nation's
greatest asset;
to be true to God and country and of lasting service to our
homes and communities.

Then they began the project lesson for the day which, during the 1920s, 1930s and 1940s, tended to emphasize cooking, cleaning, sewing, home decorating, and fashion. The women interrupted their work, but not their fun, for a large dinner at noon. In the afternoon, instruction and practice of the new technique continued until they enjoyed a light supper before collecting their children and returning home.

Including young children who could not be left at home was both a necessity and an opportunity to teach them social skills. To enable the adults to enjoy the day-long meeting, the mothers set down the rules for their children. "Before we were old enough to go to school and in the summertime, we children went to the meetings," recalled Marge about accompanying her mother in the 1930s. "And that was really where we learned how to behave socially. Before we'd go, our mother would lay down the law. You know, you don't do this and you don't do that, you clean up your plate, and you don't cause trouble, and you take what you're supposed to, and you say thank you." Two decades later, however, the Little Barre Circle Homemakers decided to exclude children from their regular meetings. In April 1959, they voted "to meet in the evenings as the number of little ones that accompanied the homemakers to meetings continued to grow. Also, tales of egg throwing in hen houses and confetti coming from upstairs heat registers made the decision very easy."[6]

Of all the lessons Homemakers undertook throughout the years, making dress forms made a lasting impression. These individualized mannequins were highly prized by amateur seamstresses of the 1920s and 1930s because dress patterns were both scarce and expensive. The time-consuming process of making a form turned out to be an amusing as well as a serious undertaking. As a youngster, Helen Hulberg helped her mother and other Homemakers with this project. She recalled, "The woman had to stand in her undies, while inch-wide gauze tape was criss-crossed over her body. Then she had to stand still and hardly breathe till two coats of shellac set." When dry, the forms were slit down the back, removed from the woman's body, and attached to a broomstick on a pedestal. Even though the end product frequently ended up in the basement or attic, the shared experience provided amusing and enduring memories.[7]

Six members of an unidentified Homemakers Club inspected their upholstery work at the end of the day, c. 1930s. A note on the back of the snapshot identified five of them as Mrs. Marvin Johnson, Mrs. Roy Rogstad, Mrs. Kenneda, Mrs. Martin, and Mrs. Bernie Anderson.

La Crosse County Extension Homemakers

During the 1950s, Extension Homemakers spent more time on issues related to community involvement, governmental affairs, philanthropy, and child welfare. Many clubs demonstrated a strong commitment to community service, devoting time and money to benefit the residents of Lakeview County Hospital and a number of nursing homes. In the 1960s and 1970s, due in part to funding cuts, the Homemakers were encouraged to depend less on the services provided by the county extension home economist and to initiate their own study topics and project lessons. There was greater emphasis on the importance of higher education for women. The county association formed a scholarship fund for young women pursuing a degree in home economics. It also gave scholarships to older women to attend the food management program at the local technical college. The association encouraged its own members to attend "College Week" for a few days of special classes in Madison. Activities placed greater emphasis on intellectual development, civic responsibility, international affairs, women's health, taxation, estate planning, and women's rights. In March 1972, the group co-sponsored the "Save A Woman" campaign with the American Cancer Society. In an effort to warn against breast, cervical, and lung cancer, it organized informational meetings for all women of La Crosse County and provided baby-sitting to make it easier for women to attend.[8]

As an adult member, Marge Gollnik gained more than improved homemaking skills. She also developed confidence and leadership skills within the Adams Valley Club and on the La Crosse County Extension Homemakers Board, where she spent seventeen or eighteen years, eventually serving as county president in 1980 and 1981. Based on her experience, she said, "Everybody should be on the board of their organization in some capacity, even if it's a small capacity because you don't really know what's going on until you get on the board." Marge also fulfilled an early dream of being a writer when she edited the group's newsletter.[9]

At the height of activity, during the 1940s, over 1,000 La Crosse County women belonged to forty-four Homemakers clubs, including nine within the city of La Crosse. By 1981, when La Crosse County Extension Homemakers published a collection of club histories, the urban clubs had died out except for the one connected with Hamilton School in La Crosse. The publication included the stories of about thirty rural clubs, including the Rockland Rock 'n' Rollers which organized in 1978.

Although Extension Homemakers served rural and urban women, project lessons rarely mentioned farming or the challenges of living on a farm. They focused instead on improving home life and the larger community. Alice Nuttleman, a member of the Table Rock Club and county president in 1951 and 1952, believed that, during the Depression, Extension Homemakers "gave us courage that things were going to be better."[10] There is no doubt that Homemakers also served an important social purpose for its members. In the words of Helen Hulberg, who joined the Brookside Club in 1925 and was county president in 1955 and 1956, "It wasn't just projects that made Homemakers special. It was almost like a sisterhood of women that had a common cause that needed to get away from their kitchens and their families for a day."[11]

"SAVE A WOMAN"

Learn The Facts About Cancer In The

SAVE A WOMAN CAMPAIGN

Sponsored By The La Crosse County Unit

AMERICAN CANCER SOCIETY

Co-Sponsor La Crosse County Homemakers

Attend One Of The <u>FREE</u>

Informational Meetings

Thursday, MARCH 16
    Holmen H.S. ....7:30 p.m.
Friday, MARCH 17
    West Salem H.S.........10:00 a.m.
    Bangor H.S. .... 2:00 p.m.
Saturday, MARCH 18, La Crosse
    Rivoli Theater.............10:00 a.m.

Free Baby Sitting Available At Each Location

3 EXCELLENT FILMS

1. Breast Self Examination

2. It's Up To You 3. Inside Magoo

Questions and Answers By Area Doctors

FOR WOMEN ONLY

This flyer advertised the 1972 "Save a Woman" campaign sponsored by the American Cancer Society and the La Crosse County Extension Homemakers.

La Crosse County Extension Homemakers

Rural Living

Three characteristics distinguished rural homemaking from urban homemaking: the physical distance between neighbors, the additional farm-related work, and, in the early years, the absence of amenities such as running water and electricity. The long distances between rural neighbors tended to isolate farm women from one another. When they did get together for a church ladies' aid or club meeting or to help one another with a project, it was a day-long affair.

In *Along the Waterloo Road*, Hazel Rahn Heider described an embroidery club formed by the women of the valley west of West Salem. Starting in 1926, Anna Miller, Clara Hauser, Marie Garbers, Minnie Heider, Emma Heider and Laura Hagen did needlework together as the Waterloo Embroidery Club. Hazel, who was unable to join the afternoon sessions because she taught school, looked forward to an invitation to join the group for supper. Some hostesses extended the event into an evening card party which included husbands. Because they played the game called 500, the evening group became known as the Waterloo 500 Club. Scheduling the Embroidery Club and the 500 Club on the same day was particularly significant for the women. Because they started their stitching in the afternoon and did not finish playing cards until late at night, this was the one day they did not have to help with the milking and other evening chores on the farm.[1]

In addition to child rearing and the standard housekeeping chores, the farmwife was also responsible for dairy chores, raising chickens, and cultivating large gardens. Besides regular family meals, the farmwife often cooked for the many workers who helped at threshing time. In order to put food on the table, she harvested from her garden, preserved the produce, milked the cows, fed and watered chickens, and gathered eggs for eating or selling. Egg money paid for the food she could not grow, the clothing she did not make, and for furnishings and supplies. Egg money was essential because the farm income barely covered the debt owed on land and machinery, the cost of supplies for next year's crop, and the price of new dairy cattle to enlarge the herd.

For most rural families in the first part of the twentieth century, running water meant running to bring it from the pump and then running

Vernetta Witte Romskog, who worked as a hired girl on the Larson farm on County M from 1930 to 1935, dressed in overalls to hoe and weed the large garden.

Vernetta Witte Romskog

outside to dispose of the dirty water. However, Irene Kreisel Schaller, born in 1922, grew up in a house on Brice's Prairie with a water holding tank in the attic. A gasoline engine pumped water up to the tank and then the force of gravity filled pipes that ran to the sink, providing water at the turn of a faucet. The Kreisels even had a limited amount of hot running water because some of the piping was routed through the stove. As long as the stove was hot, so was the water in those pipes.[2]

Urban areas of La Crosse County had electricity at the beginning of the century. However, this was not the case for most of the rural areas. Local Rural Electrification Administration (REA) cooperatives, formed in the 1930s, began to put in lines and make electrical connections to households. Utility companies supplied some rural areas, if the service was profitable, but farmers tended to shy away from the high cost of connecting to electrical lines as well as the high purchase price of electric appliances. The Trempealeau Electric Cooperative provided electricity to Brice's Prairie in 1938, but the rural electrification program did not guarantee electricity for all farms. In order to connect a valley or country road, the electric company required all farmers along that route to pay for a connection. Some farms did not particularly need the REA connection because they were generating

Mattie Larson tended the chickens on the farm that she owned with her brother and sister north of West Salem on County M, c. 1930-35.

Vernetta Witte Romskog

small amounts of electrical power with Delco Light Plants to run milking equipment or washing machines. During the Depression, many could not afford even a relatively modest connection fee.[3]

As of June 30, 1945, only forty-five percent of rural America was electrified.[4] Marge Hughes Gollnik's rural childhood home was among those that were not. Therefore, she was particularly pleased when a customer at the variety store where she worked gave her a used string of battery-operated Christmas lights. The color had chipped away from the seven bulbs, so she and her mother painted them with red fingernail polish. They wanted their tree to be special to celebrate Marge's older brother's discharge from the service at the end of World War II. Marge and her mother carefully tucked the lights into the tree. Then they tied angel hair at the top and draped it over the tree until the red light shimmered through each bough. Although their soldier did not return until after Christmas, the family left the decorated tree up in order to welcome him home. "It was risky to keep the tree up in a room with a heat[ing] stove, no water nearby, and no vacuum to remove the collecting dust, but keep it up we did," she said. When her brother finally returned, Marge triumphantly switched on the battery-powered lights to show him the beautiful tree his pending return had inspired. "What faith we had that the lights would work," Marge said, recalling that she never once checked the battery during the weeks that the tree stood.[5]

Many families worked their farm by themselves. When Howard Kinney and Minnie Christofferson became husband and wife in 1915, they began forty years of married life farming in Kinney Coulee, between Onalaska and La Crosse. Together they raised Guernsey cows, timothy, alfalfa, clover, oats and corn, plus cash crops of cabbage, peas, and sweet corn which they sold to the Onalaska Pickle and Canning Company. In addition to her household chores, Minnie did field work, milked the cows, and tended a large garden that she and Howard planted each year across the road from their house. Before their children were old enough to work alongside them, they employed a hired man during the heavy summer workload. Their daughter, Eleanor Kinney Robinson, described a typical summer day. After a breakfast of eggs, toast, potatoes, milk, coffee, meat, and sweets, the family all worked in the field, taking a mid-morning break for water. Eleanor prepared the noon meal, did the dishes and housework, and carried water to the family in the field. Minnie cooked supper while Eleanor and her brother, Tom, rounded up the cows for the evening milking.[6]

The Kinney family handled the haying on its own, but neighbors pitched in when it came time for threshing and silo filling. Whenever a large work crew appeared at a farm, the women prepared food in advance to feed the workers three times each day. For the mid-morning and mid-afternoon lunch breaks, the farmwife hauled drinking water, coffee, sandwiches, and freshly baked coffee cakes, rolls, doughnuts or cookies to the workers in the farmyard or field. The men ate the noontime dinner inside where the dining table was extended and planks were placed from chair to chair to provide enough seating. Ruth Bucklin, a farmwife from Sand Lake Coulee, usually fixed fried chicken, mashed potatoes, string beans, beet pickles, applesauce, home-baked bread, and apple pie. Myrtle Jorstad generally served home-cured sausage or beef and pork meatballs with gravy, boiled potatoes, vegetables she had canned from her garden, pickles, and poppyseed cake.[7]

When hired help was required to work the farm, the housework multiplied. A hired girl often became part of the household. Vernetta Witte

Romskog was the live-in hired girl for the Larson brother and sisters on their estate farm on County Highway M from 1930 to 1936. "There weren't buses to get to school," said Vernetta, whose family lived on a farm near West Salem. "So after graduating from eighth grade, I went to work instead of high school."[8] Vernetta helped cook, bake, can, launder, and clean. Because the barn had no electricity, the three hired hands milked the thirty cows by hand.

One day a week Vernetta did laundry for the seven people in the household with an electric wringer washer. Indoor plumbing provided a full bath upstairs plus "emergency centers" in the basement and on the first floor. "The job I really disliked was washing the separator, pails, cans, and utensils used for milking. Every morning I washed them on a wooden bench outside. During the winter, to avoid freezing, I cleaned them at a long bench in one end of the kitchen," she said.

The younger Larson sister, Clara, and Vernetta planted and tended the garden. The older sister, Mattie, tended the chickens. Vernetta also mowed the lawn with a push mower. "I often mowed after supper. The workers came in for supper at 4:30 so I always had the kitchen cleaned up by six. Sometimes the family would tell me to stop mowing for awhile because it was too hot and my face was all red. They treated me like family," she recalled.

In addition to doing labor-intensive work on the farm, Shirley Dummer became involved in the National Farmers Organization (NFO), which she described as "the original bargaining organization for farmers."[9] When she married in 1951, her husband, Francis, was farming with his brother and father. Shirley was responsible for the children, lawn mowing, household chores, gardening, canning, sewing and the "everlasting thankless job" of mending. When her brother-in-law went into the service a few years later, she added milking the cows seven days a week to her list. Her first job in the morning was milking, followed by feeding the cattle and cleaning the barn. She returned to domestic tasks in the house about 11 a.m. From 4:30 to 7:30 p.m. she was back in the barn for milking, feeding, and cleaning. The Dummers fed their family of six children with the meat they raised, berries and vegetables from their garden, and raw milk. They bought staples, such as flour, sugar and salt, and some fruit to round out the diet.

The Dummers joined the NFO in the early 1960s and became more active in the organization as their children grew and assumed more responsibility at home. They participated in the March 1967 milk dumping action when NFO members across the state "opened the spigots on their bulk tanks, fed hogs, calves and cattle with the milk, took baths in milk, and made butter and ice cream."[10] Some non-NFO farmers also joined in this one-week effort to achieve higher prices for milk producers. Some members of the community were "horrified" but others, including the Dummers' banker, were sympathetic.

Shirley Dummer was a Wisconsin delegate to the 1972 convention of the National Farmers Organization.

Shirley Dummer

Francis served as La Crosse County NFO president from the late 1960s to the late 1970s when their son Mike moved into that position. Shirley handled public relations for the group. Her job was to get farm and NFO issues covered by the news media. She remembered being really nervous the first few times a TV reporter came to the farm for an interview or a radio news director called to ask her opinion about a story that had just come over the wire service. "But the more I did it, the more confident I became. I learned to tell an interviewer or reporter, 'Don't use that. I want to reword it,'" she said.

During the meat boycott in the winter of 1973, the Dummers held livestock at home rather than sell them. While distributing leaflets in La Crosse supermarkets to explain the NFO position, Shirley received mixed reactions. "Most people thought the farmers must be getting rich. They didn't realize what the middleman was adding to the cost of meat in the stores," she said. The NFO held farmer-to-consumer hamburger sales several weekends during that winter. Business was slow the first day at the Causeway and Copeland location in La Crosse. The next day, however, when people saw a photo and story in the *La Crosse Tribune*, sales increased significantly. "Farmers trimmed out whole cows and turned all of the meat into hamburger for direct sales to customers. People said they didn't know it could taste so good," Shirley recalled.

Shirley's local activity led to a seat on the Wisconsin NFO board in 1974 where, for 20 years, she handled the group's public relations and also served as its chief editor for five years. Her responsibilities included speaking one-on-one and to large audiences, trying to keep NFO issues in the news, producing program booklets for state conventions, and working on the cookbooks which successfully raised money for the state and county organizations to carry on their work. She also wrote the state NFO history, *NFO in Wisconsin: A Dream, A Challenge, A Reality*, which was published in 1984.

Over the years the cost of farming increased because of high-priced equipment, higher taxes resulting from increasing land values, and high interest rates. In order to afford to continue farming, many farm wives added a job in town to their daily housework and farmwork. A 1983 survey of eight southwestern Wisconsin counties, including La Crosse, found that thirty-seven percent of farm wives worked "off-farm."[11] At the same time that the Homemakers Clubs were broadening their scope outward from the home into the community, these jobs took farm wives beyond the sphere of the family farm into their communities as well.

Making Do

During World War I, Americans had a taste of rationing when they conserved fuels and foods. To conserve oil and grease, West Salem garages discontinued all unnecessary and free service and inspections for vehicles.[1] Patriotic citizens observed wheatless Mondays, which meant no bread, and meatless Tuesdays. They also preserved the bounty of their gardens to keep their larders stocked. Even the La Crosse Normal School had a victory garden on its campus.

Cora Olson had charge of the sugar distribution in the twenty-first ward of La Crosse during World War I. Because that ward had the largest families, it had more children, 532 under the age of sixteen, than any of the other wards. She said, "Naturally [they] needed more sugar than our general allotment. I had more than one squabble with our sugar man, Mr. [Gysbert] Van Steenwyk. From five o'clock in the afternoon until ten in the evening I would be busy writing sugar orders. My porch and living room would be filled with fathers of these large families and smoke — also a lot of war talk."[2]

"Making do" was a way of life for everyone from 1929 to 1945. Incomes plummeted during the Depression. People had little money because they did not have jobs or because their customers and patients could not pay for their goods and services. Town people paid what they could or bartered. Farm families generally paid their medical bills with produce. Carroll Gundersen, whose husband was a urologist with the Gundersen Clinic, used their garage as a receiving station: "The medical profession got paid in potatoes and apples and turkeys and chickens and things like this.... someone [would] call and say 'I am bringing fifteen turkeys in.' Then when they came to the garage it was my job to call the clinic and say 'I have fifteen turkeys.' Then the turkeys would be distributed around to the doctors as far as they went [or] they would come with two or three bushels of carrots. Then I would say, 'Get the word out, if anyone wants carrots I have them in the garage,'" she said.[3]

Dr. N. Philip Anderson of Grandview Hospital also received payment in produce. In addition to feeding their large household which included seven children, his wife used the abundant food to feed the hungry. Job hunters and transients hopped off the train at Cass Street just east of Losey Boulevard and walked the few blocks to the Anderson home at 2027 Cass. The Andersons' daughter, Priscilla Dvorak, remembered there was a white

"X" marked on the curb which indicated this house was a place to get a meal. "I remember the men lined up at our back steps for soup or whatever my mother had prepared," Priscilla said.[4]

Money for new clothing was scarce, too, so women did their best to alter and to mend as their families grew and wore out clothing. Florence Munson sewed underthings for herself and her daughters from flour sacks.[5]

The U.S. economy began to recover in the late 1930s as the nation produced supplies for the European countries already at war. People found work again, and they had money to spend. However, as soon as the United States entered World War II, there were fewer and fewer domestic goods to purchase with that money. Instead, people were encouraged to invest in defense stamps and bonds.

Rationing during World War II complicated household life. The first commodity to be rationed after the United States declared war on Japan in December 1941 was rubber which was imported from the South Pacific. Tires for cars and bicycles became scarce. People kept their cars in the garage and walked or took the bus or streetcar. Kathy Schnur Witzke's father sold the family car in 1941 and did not get another until 1948. "We biked or walked," she said of those years.[6] Delivery service was cut back. In January 1942, local milk dealers reduced home delivery of milk, and grocers restricted home delivery to two times per day. Orders called in by 9 a.m. would be delivered by noon. There was a 3 p.m. deadline for late afternoon delivery.[7]

Fuel rationing cut down automobile travel and reduced home heating temperatures. Gasoline purchases were limited to four gallons per week beginning November 30, 1942, and restricted even further the following summer. La Crosse homes connected to city heat continued to receive seventy degree steam heat. People who depended on fuel oil received coupons entitling them to the number of gallons needed to achieve sixty-five degrees. Allotments varied with the number of people in the family, the number under four years old, and the number of rooms that could be closed off.

Food rationing began when, in early May 1942, seventy-six centers opened to register the county's population of 70,000. To register, one family member (usually the mother) gave names, addresses, height, weight, color of hair and eyes, age, and sex of each member of the immediate family who required a ration card. Since the first commodity covered by this ration system was sugar, each registrant also reported the amount of white and brown sugar on hand in her home.[8]

As more and more foods such as meat, coffee and canned goods were rationed, the housewife not only needed to budget money for food, but she also had to figure out how to get the most benefit from the ration stamps. In a March 1, 1943, *La Crosse Tribune and Leader-Press* article, housewives were advised to study the shopping list and the point value chart before leaving the house.

> *The real trick of 'point rationing' is for each family to figure out,*
> *considering the point values of each item, just what it wants to*
> *get with its 48 points per person during March [and] to space*
> *purchases so that points will be left for month-end needs.*[9]

Coffee and sugar were rationed because they were imported. Other items, such as meat and canned fruits and vegetables, were in smaller supply for the civilian population because the U.S. military had first priority. Because leather was needed for military boots, civilian shoes made of leather were rationed although shoes made of fabric did not require ration stamps.

Shoppers dealt not only with the rules and regulations of rationing but also with the attitude of others who watched them and the purchases they made. Ruth Snodgrass described the rude treatment she received from a store clerk while buying bananas: "I bought five bananas [for my mother who lived next door with three others and for me] and [the clerk] thought it was terrible I bought that many bananas. Well it was just one apiece but I remember the clerk yelling at me like I was buying the store."[10]

Newspapers carried suggestions for conserving soap. An article from a series prepared by the local branch of the American Association of University Women described the advantages of buying soap in quantity, the proper type of soap to use for each household purpose, the variation in price and general tips on prolonging the lifetime of a single bar.[11]

In another effort to waste nothing, women saved and reused cooking fats and oils. Muriel Mitchell decided to use rendered chicken fat in her cookie recipes. She tried it once or twice before giving in to her family's objection to the taste.[12] Karo corn syrup, molasses and honey were used as substitutes for sugar in baking.

Even before Pearl Harbor, housewives surrendered aluminum pots and pans they used infrequently to be reused in making parts for airplanes, tanks, battle ships, and other defense material. Tin cans were also saved for munitions production. Boy Scouts collected the scrap metal in La Crosse. Women's groups organized the collection effort in other parts of the county. In early 1943, the Girl Scouts collected 12,000 pairs of discarded nylon and silk stockings which were shipped off to be made into powder bags and parachutes. In their place, women could buy rayon hosiery described as "victorious and glorious" in advertisements but "crawly" by those who wore them.[13] Ruth Snodgrass remembered how scarce nylons were during the war: "Every Saturday morning you could ride up to Winona. They had a nylon factory there. You had to stand in line, and it was a block long for one pair of nylons."[14]

Women learned to cope with other wartime shortages as well. Because worn-out tools and furnishings could not be replaced, repairs had to suffice. Women enrolled in classes at La Crosse Adult and Vocational School to learn how to solder kitchen utensils, make simple furniture, fix faucets and locks, and repair appliances.[15] They also attended home nursing classes sponsored by the Red Cross. Doctors and nurses were at a premium, and these classes were an attempt to reduce the number of incidents which required medical attention by teaching about good health and safety practices, communicable and other diseases, and procedures for taking care of a patient at home and home births. Several qualified people, usually nurses, taught these courses throughout the county. Lilly Hendrickson already was working long hours at the La Crosse Hospital plus, with her husband, raising three young children. Nonetheless, she volunteered to teach adults about nutrition, taking care of minor emergencies, giving bed baths, and living with rationing. "I really enjoyed the evening students because they were eager to learn how to take better care of their families and themselves. I still have the Certificate of Appreciation from President Truman for my Red Cross teaching," she said.[16]

No one seemed to begrudge the wartime concessions, and it was not all drudgery. Groups of young single women attended USO dances at Camp McCoy. Once or twice a week they boarded a bus from the vocational school in La Crosse to attend the well-chaperoned events at the camp. Priscilla Anderson Dvorak remembered attending the dances with friends. Her parents did not like the idea, but they did not stop her from going. "Everything was so well chaperoned, there was no need for concern," Priscilla recalled. Because many of the local young men were gone, this was a chance to dance and talk and laugh "with fellows just as nice as the ones from home," she said.[17]

Housing was at a premium during and after World War II. Soldiers' wives strained the already tight supply of housing in La Crosse because Camp McCoy was a last stop for military training before servicemen left the country. The wives wanted to be close to their husbands before they were shipped overseas. Some of these renters, who generally came from the warmer climates of southern states, suffered from insufficient heat in their living quarters. The drafty apartments were caused not so much by stingy landlords as they were by fuel conservation.[18]

There had been very little construction during the Depression, and it took a while for manufacturers to shift from defense to domestic production after World War II. Wartime marriages increased the number of families looking for homes of their own after the war. Some families doubled up until a dwelling became available. Della (Feak) and Oscar Berg and their young daughter alternated living with his parents and her father until Oscar found a house for them near downtown Bangor. Knowing that others wanted that house, or any house for that matter, he bought it quickly without waiting to consult his wife. As soon as they moved in, another young couple asked to rent their upstairs rooms even though they were not partitioned into a separate apartment.[19]

In 1941, Eleanore Wollschlaeger and her husband bought property on the east edge of La Crosse adjacent to the golf course and developed plans to build a new home. Every January their contractor put in a request for a permit to build in the spring. Each year, until 1946, the request was denied. One day their contractor called and excitedly declared, "We can build, we can build, we can build."[20] The Wollschlaegers had planned for one bath on each floor of their two-story house, but their permit allowed only a single bathroom for their family of three. They had a hard time finding oak flooring until their contractor managed to swap materials he had on hand for oak from Erickson Hardwoods.

Florence Olson Whiting returned to La Crosse with her husband and their two sons at the end of the war. They made plans to build a new home at that time, but instead extended their stay with Florence's mother while they waited for various building materials to become available. Florence said, "We went all over the state to get the hardwood … we got the only bath tub left in La Crosse … it was a big tub and that suited us just fine because we had tall boys…. We had such a time to get lumber. The lumber was quite green…. Finally, when it came, I said, 'I'll ride out with you on the truck' because I was afraid somebody else would get it. And they said, 'You can't, they won't let you.' And I said, 'I'm going to anyway,' and I did, I rode on the truck…. The kids and I helped take the lumber off and placed it so air would go through so it would be weathered and not so green."[21]

The years 1929 to 1945 were challenging for homemakers. During the Depression they did their best to prolong the usefulness of every garment and household gadget because they did not know when there would be money to replace things. During World War II, it was the shortage of commodities and services, not of money, that posed the challenge to taking care of the family. Even after the war ended, it took time for factories to convert from wartime to domestic production.

Beyond the Home

La Crosse County women cite two significant developments that expanded their world in the twentieth century — driving and entering the work force. Although cars were not plentiful in the early part of the twentieth century, women who owned and drove them experienced a new sense of freedom. Florence Olson (Whiting) purchased a Model-T Ford in 1922. She had just graduated from the La Crosse Normal School and still lived at home on South Avenue with her parents and younger sister. No one else in her family owned a car. Her father rode his bicycle to work at the Hotel Stoddard Barber Shop in downtown La Crosse. Florence, her mother, and her sister walked or took the streetcar wherever they went. She recalled,

> I bought the car and I never had driven a car and one of my church boyfriends went along with me ... out to Salzer Field ... that's where I learned how to drive. That very late afternoon I went downtown, imagine, and I picked up my father — he didn't know I had a car. Papa sat in the front seat and he had one leg out. He was scared to death because I'd never driven before. I had to borrow some money from the bank — the old Batavian Bank — I was just a young person teaching. (I had a contract to teach the next year but that wasn't money right there.) Of course they wanted to know who would be responsible for me, and I said, "I've got my father," and they got a big kick out of it because they knew my father, and I said, "Well, I've got a perfectly good father." I got the money all right. I think I paid $500. It was almost a brand new car.[1]

Florence used her car to travel back and forth on weekends between her teaching position in Sheboygan and her home in La Crosse. When she finished with it, she gave the car to her sister who used it to travel between La Crosse and her teaching job in Watertown.

The second significant development that affected women's view of themselves and their abilities occurred during the world wars when they entered the work force in larger numbers than ever before. Women whose mothers had never left their homes found the boundaries of their lives widening into the workplace where they, along with many others, gained new skills and earned paychecks. Many young unskilled women who found better pay and work schedules in factories during World War I did not return to domestic service in private homes after the war. Before World War II, most working women were young and single. By VE-Day, the majority were married.[2] They were doing their part for the war effort and waiting for their husbands to return from the service. At the end of World War II, there was an effort by government, media, and social scientists to move women out of the labor force and back into their homes.[3] Those who could live comfortably on their husband's income did stay at home, at least until the youngest child started school. Some women continued working both inside and outside the home because their families needed the additional income.

Despite changes in mobility and work status, women, for the most part, remained the primary caregivers and housekeepers throughout the century. Between World Wars I and II, in an effort to combat infant mortality, mothers were encouraged to watch scrupulously over their children's health. Their efforts, in conjunction with medical advances, paid off. The national infant mortality rate, which was 100 per 1,000 live births in 1915, dropped to 55.7 in 1935 and to 13.8 in 1978. Changing child-rearing standards also added the social and mental development of the child to the mother's traditional concerns of cleanliness, health, and discipline. Mothers attended child-study meetings, became involved in their local schools, read books and magazines about children, and supervised them in playgrounds. They chauffeured their children to medical and dental appointments, piano lessons, baseball practice, and social events.[4]

It would be logical to expect that timesavers such as running water, gas and electricity, modern appliances, convenience foods, and fast food restaurants would have made a housewife's life less demanding and time consuming. Studies showed, however, that full-time homemakers spent approximately the same amount of time taking care of children and keeping house throughout the twentieth century.[5]

In 1924, the typical housewife who was not employed outside the home spent fifty-two hours each week on family care, home care, clothing and linen care, food preparation, shopping, and managerial tasks. Her counterpart in the latter half of the century spent less time preparing food and cleaning up after meals but more time managing the home, caring for her family, and traveling to and from her home to obtain goods and services. As more food, clothing, and cleaning products were produced outside the home, women spent more time shopping, comparing, and deciding what purchases were best for the family. Supermarkets that stocked a larger variety of items often offered lower prices than the small neighborhood stores but usually were more than walking distance from home. The appearance of the two-car family made it possible for the housewife to travel greater distances to shop for food, clothing, and household items. It should be noted, however, that even into the 1970s and 1980s, the second "car" for some local families was not a car. Some women, like Beth Roskos, rode a bicycle with baskets and an extra seat to carry parcels and young children.[6] Others pulled their children in a wagon or sled as they went on errands close to home.

The one household task which changed little in terms of the time required was laundry. For most families in the early part of the century, wardrobes contained the basic necessities, and clothing was worn for several days. Bathing and laundry, and sometimes baking, seemed to go hand in hand. Marian Ramlow recalled that as a child in the 1920s her family put on clean clothes after a bath and wore them until the next bath. In her childhood, Margaret Fish associated baths with the smell of baking bread because her mother always baked on Saturday to warm the kitchen for the weekly baths that night. Indoor plumbing, washing machines, and vacuum cleaners increased the standards of cleanliness and, therefore, the time spent cleaning people, clothing, and the home. For example, as machines and wrinkle-free fabrics alleviated the drudgery of wash day, people became accustomed to larger wardrobes and wearing only clean clothing. Therefore, just as much, if not more, time was spent doing laundry at the end of the twentieth century as at the beginning.

All in all, the total time spent by a full-time homemaker fluctuated very little throughout the course of the century. In fact it rose slightly to fifty-five hours a week in the 1960s. However, for the married woman who also worked outside the home, modern conveniences made it possible to maintain decent standards in the home without the help of assistants and without a full-time commitment to housework. Women working forty hours a week outside the home in the 1960s spent twenty-six hours a week on household tasks, nearly fifty percent less than housewives who worked in their homes full-time.

The woman's role as responsible consumer became increasingly important as more products appeared on the market and as advertising in newspapers, magazines, radio, and television bombarded the citizenry. For example, disposable paper products such as cups, plates, napkins, diapers, even dresses and curtains, reduced some household chores but later raised concerns about the environment and the use or overuse of natural resources. Sunday drives, a favorite family pastime that resumed when World War II gas and rubber rationing ended, were cut back once again by the oil embargo of 1973. Americans shopped for smaller, fuel-efficient cars, turned down thermostats to conserve home heating fuel, and started recycling more and using less so they would be less dependent on imported oil.

Women in La Crosse County have long distinguished themselves as homemakers. That term has always included more than raising children and keeping a clean house. Many women have taken the morals, values, and skills they cultivated in the home out into their communities to benefit others. Sewing skills honed on family garments, for example, were used to sew quilts and comforters for the needy either in their own communities or in distant missions. If a woman didn't enter the workplace, she turned her energies to community causes such as libraries, school policies and funding, and to social services for the young, the aged, and the disadvantaged. By 1965, twenty-two million women throughout the United States (three-fourths of whom were married) produced about fourteen billion dollars worth of unpaid services in their roles as PTA heads, scout leaders, hospital aides, museum guides, and fund-raisers for worthy causes.[7] A La Crosse County woman of the twentieth century who described herself primarily as a homemaker more than likely had spent time in the workplace and/or had been active in the larger community through her church or as a member of a cultural or civic improvement club.

In the
Workplace

[If] a woman could contribute more by her earning power than by her attempts to stretch the scarce resources of a household, then a job was a practical necessity. Women who need to work for economic reasons have constituted and still constitute the vast majority of wage-earning women in America.

Alice Kessler-Harris[1]

Women have always been a crucial component of American labor. Their jobs changed as the nation shifted from a primarily agrarian society to a predominantly urban one. In pre-industrial society, nearly every man, woman and child worked, but rarely for wages. Within the home, each member of the family labored to produce the food, clothing, and furnishings necessary to sustain the household. During the century-long industrialization process of the 1800s, several production activities moved from the home to the factory. When the twentieth century began, domestic servants and waitresses accounted for about thirty-three percent of women in the workforce. Nearly twenty-five percent were factory workers. Ten percent worked in agriculture. Approximately ten percent were salesclerks. Another ten percent were professionals in fields like nursing, library science, social work, medicine, journalism, and law. Women who worked in their own homes as laundresses, seamstresses, and boarding house keepers comprised the remaining twelve percent.[2]

When there was a shortage of men available for work during wartime, women were encouraged to enter the workplace. When jobs were at a premium, women were urged to stay at home. For example, during the Depression, social thought and public policy pressured women to give up their jobs to men. That happened again at the end of World War II. Women who enjoyed their work outside the home as well as the paycheck that went with it were reluctant to leave their jobs to make way for returning soldiers and sailors.

It was an irony of the post-World War II advertising culture that, at the same time it promoted the home as the domain of women, it also influenced them to join the workforce in order to afford more products and services which resulted from increased expectations and an increased standard of living. In the 1960s and 1970s, women began to lobby for changes in public policy which would improve their employment and career possibilities.

Healers and Helpers

Women's traditional role of caregiver translated into employment in the field of health and medicine. Women cared for others as nurses and midwives. They also became physicians, although in much smaller numbers. As medical knowledge and technology expanded, so did the need for supporting services in health and medicine.

Nursing

Traditionally, nursing was viewed as an extension of a woman's domestic responsibilities, and, prior to the 1850s, nurses usually were members of the servant class.[1] In the mid-nineteenth century, nursing leaders began to define nursing as a womanly service of self-sacrifice and religious devotion. Thus, nursing developed as one of the few opportunities for women to pursue paid work that was considered inherently feminine and acceptable to the larger society. From the 1860s onward, nurses received their training in hospitals, for the most part in hospital schools of nursing that combined classes with on-the-job training.

Physicians trained five members of the Franciscan Sisters of Perpetual Adoration (FSPA) to serve as nurses for St. Francis Hospital when it opened in La Crosse in 1883. They were the first nurses in western Wisconsin.[2] In 1901, two lay women entered the training program. The following year St. Francis Hospital formally opened its school of nursing. Within a few years, La Crosse had three more nursing schools connected with local hospitals: Lutheran in 1902, La Crosse in 1903, and Grandview in 1915. Many local and area women throughout the twentieth century chose to enter nursing because training was so accessible. These nursing graduates served in local hospitals, did private duty nursing, served overseas during both world wars, had careers in public health, and worked in industry.

Just after World War I, a 1919 St. Francis Alumnae Association publication described the efforts of its members on both sides of the Atlantic Ocean: "Our graduates are wrestling with disease and death on this side and the ravishing destruction of war on the other." While some served soldiers in Europe, others cared for local victims of the deadly influenza pandemic of 1918 and 1919, which claimed half-a-million victims in the United States. Marie Ruetten Flynn, class of 1921, remembered her student years, "The Franciscans worked side by side with their nurses, putting in the same incredibly long hours on crowded hospital wards and at the bedside of sick and dying patients. Their feet swelled, blistered and bled after grueling hours on duty."[3]

Almost every aspect of the nurse's life was under the control of her nursing supervisors and instructors. In the fall of 1994, alumnae of the La Crosse Lutheran Hospital Training School for Nurses, which closed in 1932, reminisced about their schooling and subsequent nursing assignments in the 1920s and 1930s.[4]

Margaret Steuernagel Griffel chose her school because of its Lutheran affiliation. "We started each day just before seven in the morning with chapel," she said. Morning duties followed chapel. Each student had four patients. Dorothy Ahlstrom Harman recalled, "We mostly gave bed baths, but we also learned to give enemas and, after our first year, we gave hypodermics or injections. They mainly were sedatives — sleeping medication, pain medication." The students had to have the patients and their rooms looking their best by the time the doctors made rounds. Nursing students were expected to clean the rooms, dust the transoms, and polish the doorknobs. Although they did not have to mop the floors, they occasionally aired mattresses on the porches of the old Lutheran Hospital building.

Nurses were expected to be deferential to the physicians. "When a doctor approached the desk, you stood up, said, 'Good morning, Doctor,' and gave him your chair," Dorothy recalled. Nurses had very little decision-making responsibility. They were to make patients as comfortable as possible given their limited medicinal arsenal. "Before penicillin, fevers were always a problem. All we could do was give aspirin, sponge baths, and fluids," Dorothy said. If a patient recovered from pneumonia, credit was due to the nursing care because there were no miracle drugs to treat the illness.

In exchange for their work, nurses-in-training received room and board, laundry services, a small stipend — it was so small they called it "stamp money" — and afternoon classes. After class the students returned to the hospital wards and rooms for an evening shift.

During their three years of training, the students were closely supervised. They lived in the hospital's nurses home and were allowed to visit their families at home one day a week. They could go out socially on weekends but had to respect a curfew. Third-year students were allowed to spend Christmas Day with their families. Freshmen had to wait for seniors to return before they could leave to visit their families. Despite the restrictions, the alumnae fondly recalled a holiday tradition at Lutheran Hospital, "We were up and in uniform very early on Christmas morning. We paired up and carried lighted candles through the hospital as we sang carols to the patients. There were tears in their eyes and tears in ours, too."

Prior to World War II, hospital schools' student nurses provided a pool of cheap labor. While financially beneficial to the hospitals, that practice precipitated widespread unemployment and under-employment for trained nurses. Upon graduation,

Airing mattresses was one of the student nursing chores at Lutheran Hospital in La Crosse, c. 1920.

Gundersen Lutheran Medical Center

a few were hired as supervisors or charge nurses for a hospital floor. Most graduates left the hospital, diploma in hand, to work as private-duty nurses. Before intensive care units existed, a patient who needed round-the-clock care hired a private duty nurse. She would set up a cot in the patient's hospital room or sickroom at home and provide twenty hours of care for four or five dollars a day. The Lutheran Hospital nursing alumnae recalled, "We napped while the patient slept. We got a four-hour break when the family came to visit. That gave us enough time to bathe and change our uniform."

Margaret Steuernagel Griffel graduated in 1930 and went to work as nursing supervisor and obstetrical supervisor in the Spring Grove, Minnesota, hospital. "I made my own surgical packs and OB [obstetrical] packs, but I felt overpaid at seventy-five dollars a month," she said.

Clarissa Larson Espeland did private duty nursing in small communities in Minnesota from the time she graduated in 1930 until Lutheran Hospital called her back in August 1934. "They offered me a job as a night duty nurse. I worked from 7 p.m. to 7 a.m. and that included three hours for sleep. I was paid forty-five dollars a month plus room and board," she recalled.

Upon graduation in 1931, Agnes Burt Garthus Amble returned to her parents' farm in Independence, Wisconsin, because there were no positions open at Lutheran Hospital. A month or so later, however, the hospital hired her as a general duty nurse for thirty-five dollars a month plus room and board. "I was glad to have a good place to stay, very good work, and good food," she recalled. Agnes left nursing work when she married A. S. Garthus in 1935.

Lutheran Hospital decided to close its school of nursing in 1932. The students had given much free service to the hospital. However, increased class requirements recommended by the state review board meant the students would have less time to give nursing care. In addition, the state nursing board gave notice that, unless certain standards were met, the nursing school would be removed from the list of accredited schools. Closing the school turned out to be an expensive decision. Without it, Lutheran Hospital no longer had a pool of student nurses upon which to draw. Instead it had to hire and pay graduate nurses. Dorothy Harman remembered Dr. Gunnar Gundersen saying, "That was the biggest mistake we ever made."

During the Depression, the move toward hospital care, the lack of money for everything including health care, and the oversupply of nurses essentially destroyed the private-duty market and led to widespread unemployment.[5] Employment opportunities rapidly improved, however, with the approach of World War II and the continued expansion of hospital care. The war demanded nurses and doctors to serve soldiers in the European and Pacific theaters. It also required more from those who remained on the homefront.

In 1943, Evelyn "Evie" Helgerson Hoover, a member of the Army Nurse Corps, was shipped to a field hospital in England. On D-Day, her unit of Red Cross nurses was on the coast watching Allied forces head across the English Channel. Her group left a day or two later to serve with the 100th General Hospital which was operating as an evacuation unit in France. During the Battle of the Bulge, Evie recalled, "The hospital had been set up too close to the front so we were ordered to pack up and move back." Evie saw the use of new and old techniques. Penicillin, the new wonder drug, for which the military had top priority, "saved many, many lives during the war." The ancient debridement technique of using maggots to clean out wounds was "kind of a sickening sight but did a surprisingly good job of cleaning up the infected area." After the war ended in Europe, the nurses were sent to a staging area in Marseilles, France, where Evie and others waited, apprehensively, to be shipped to Japan. One nurse, determined not to go, took the drastic action of having all her teeth pulled. While Evie was on a truck headed for the ship, word came that the Japanese had surrendered. "We had celebrated for days when the war in Europe was over. Now we celebrated even longer and harder," she recalled.[6]

Evie took a leave from nursing when she married and had three babies. In 1958, she succumbed to repeated calls from a friend and nurse at Lutheran Hospital, Hannah Olson, who kept telling Evie her help was needed because there was a shortage of nurses. Evie started part-time on the hospital's pediatric ward and eventually became head nurse in charge of the evening shift on that ward. At the time she was hired, few nurses had pediatric training or were willing to serve in pediatrics.

Despite an unwritten rule that nurses were not to move from hospital to clinic or vice versa — in other words, no raiding allowed — the Gundersen Clinic pediatricians invited Evie to come to work with them in 1964. She made the move. Nine years later, she was ready to forge another new path. Twice a month for a year, she traveled to Madison for training as a pediatric nurse practitioner. For ten more years, she worked at Gundersen Clinic as a fully qualified independent practitioner. Considering the restrictions of the past, when nurses were not even allowed to take blood pressures, Evie had come a long way. She performed complete physical assessments, consulted with physicians, and wrote orders. After retirement in 1983, Evie continued to practice nursing, working part-time for the Visiting Nurses Association.

Myrtle Onsrud, who graduated from Lutheran Hospital Training School for Nurses in 1932, served in the Pacific theater during World War II. First she was assigned to a platoon of ships and then to a floating hospital, the U.S.S. Comfort. The brother of Myrtle's classmate, Marguerite Schroeder Figge Goodermote, was wounded in battle in the Pacific and ended up on the U.S.S. Comfort. When he was told there was a nurse from Wisconsin on board, he said, "I bet her name is Myrtle." According to Marguerite, "Myrtle visited my brother every day. He was served ice cream and got the royal treatment."

Myrtle, who later was seriously injured during an attack on the U.S.S. Comfort, recalled, "We were involved in about seven invasions, picking up and treating patients, before a kamikaze dove into the ship in Okinawa."[7] She spent a year recuperating, first on Guam, then in the United States. Eventually she returned to Lutheran Hospital where she served as assistant director of nursing in the 1950s and 1960s.

Local hospitals were severely understaffed during World War II because so many doctors and nurses were serving in the war. Those who worked on the homefront often worked longer than normal shifts and carried extra duties. For example, the nurse in charge of obstetrics at La Crosse Hospital also was responsible for stoking the furnace with coal. Lilly Hendrickson, a supervising nurse at La Crosse Hospital during the war, recalled, "We had to do things we weren't really trained to do." Although she had not been trained, she did have the experience of starting IVs and doing male catheterizations — procedures that were usually done only by doctors or interns in those days.[8]

Many of the La Crosse Hospital patients were GIs from Camp McCoy, Lilly recalled: "Some of them were disturbed. One time, one was headed out the door in the middle of a cold night with just his gown on. A nurse grabbed at him, but he slipped out of his gown and the hospital. We called the police, but they couldn't find him. Later there was a rapping at the window and he was outside asking, 'Can I come in? My feet are cold.'"

After the war, Lilly tried something different. "Sig Wateski in personnel at Auto-Lite called to see if I'd like to be an industrial nurse. 'You'll have good hours and weekends off; it would be a nice break for you,' he said. And I just loved it. I was on my own. I had to make quick decisions. There were serious injuries to take care of. Sometimes a worker would be going too fast and have an accident and lose some fingers or part of his hand. When one of the roofs leaked, the rain was dripping in. When it hit the electric machinery, it seriously shocked two of the workers." Lilly treated medical problems, like rashes and infections, and bandaged slivers and cuts. "I also did a little counseling if people were careless about their personal hygiene," she added. She dealt with the union and management, too. If management wanted an employee who had been ill or injured to return to work and the union did not think he was ready, Lilly consulted with the doctor who had treated the employee and worked something out to everyone's satisfaction. "Sometimes I got caught in between, but they all respected the nurse," she said.

Before 1950, many hospitals used the constant turnover of recently-trained nurses to keep skills up-to-date on the wards. This system proved less effective after 1950. More graduate nurses were working on the wards, more nurses remained on the job for longer periods of service, and more nurses continued to work after marriage. Nursing required more breadth and flexibility than hospital schools of nursing generally provided.[9] National nursing leaders pushed for a unified standard of education that demanded the baccalaureate degree for all nurses. They were only partially successful in achieving this goal and were compelled to accept a two-tiered system in which a baccalaureate nurse exercised authority over her colleagues who continued to train in hospitals or technical/vocational schools.[10]

Baccalaureate Nursing Program

Because of the vision and persistence of Sister Grace Clare Beznouz, the first chair of Viterbo College's Nursing Department, La Crosse County gained a baccalaureate program in nursing. La Crosse Hospital closed its nurses training school in 1925, Lutheran Hospital in 1932, and Grandview Hospital in 1934. As sponsors of the last existing training program, the Franciscan Sisters were conscious of their responsibility to provide nurses for the La Crosse community. Therefore, the closing of St. Francis' school in 1970 was timed to coordinate with the first graduating class of baccalaureate nurses from Viterbo College in 1971.

Sister Grace Clare graduated from the St. Francis School of Nursing in 1943, served as a nurse, and then taught at Viterbo from 1955 to 1965. "During those ten years, I saw the direction nursing was taking," she said. "I came to believe that nursing had to get into higher education. Nurses had been taught skills, but they were not liberally educated."[11]

Sister Grace Clare's proposal to develop a baccalaureate nursing program met opposition. "The biggest problem I encountered was that St. Francis graduates were highly respected in this community. They were considered skilled practitioners, and no one — patients, adminstrators nor medical staff — saw why things should change," Sister Grace Clare recalled. Hospital administrators eventually realized that the existing diploma program could jeopardize insurance income. Health insurance companies began to question whether they should pay for care given by nursing students rather than by nurses.

Using her public relations and negotiating skills, Sister Grace Clare spent three years meeting with small groups of doctors and adminstrators to convince them the change would be beneficial. "My conviction was that education is important for everyone, and I love nursing so I wanted nurses to be educated women.... We kept the best part of the St. Francis diploma program." In the mid-1960s, a typical day for a St. Francis nursing student began at 7 a.m. sharp when she received reports and instruction from the head nurse. In daily conferences, student and teacher shared ideas, formed new care plans for patients, and practiced skills and techniques. The freshman students took frequent exams in anatomy and physiology, biology, and chemistry. Junior students began caring for medical and surgical patients, giving them baths and injections. Senior students learned about childbirth and worked in pediatrics. Each afternoon until four, students attended classes that ranged from Christian marriage to pharmacology. Study time followed supper with lights out at 9 p.m.[12]

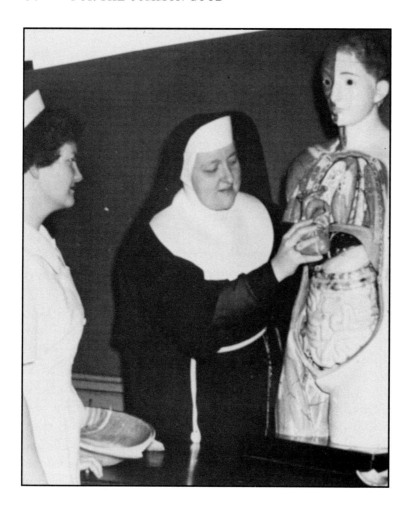

Sister Grace Clare
Beznouz, who became
the first chair of the
Viterbo College
Department of
Nursing, taught
anatomy and
physiology to the
St. Francis nursing
students, 1955-1965.

*Franciscan Skemp
Healthcare*

In accordance with Sister Grace Clare's proposal, the Viterbo program added liberal arts and supportive classes so each graduate would be a skilled practitioner and well-educated. When the baccalaureate program received criticism for not having enough clinical time, Sister Grace Clare's response was, "'It's not length of time but quality.' Our clinicals were very structured. The students were to receive an education not just to give service. We had clinicals at both St. Francis and Lutheran from the start. The two hospitals were very different; we recognized that as a strength."

There were other differences between the diploma program at St. Francis and the baccalaureate program at Viterbo. St. Francis had not admitted married women because students were to study, work, and sleep on the premises. Viterbo had no such restriction. St. Francis' program was for women only. Men were accepted into the college's nursing program starting with the 1969-70 school year. Although Viterbo was not co-educational at the time, a study in the spring of 1969 "revealed that hospitals were eager to have male nurses and that the [Viterbo] faculty favored admitting men to the collegiate program."[13] Also, there were men who had served as medics in the Vietnam War who were interested in becoming nurses, and the federal government awarded grants to co-educational schools.[14]

Practical Nursing Program

At the same time that the St. Francis School of Nursing was phasing out its three-year diploma program and Viterbo College was developing its four-year baccalaureate program, Coleman Technical Institute (CTI, now Western Wisconsin Technical College) was establishing the first practical nursing program in La Crosse County. This new nursing program had been on the drawing board for several years when Maddeline Schuldes was hired to launch it. Maddeline was a graduate of the hospital nursing program at Johns Hopkins in Baltimore. She earned her degree at Ohio State University and taught there before moving to La Crosse where she became active in the Medical Auxiliary and a member of its Scholarship Committee. It was when this committee decided to give a scholarship to a nursing student at CTI that Maddeline discovered there were no students because the program did not yet exist. She contacted the school's administrator, Arthur Jordan, to ask how she could help. In late 1964, with three young children and a husband with a very busy medical practice, she reluctantly accepted responsibility for planning and implementing a program to train a new breed of nurses.[15]

Florence Campbell, the first instructor Maddeline hired, brought to the program academic credentials from the University of Iowa School of Nursing as well as her teaching and professional experience. At the time, she worked at Lutheran Hospital training nursing assistants in a two-week course. Sometimes, the hospital's staffing shortages became so acute that Florence had to put aside her teaching duties and fill in as a nurse. When that happened, she sent her students to the hospital wards to observe experienced nursing assistants. Though the students seemed to be learning, Florence was frustrated with the fragmentation of their training. She looked forward to the chance to address this problem through nurse education.[16]

In 1966, after a year of preliminary work, Maddeline and Florence began training their first class of practical nurses — a group of women they both described as "exceptional. Many of these bright, mature, and highly motivated women already had raised a family or had been working in a hospital and had long dreamed of becoming qualified nurses." Following Wisconsin state regulations and guidelines from the National League for Nursing, Florence and Maddeline developed a program that included intense classes and clinical experiences. The schedule for this one-year program took place during the normal working day unlike the three-year hospital programs which frequently required students to work split p.m. (3 to 11) and night (11 to 7) shifts. Practical nursing, therefore, provided a new career option for women who, because of family responsibilities, could not devote themselves to the demands and inflexibilities of hospital school training.

Both Maddeline and Florence admitted they "overtaught" these first students, "We tried to teach them everything in one year that diploma nurses covered in three." Their zeal paid off. All of their students passed the state board exam for practical nursing and found gainful employment.

One member of the first class of practical nurses was Dorothy Mercier. Dorothy worked as a nurses' aide at Grandview Hospital for fifteen years before enrolling in CTI's program. Upon her graduation in June of 1967, she went to work part-time with patients in the clinical areas of Lutheran Hospital. By 1968, she was working as a scrub nurse in the hospital's operating rooms. In order to anticipate the surgeon's requirements and use of instruments so she could hand them over during an operation, she needed to understand the surgical procedure. Although Dorothy "scrubbed" for many surgeons, she worked primarily with neurosurgeon C. Norman Shealy.[17]

As the program flourished, Florence and Maddeline counted on assistance from Ruth Anderson, Dorothy Beers, and LaVerne Ness to prepare practical nurses for the community. In 1969, Maddeline moved on to other challenges in nursing; Anita Smith became the new head of the Health and Occupation Division. Florence remained with the program until her retirement in 1980.[18]

Nursing Administrators

At the formal ceremony to celebrate the opening of La Crosse Hospital in May 1901, administrator Edith M. Briggs and her assistant, Ella C. Ingwersen, answered questions about the management of the hospital and the prices it would charge. The visitors were reassured when they were told "the prices are to be here the same as those charged in other institutions of this character though the accommodations are unusually fine."[19]   The following year, Ella became superintendent of the hospital. For forty more years, she supervised the teaching of nurses and dedicated herself to serving "poor and rich alike who entered its doors as patients."[20] When Ella died in 1942, Martha Horn was hired as the new superintendent of La Crosse Hospital. Martha had been a Red Cross nurse volunteer during World War I, serving in a group that worked just behind the shifting battle lines. She remained overseas until January 1919, nursing soldiers who had contracted influenza.[21] After the war, she was a nursing administrator in Pennsylvania hospitals for twenty-three years before returning to her native state, Wisconsin. Martha wanted to be closer to her sister and brothers and looked forward to having some leisure time which she thought would come with working in a smaller hospital. However, the shortage of nurses and other staff in the years during and right after World War II called for more than her administrative skills. Evie Hoover, who at that time lived a block from the hospital and could fill in on short notice, recalled that if she could not find the superintendent in her office, "I would look for her baking bread in the kitchen or working in the garden. Miss Horn also took all the X-rays and ran the laboratory."[22] Martha also supervised extensive improvement and remodeling of the hospital building during her fourteen-year tenure.

Nancy Fitzpatrick was nearly fifty years old when she became director of nursing at Lutheran Hospital in 1965. She brought wisdom, maturity, excellent education credentials, and a wealth of management experience to the job. When a friend encouraged her to apply for the position, Nancy was reluctant to consider moving away from Kansas City, which had always been her home. Eventually she submitted an application and received a job offer from the hospital's administrator, Stanley Sims. Nancy named a salary that she thought would be out of the question — $10,200. Sims, who was convinced she was the right person, countered with an even higher $10,500. Still reluctant to move to a new community and take on the challenging position, she bargained for air conditioned housing that would allow a dog. The hospital met her requirements, and she made the move.[23]

Nancy was well-suited to the director of nursing position during a time of change in nursing education and in nurse-doctor working relationships. As one doctor said to her, "You're the first nurse with guts to stand up to doctors." One of her first big hurdles was getting doctors to sign their orders. In one instance, she literally stood behind a nurse and told "both the doctor and the nurse that the orders couldn't be carried out without his signature. The doctor finally signed the orders," Nancy recalled. She also stood up to doctors over the issue of uniforms. At that time, everyone was wearing white uniforms. "You couldn't tell a nurse from a scrubwoman, the office staff, a ward secretary, or a housekeeper," she said. On several occasions, she made it known to Dr. Adolf Gundersen that she wanted only nurses to wear white uniforms. The practice finally changed when a patient complained about something he had been told by a "nurse" who turned out to be a clerical worker dressed in white.

Nancy Fitzpatrick believed nurses could be patient advocates and educators as well as care providers. "I tried to teach nurses they were important; that, after all, they had brains and could think. 'If you have all your facts when you call the doctor,' I would say, 'they're not going to argue with you.'" Nancy's tenure coincided with a time of rapid change, and, when she saw the tempo picking up, she decided to resign in 1977. "I knew the changes that were coming required someone younger with more modern experiences," she said.

One of the nurses Nancy encouraged to improve her own education and that of others was June Kjome. June, who came to Lutheran Hospital in 1965 to work in pediatrics, had spent the previous twenty years as a midwife at a mission hospital (which was "more like a first aid station") in Zululand, South Africa. During her World War II-era training in Minneapolis, June had seen the trend toward focusing on patient care. Twenty years later at Lutheran Hospital, she observed that nurses were still performing many non-nursing jobs: "Other departments like PT [physical therapy], OT [occupational therapy], X-ray, and dietary went home at five or seven in the evening; after that time, nurses had to take patients to emergency X-ray or return food trays to the kitchen. Also, nurses were serving as receptionists — answering the phone, directing traffic."[24] About 1970, when Lutheran Hospital became interested in enlarging its nursing in-service department, Nancy Fitzpatrick asked June if she would be willing to go back to school to complete her degree and to learn more about in-service training. Some of the courses June took in the 1970s in Madison were familiar, because of her original training, yet new, because of research and development in medicine. "In physiology class, I said to the professor, 'I don't remember hearing about enzymes when I was in nurses training.' The professor looked at me and said, 'Well, I don't think we knew about them then.' We all laughed at that. Anatomy hadn't changed but physiology had," June remembered.

While June was in Madison, she arranged for an in-service practicum at St. Mary's Hospital and worked with the education director, Barb Nichols, who told her, "I've never had anyone so eager to learn." June responded characteristically, "You never had anybody with so great a need." When June returned to Lutheran in 1973, she reorganized and enlarged the nursing in-service into a hospital-wide education program. In addition to providing orientation, development, and continuing education for all hospital staff, the education department looked for community needs that were not being met. "We were the first to offer CPR [cardio-pulmonary resuscitation] in the community," she said. "We trained the ski patrol and firemen. As soon as another group would pick up the idea, we would let it go" and look for the next need. During this time, area hospitals were doing cooperative buying, and directors of nursing and administrators were getting together to share ideas. June suggested that directors of education do the same, and they formed "a collegial group with innovative ideas." Because education departments had started as nursing in-service, most of the education directors were women who had come up through nursing. In 1985, at the age of nearly sixty-five, June looked at the changes in medicine and education and decided the education department could use new vision and leadership. "I've always said people should give up when they're ahead — they should know when it's time to change, to move on," she said. "Besides, I wanted to do a lot of volunteer work while I still had the energy and wits to do it. I looked forward to programming my own time instead of having people say, 'You should do this, you should do that.' I used to say, 'Don't you should on me.'"

Public Health Nursing

In the 1920s, public health nursing emerged as an alternate form of nursing practice. Employed by charitable or governmental agencies and largely removed from the control of doctors, these educated, independent practitioners spread the "gospel of health" to almost every American home. Rather than transform nursing, the public health nurse essentially extended its scope, bringing medical expertise to bear on almost every aspect of daily living.[25]

For many longtime La Crosse residents, the word "quarantine" went hand-in-hand with the name Augusta DeFlorin. As a public health nurse working for the city of La Crosse from 1926 to 1964, Gusta, as she was called, posted the "No Admittance" signs warning people of the presence of a contagious disease within a household. Gusta received her training at Grandview Nursing School. She was class speaker at her 1926 commencement.[26] The moment her small official car appeared, neighbors knew someone was ill. When children were absent from school for three consecutive days, it was her job to visit the home to investigate. If the short, sturdy woman in a dark blue uniform determined the illness was contagious, she pulled out her hammer and nailed the quarantine sign to the home. Passersby could identify the disease by the color of the sign. People hated quarantines which prohibited them from leaving home, or others from entering, until the disease had run its course. Before immunizations and antibiotics, quarantine was one of the few tools available to attempt to control contagious diseases such as whooping cough, measles, scarlet fever, mumps, and chicken pox.

For almost forty years, Helen Hanson served as La Crosse County's primary public health official, the county nurse. She dedicated herself to improving standards of health care primarily through prevention. After graduating from La Crosse Central High School, Helen found work at St. Francis Hospital as the only records librarian in the medical records room. "The interns would dictate the histories of all the patients who came into the hospital and then I'd go to the surgery area and take dictation from the doctors about the operations," she said.[27]

Fascinated by the work of doctors and nurses, she enrolled in the St. Francis School of Nursing in 1927. Upon graduation three years later, she and her classmates faced an uncertain future. Unable to find work in the depressed economy, Helen returned to her former position as records librarian at St. Francis. Finally, in 1934, she was hired to be the La Crosse County Nurse, succeeding Elsie Burkhardt (1919-1921), Mary E. Regan (1921-1926), and Eva M. Stifter (1926-1934).

In the early years, Helen spent much of her time on the road visiting each of the seventy-five rural school districts in the county. During these visits she inspected children's teeth, skin, hair, posture, and overall health. Barbara Schieche Frank, who attended Elm Grove School in the 1940s, remembered "Miss Hanson as extremely competent, and kind, but mostly as an example of a professional woman who showed girls the possibilities for themselves." Elvern Ericksen Nyseth, who attended Maple Shade and Halfway Creek schools in the 1930s, commented on Helen Hanson's tenure, "She was the county nurse when I was a student and she still was the county nurse when I became a teacher."

After a school inspection, Helen often scheduled home visits to inform parents about her concerns and, if necessary, make arrangements for further care. She would put herself in their place and think, "How would I feel if someone came and told me my child needed to go to the dentist?" Fortunately, she had funds at her disposal to help families in need. "If a family couldn't afford to take their child to the doctor for an eye exam or dental care or if the child needed eyeglasses or to have tonsils removed, the service was paid for by the County Nurse's Corrective Fund." In 1942-43, the corrective fund provided $200.00 for dental care, $75.25 for eye care, and $325.50 for twenty-nine tonsillectomies.

In an effort to combat the spread of tuberculosis (TB), Helen tested all children and adults associated with rural schools. She described why she started the state's first county-wide tuberculin testing program: "There was a teacher in another part of the state who was found to have active TB. As a result there were quite a few children with a positive tuberculin test in that school. I decided to test everyone — that included the teachers, the janitors, the bus drivers, the cafeteria workers, the office secretaries, everybody associated with the schools."

With each passing year, Helen Hanson's duties changed and expanded. She worked to ensure that all children in the county were immunized against diphtheria, whooping cough, tetanus, small pox and, eventually, polio. Polio, though not as prevalent as tuberculosis, was both a killer and a crippler. During an outbreak of polio cases in September 1945, the city of La Crosse's board of health prohibited all city children under the age of sixteen from congregating except for attending school. The board unanimously adopted a resolution that "all recreational centers, school dances, weekly gatherings of all kinds be prohibited for the present, or until this wave of infantile paralysis has passed." The resolution's prohibitions included gatherings in private homes as well as going to movie theaters and other amusements, but the ban did not include football games.[28] In 1954, La Crosse County was one of eight in Wisconsin chosen to participate in wide-scale testing of the Salk polio vaccine. Of the 822 first through fifth grade children (624 in the city and 198 in the county) who received the vaccine, none contracted polio. Overall, the vaccine proved to be 94 percent effective.[29]

Helen's role as health educator was a continuing one. Before she retired in 1971, life expectancy had increased to about seventy years. Therefore, near the end of her career, she devoted more of her time to adult health and topics such as "To Smoke or Not To Smoke" and "Breast Self Examinations."

While Helen Hanson was combating tuberculosis by identifying carriers of the disease, Myrtle Carlson was nursing TB patients at Oak Forest Sanatorium in Onalaska from 1957 to 1978. She remembered many happy times when patients and staff enjoyed birthday parties, ice cream socials, and making popcorn in the evenings. "There were even weddings in the san," Myrtle recalled. However, few people visited. "Outsiders were afraid of people in the san. They were even afraid of those of us who worked there," she added.[30]

In 1908, more than 2,500 people in Wisconsin died of tuberculosis and, as late as 1950, TB remained the most common communicable disease for people between the ages of fifteen and thirty-four. In 1917, the La Crosse County Board of Supervisors voted to build the Oak Forest Sanatorium, and, in so doing, established the first county-operated tuberculosis sanatorium in the United States. To prevent the spread of this contagious, deadly disease, those found to be infected were quarantined, that is, committed to a TB sanatorium. Only adults were admitted to Oak Forest. Children had to go to Madison for treatment. Prior to the advent of streptomycin in 1947, treatment involved rest, plenty of fresh air, sunlight, and a good diet rich in protein, vegetables and whole milk, and, of course, good nursing care from dedicated, compassionate nurses. At Oak Forest, Myrtle recalled that both staff and patients ate the same rich diet which, in turn, resulted in unwelcome weight gains for nurses and nurses' aides. In the early years, windows were always kept open, even in winter. "Sometimes it was 25 below. The patients had double pajamas. They'd have a 'pig' — a crock filled with hot water — wrapped in bed with them. They slept in caps, mittens and socks, and they'd come inside from the sleeping porches to dress and undress," she remembered. Myrtle, who graduated from the Grandview School of Nursing in 1935, taught her staff how to protect themselves by wearing masks and gowns, by washing frequently, and by boiling dishes used by the patients. "Masks and gowns became a part of me," she said. Despite the threat of contagion, she witnessed very little turnover in staff which included both nurses and nurses' aides. "I generally hired people in their twenties," she said. "They quickly became accustomed to the work and stuck with it."

Although TB continued to be a major threat throughout the 1950s, the tide finally began to turn in 1960. As the number of cases waned, Oak Forest was converted to a nursing home and eventually closed. The grand building, which boasted beautiful woodwork and stained glass windows overlooking idyllic grounds with a goldfish pond, was razed in 1982.

Midwifery

The practice of midwifery was a thriving occupation in Wisconsin by the early part of the twentieth century. Midwives were often motivated to practice because of the financial needs of their families. Most were informally trained through their own labor and delivery experience and by assisting other midwives.[31]

Mary Friedrich Gerrard practiced midwifery in the La Crosse area from 1878 to 1913.[32] She was one of approximately twenty women listed as midwives in city directories and telephone books between 1870 and 1915.[33] Mary emigrated to the United States from Luxembourg in 1872 and settled east of La Crosse in St. Joseph's Ridge. A year later she married another Luxembourg immigrant, Michael Gerrard, and they settled on a farm on the ridge. While working as a stonemason for the John Paul Lumber Company, Michael was severely injured, and eventually blinded, when a stone chip flew into his left eye. Support of the family fell on Mary's shoulders. Because she had served as a midwife for friends and neighbors on the ridge, it seemed natural for her to turn to midwifery to earn a living. Leaving her baby son in the care of a young cousin, Mary spent five months in Milwaukee attending midwifery school.

During her career Mary Gerrard delivered 3,932 babies. Five were her own grandchildren. Mothers loved her for her compassion and kindness and considered her a special woman. Her work took her as far away as Hokah and Brownsville, Minnesota. She traveled alone in a surrey with a fringe on top in warm weather and in a sleigh, wrapped in a buffalo robe, in the winter. She required patients to reserve her services prior to delivery and to note an approximate due date. She visited her patients each day for nine days after delivery to bathe the baby and mother and to check on their progress. She kept a record book as proof of birth long before the state began to record births. Parents of the newborn paid the $3.00 fee for total services in cash or goods such as fruit, vegetables, or home canning. Some paid with freshly slaughtered meat which was kept in a smokehouse at the rear of the home to which the Gerrards had moved in La Crosse. It was often necessary to keep the meat safe from the wolves that roamed the city looking for food.

Mary did well as the breadwinner of her family. Somehow she found time for homemaking — mothering her family of seven children (two of whom died in early childhood), sewing, baking bread, making jelly, and rendering lard.

She loved playing cards and enjoyed church, politics, and her grandchildren to whom she gave generous helpings of ice cream when they came to visit. She died in 1915, a few months after suffering a stroke.

During the years of Mary Gerrard's practice, the medical profession was growing in power and using that power to eliminate the practice of midwifery. The medical profession blamed the prevailing high infant and maternal mortality rates on midwife-attended births and began to advocate childbirth attended by obstetricians.[34] In 1900, more than half of all births in the United States were attended by midwives, most in the mothers' homes. Thirty years later the medical profession's idea that childbirth was a dangerous process that mandated technical intervention had taken hold and virtually eliminated midwives as birth attendants.[35]

Dorothy Ahlstrom Harman, who graduated from Lutheran Hospital's nursing school in 1926, was interested in post-graduate training in obstetrics. Because Lutheran Hospital did not have enough obstetrics cases to qualify for state educational standards, she took her post-graduate work at Chicago Lying-In Hospital. The philosophy at Chicago was to let nature take its course during childbirth. Later, while working at a hospital in Cleveland, Ohio, Dorothy saw the effects of a different philosophy and practice. Sedation administered to women during labor and delivery induced "twilight sleep." Dorothy observed that heavy sedation was not good for the baby. "I saw so many instances where babies needed to be resuscitated," she recalled.[36]

When Kathy Schnur Witzke was born in Geneva, Illinois, in 1939, she and her mother stayed in the hospital for the usual two weeks. "They wouldn't even let my mother out of bed, so she was very weak from lack of any activity. My father had to carry her into the house, and people came to help take care of her and me," Kathy said.

In the spring of 1969, while Kathy and her husband, Terry, awaited the arrival of their first child, she read and thought about natural childbirth. However, sedation for labor and delivery was still the practice in La Crosse. She recalled, "I had requested no anesthesia, but when I got into the delivery room, they knocked me out. I was so mad!" It was not until she regained consciousness that she learned she had a healthy son. When the Witzkes' third son was born in 1974, Kathy experienced natural, unhindered childbirth and also noted a change in attitude toward breastfeeding, "When I nursed my first baby, I was looked upon as doing something uncommon. But it was finally starting to become accepted by the time my third came along."[37] It should be noted that twenty years earlier breastfeeding was recommended to new mothers although the decision was left to them. Government publications pointed out the benefits of mother's milk to the infant.

When Joyce and Bob Arthur moved from Long Island, New York, to La Crosse in August 1969, Joyce was eight and one-half months pregnant. Wanting to use the La Maze childbirth method, to have her husband with her during labor and delivery, and to keep the new baby in her room, Joyce wrote to the only La Crosse physician on a "natural childbirth" list she had obtained. That doctor, J. R. Richter, wrote back to say he would be on vacation during September and to recommend another physician:

> *The La Maze technique is not used by any other physician in*
> *this locality. I can give you the name of an obstetrician who*
> *will use a cervical block and local [anesthetic] for an*
> *episiotomy so that you can be awake when your babe is born.*
> *You may have your husband in the delivery room, and I am*
> *sure rooming in can be arranged.*[38]

On her first visit to the recommended obstetrician, "he made it clear that he would make all the decisions concerning the birth — whether a local anesthetic or general was to be used — and there would be no husband present nor consultation of my wishes," recalled Joyce. Fortunately, she also received a letter from Maureen Guillan, president of the La Crosse Chapter of La Leche League. Maureen, who was expecting a child in October, recommended Dr. Ubaldo Alvarez. She also wrote that the La Maze method "is not well known around here ... perhaps with the two of us using this method in La Crosse, we'll be able to get something started."[39] On September 6, 1969, Dr. Alvarez assisted the birth of the Arthurs' first child, without anesthesia and with both mom and dad present. Their son was one of the first babies, if not the first, born using La Maze methods in La Crosse.[40]

Obstetrical care supervised by certified nurse-midwives gained increasing acceptance during the last quarter of the twentieth century. The American College of Nurse-Midwives reported rapid growth of nurse-midwifery practice in the United States since 1975. That is the year Gundersen Lutheran Medical Center first offered the service. Nurse-midwifery was seen as a step forward, not backwards, because: pregnancy, by then, was seen as a normal event not a pathological model; nurse-midwives, because of their education and training, were accepted as part of a team; and, "the fact was, women still needed women when in labor," observed Linda Hirsh, the head of Gundersen Clinic's midwifery program.[41] In the mid-1970s, Gundersen Clinic patients were starting to ask for midwives. The obstetricians, all of whom were male, generally supported the hiring of Cynthia Thompson Delano who had just graduated from Yale. "In

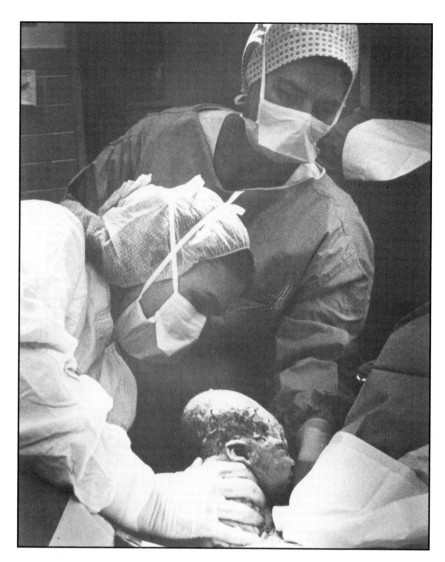

Certified nurse midwife Cynthia Thompson, left, and obstetric technician Arlys Noben welcomed a new baby to the world, 1976.

Cynthia Thompson Delano

1975, women in the high risk pregnancy clinic got lots of attention. I thought every woman should receive attention and reassurance," she recalled. Cyndy was instrumental in establishing the first birthing room at Lutheran Hospital. Before long, patients of obstetricians wanted to use it, too. In 1995, six birthing rooms had completely replaced the operating room style of tiled delivery rooms.

    "Cyndy paved the way by working hard, so I was welcomed with open arms two years later," said Linda, a Columbia University graduate and the clinic's second nurse-midwife. As Cyndy and Linda reflected on the similarities and differences between nurse-midwifery in the latter part of the twentieth century and the practice of the granny-midwife in the early part of the century, they stressed the nursing-based education. Long ago the granny-midwife was a friend, neighbor, or relative who had learned by experience and operated on her own. Today the nurse-midwife is a professional who manages the labor and delivery. She is part of a team and can, when needed, call upon a nurse and an obstetrician to assist her. Today's nurse-midwife, like yesterday's granny-midwife, provides a warm, personal touch. She is still at the bedside, rubbing the back, a woman helping a woman in labor. No matter how technical society becomes, the expectant mother still needs comforting reassurance, someone to say "I'm here with you. This is what is happening," Linda said. Some things never change.

Physicians

Even with the advent of women's medical colleges in the 1840s, many fewer women than men became doctors. Education was considered an investment and not a particularly wise one for women because society expected them to marry, have children, and stay at home. Marguerite Schroeder Figge Goodermote became very interested in medicine during her nurses training at La Crosse Lutheran Hospital from 1929 to 1932. Because her parents thought medical school was inappropriate for women and because she could not afford the fees during the Depression, Marguerite settled for a career in nursing. When medical schools began to admit women in the 1870s, they did so in very small numbers and with tougher entry standards for women than for men. That practice continued until the 1970s, when such actions became illegal. The American Medical Association (AMA) further restricted the number of women in medical practice by not admitting them to the AMA until 1951.[42]

By the mid 1850s, there were approximately twenty female medical doctors in the nation.[43] Only four were in practice, three in the East and Dr. Mary E. Parker Finney Lottridge who opened her medical office in La Crosse in 1855.[44] She was the first woman with a medical degree and license to practice in the heartland, and she spent her entire forty-five-year career in La Crosse County. Mary Elizabeth Parker, born in 1826, married Dr. Noble Finney in 1846. She became involved in his practice in Ohio and often accompanied him on his rounds. During this time she realized she had not only the interest but also the aptitude for medicine. When her husband died in 1853, Mary entered the Eclectic Medical College of Cincinnati. After she graduated in 1855, Mary moved to La Crosse, opened a medical office on Fourth Street and, in December 1855, placed an advertisement in the newspaper as a "Female Physician." Local newspaper accounts described her as "tall, black-eyed and distinguished looking" and as "a lady of talent and mind, worthy of the profession she has chosen, and well-fitted for the discharge of her duties." A listing in an 1861 directory said, "Special Attention Paid to Pathology and Treatment of Uterine Diseases."[45] In 1862, she married Leonard Lottridge, a widower who owned and edited newspapers in La Crosse and West Salem. The two daughters from her first marriage died at an early age, but a daughter, Hope, was born to the Lottridges in 1868.

Six years later they purchased and moved to the octagonal house in West Salem built by Dr. Horace Palmer. One of its attractive features was the barn which was conveniently attached to the house. It afforded protection from inclement weather when she hitched up her horse and climbed into her enclosed buggy. Her husband must have appreciated that, too, because it has been said that he would not get up to help his wife prepare for a night call; he thought her perfectly capable of handling it all herself. She had a large following as a general practitioner and reportedly delivered 600 babies that she often referred to as "her babies." She died just shy of her eightieth birthday in June 1906.

Toward the end of Dr. Mary Lottridge's practice, the life of another West Salem woman who would make medicine her career was just beginning. Edyth Claire Swarthout was born in 1891 to Dr. Ezekial and Sarah Swarthout.[46] She graduated from the Johns Hopkins University Medical School in 1913 and did an internship at Bellevue Hospital. Afterwards she returned to La Crosse to join her father, who practiced medicine until 1922. At that time he retired to manage the family land holdings and business concerns acquired by his father. Edyth kept very busy with both her medical practice and, after her father's death in 1943, the Swarthout family business accounts. She commuted back and forth from the family estate on Lake Neshonoc to her office at 609 St. James Street in La Crosse. A tragic car accident in 1953 injured her spine, confined her to a wheelchair for the rest of her life, and forced her to retire from her medical practice. From that time on she joined her older sister, Susan, in managing the family business matters.

In the early part of the twentieth century, students in Wisconsin normal schools received health services from a traveling physician. Dr. Sarah Garrett spent three years as a "circuit rider," traveling from campus to campus conducting physical examinations, before marrying Andrew C.

Bangsberg and settling in La Crosse in 1918.[47] That year, Dr. Sarah Garrett Bangsberg became the full-time physician at the La Crosse Normal School. She kept office hours and made house calls. One time the doctor, who was described as "about five by five and very tough," actually carried a sick female student across the street to Grandview Hospital. Common health problems during her tenure ranged from athletes foot to tuberculosis. It seemed, to at least one student, that no matter what the medical problem, the doctor always prescribed iodine. The student recalled having her nose swabbed by the doctor to deal with a terrible chlorine allergy and sinus infection. The school's physician enjoyed her work with students until her retirement in 1944 because, she said, "Youth responds so quickly and so beautifully to treatment."

Lilian B. Tracey was another local physician who demonstrated pioneering qualities. During the years of her medical practice, 1929 to 1973, she promoted birth control, care of the elderly and handicapped, and stressed the importance of controlling alcohol abuse. Although she was ridiculed for her progressive views, she never compromised her beliefs during her forty-four-year practice as an osteopathic physician and surgeon. Born in 1900, she graduated from the La Crosse County School of Agriculture and Domestic Economy in 1919 and the La Crosse State Normal School in 1922 before taking nurses training in Madison. In 1929, she graduated from Still College of Osteopathy in Des Moines, Iowa. Not only was she the only woman in her class, but she also was class president during her senior year. It had been her hope to practice obstetrics, but she changed her mind after delivering sixteen babies and being paid for only three. "Doc," as she was known to her friends, was a woman ahead of her time. With a genuine concern for women and their health problems, she opened a birth control clinic in the 1930s. She was not an abortionist, but other physicians sent their patients who were seeking abortions to her. She believed they did so in an attempt to besmirch her reputation. In an effort to treat drug addiction and alcoholism, she purchased an old La Crosse hotel to provide a haven for individuals with

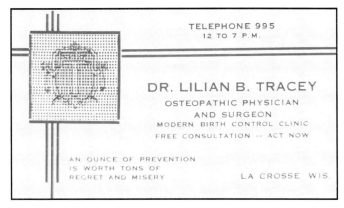

Dr. Lilian B. Tracey's business card.
John L. Dolbier

such problems. Her plan was sound and her intentions sincere, but the project failed because it was too much for one person to accomplish alone. Some people thought she was opinionated, caustic, and argumentative. Others discovered under her gruff exterior a woman who "loved children, her community, the beauty and nature of God."[48] She practiced osteopathy from an office in her Onalaska home until illness forced her to retire in 1973.

When Gretchen Guernsey entered medical school in Kansas in 1934, she was one of eight females in a class of sixty-eight students. "We were considered a bunch of pioneers," she said.[49] As a senior medical student and again as an intern, she saw an anesthesiologist lose a patient. Both incidents had a profound effect on her and influenced her decision to pursue this specialty which was still in its infancy. During World War II, she practiced pathology, but, after the war, she taught anesthesiology at the University of Kansas and then went into private practice. After her husband's death she took the advice of friends and moved to La Crosse in 1960 where she joined the Gundersen Clinic as its only anesthesiologist. She was responsible for supervising the nurse anesthetists who assisted with the twenty surgeries performed in Lutheran Hospital's four operating rooms each morning. She was also on call and administered anesthesia in complex cases. When asked about the demands of a career in medicine, from which she retired in 1979, she said, "I don't think you can do it all, but, on the other hand, I don't feel like I gave up much. You need to make room for what you like to do and for what's important to you."[50]

Mary Scheurich Maney did not have the same kind of support that Gretchen Guernsey received from her family. Although her physician father influenced and encouraged her interest in becoming a doctor, her mother did not. "My mother thought I should go into nursing because then I could still marry," Mary said.[51] The school counselor was equally discouraging, advising that "I could not be a doctor because I was a girl." Despite these obstacles, she graduated from Marquette Medical School in Milwaukee in 1951. She was one of six women in a class of eighty-five. Most of the men in the class were World War II veterans. Although her original interest was in obstetrics and gynecology, she chose pediatrics because the residency was shorter and, at the time, she was engaged to be married.

When Mary arrived in La Crosse in 1954, she joined the La Crosse Clinic. She earned $700 a month. Her rent was sixty dollars and the monthly payments for her new car were $300. "I don't think I earned my salary that first year," she said. "I saw five or six patients a day at three dollars an office visit. But, after a couple of years, I had a full practice. There really was no competition because there were so few pediatricians." Early in her practice, Mary, who was on call every night "always gobbled down supper and then stayed up until one in the morning thinking I might be called."

Mary described her career as coinciding with the golden age of medicine. There was a change in the prevalence of certain diseases, there were major developments in antibiotics, and people looked up to doctors. At the time she started her practice, there was "lots of polio, chicken pox, measles, encephalitis." The development of vaccines was "wonderful. No measles, no encephalitis. Polio was practically non-existent one year after the vaccine." While there were only a few antibiotics — penicillin, sulfa, tetracycline — to rely on early in her practice, "the last ten years had as much progress as the first ten thousand," she said. She felt she was doing a good job, too. "Malpractice wasn't a problem because people trusted you and knew you would do the best you could." When she retired in 1986, the use of CT scans and MRIs was becoming prevalent. "Medicine had been much more exciting, much more of an art before this technology," said Mary who had an excellent reputation as a clinician. "You just had to figure it out, and it was so exciting."

Ruth Dalton decided to become a doctor despite her parents' view that such a goal was unattainable. Her mother thought college and medical school would be too hard. Her father knew he could not pay for the education because he had lost his job. Ruth remained steadfast, and a part-time job in a hospital laboratory led her to the field of pathology. Competition for admission to medical school was stiff in the late 1940s because "lots of vets were coming back," so she attended night school and worked days for one year before entering the University of Illinois Medical School in Chicago. One of nine women in a class of 160, she found the first couple of years were very hard. "Some faculty did not want women in medicine. They figured women would get married and have kids and not practice medicine," she said.[52]

During the last of her eight years of internship and residency in pathology, she sampled La Crosse for two weeks and found she liked the variety awaiting her. In 1958, she joined Dr. Paul C. Dietz in a private pathology practice and taught at the St. Francis School of Medical Technology and at the St. Francis School of Nursing. In the early days, these two doctors alternated weekends and weeks on call. They also consulted on medical/legal cases such as suicides, homicides, and accidents. By the time Ruth retired in 1986, the practice included five pathologists and contracted with eight hospitals. For Ruth, pathology was the most rewarding and challenging field in medicine because "making the correct diagnosis was always the challenge. You discovered more in diagnosis than in treatment."

More Healers and Helpers

Pharmacist

In 1929, when the Gundersen doctors built their clinic on South Avenue in La Crosse, it included a pharmacy. The clinic's first in-house pharmacist was Oliver Young. When he entered the armed forces during World War II, Louise Cook was hired to replace him. "They knew I wouldn't be drafted," she said. Louise had trained at the University of Wisconsin, graduating from the two-year course in 1921. She worked as a pharmacist until her marriage in 1931. When her husband died eleven years later while they were living in Michigan, she returned to Wisconsin where she was licensed.[53] According to Louise, the Gundersen Clinic pharmacy was a small "one-man" operation: "We had a compounding room [for preparing medicines, ointments and solutions] ... we did a lot of compounding in those days. We made whatever we couldn't buy cheaper." She also made all the mouthwash for Lutheran Hospital in a twenty-gallon crock. In the process of serving both Gundersen Clinic and Lutheran Hospital, she used so much distilled water that she got permission to buy a still.

When Lutheran Hospital formed a pharmacy department in 1944, Louise Cook was placed in charge of both the hospital and clinic pharmacies. During her later years, Louise also provided practical experience and training for student pharmacists. Penicillin was just coming into use in the early 1940s when Louise Cook reentered the field of pharmacy. By the time she retired in 1963, the pharmaceutical line had expanded tremendously. She cited antibiotics, antihistamines, vitamins, hormones, and cortisone as new and important developments for treating patients.

X-ray Technologist

Leona Goetzinger graduated from the St. Francis School of Nursing in 1932 and later joined the St. Francis Hospital radiology department. In 1943, she became the first La Crosse area professional to pass a national registry exam and become a registered X-ray technologist. She helped establish the St. Francis Hospital School of Radiologic Technology. After her retirement in

1981, which capped a career of more than fifty years of service to St. Francis Medical Center, she continued her connection with the hospital as a volunteer and as a member of the St. Francis Auxiliary.[54]

Hospice Worker and Volunteer

In the late 1970s, local hospitals were considering better ways to serve terminally ill patients and their families.[55] In the fall of 1978, Lutheran Hospital employee Dorothy Wetterlin began visiting hospices in the midwest. She and the hospital's chaplain, Dan Vinge, spearheaded a task force to form a hospice program. The Lutheran Family Hospice officially opened in April of 1980 with June Knutson as director. It started as a hospital/home care program with beds scattered throughout the hospital.

In the spring of 1979, St. Francis Hospital oncology nurses Paul Geronime and Sandy Hinders heard an English physician who was making a lecture tour of the United States speak of a new method in his country for caring for the terminally ill. Sandy and Paul became enthusiastic about starting a hospice at St. Francis. They took their plans to Sister Celesta Day, the hospital's director of planning, who helped launch the program.

On May 1, 1980, one year and many hours of labor later, the St. Francis Hospice admitted its first patient. Members of the original hospice team included Dr. Jim Murphy, physician director; Sandy Hinders, head nurse-program director; Dorothy Beers, a dedicated registered nurse who had been recently widowed and had a keen interest in helping the dying and their families; and Sister Catherine, the pastoral care coordinator. Social workers, dietitians, recreational therapists, a home care coordinator, a public health nurse, and volunteers, most of them women, completed the hospice staff. Because the hospice programs depended heavily on the services of volunteers, Marilyn McElligott and Elaine George, directors of volunteers for Lutheran and St. Francis hospitals, respectively, spent much time together planning and developing the volunteer aspect of the programs.

In the beginning, St. Francis Hospice was a place as well as a philosophy. A corner of the fifth floor of the hospital was remodeled into a comfortable unit with private rooms for patients and a living room for relatives where the coffee was always brewing. There was an alcove with a piano, potted plants, and an aquarium. Volunteers like Dorothy Lawrence read to patients, prayed with them, helped the nurses with simple nursing tasks, or even became the "patient" so nurses could demonstrate bathing techniques to new volunteers. Volunteers often became quite close to the families and shared vigils with them. A patient might surprise everyone, volunteer Viki Ott recalled, by requesting "some lively music, please! Can anybody play 'The Tiger Rag'? I used to play with a jazz band."

Patients made various requests: "Read to me." "Pray with me." "Stay with me; I'm afraid to be alone." Sometimes just an outstretched hand reached for physical comfort from another human being. Staff and volunteers reaped intangible rewards from knowing they had helped relieve the suffering of a fellow human being. The tasks called for a high degree of compassion, and detachment was difficult. There was some burn-out among both staff and volunteers, but many dedicated people persisted with hospice, giving countless hours since its inception in 1980.

Educators

*It is woman fitted by disposition, and habits, and
circumstances for such duties, who, to a very wide extent,
must aid in educating the childhood and youth of this
nation ... Most happily, the education necessary to fit a
woman to be a teacher, is exactly the one that best fits her
for that domestic relation she is primarily designed to fill.*
Catharine Beecher[1]

Until the mid-1800s, most teachers in the United States were male. In
the 1840s and 1850s, Catharine Beecher waged a campaign to shape
teaching into a respectable profession for women. She was an educator, a
writer, and a crusader. In her standard speech, she called upon women to
save their country from ignorance and immorality. During the Civil War
years, the balance shifted, and, from that time on, women comprised the
majority of teachers. Catharine Beecher's efforts were aided by the fact that
school boards and administrators realized that women could be paid less
than men.[2] Although teaching never ranked first, it always was included in
the top five of the ten most female jobs for each decade from 1880 to 1980.[3]

The first year of public schooling in La Crosse is recorded as 1851-52.
When enrollment grew to 102 students in the fall of 1852, Mary Bagley, age
eighteen, was hired as assistant teacher for the spring 1853 term and was
paid fourteen dollars a month. The teacher, Robert Whelpley, received
thirty.[4]

Maria Serviss Allen operated West Salem's first public school, in
1853-54, in a private home. However, West Salem's earliest school was a
private one. In 1852-53, Mrs. Chauncey (Catherine Preston) Elwell opened
her log cabin to teach twelve children from ages eight to sixteen.[5] The
Elwells' daughter, Ida, was born in that home in 1854. Ida's education began
when her mother taught her the alphabet at the age of two. She continued
her education in West Salem and then graduated from Ripon College in 1873.
The title of her graduation paper was, "The Place of Women in Agriculture."
Ida taught in Mississippi and then in Chippewa Falls, Wisconsin, where she

met and married Edmund Tilson. When he died in 1878, she taught for three years at the then new West Salem High School. Through the 1880s and 1890s, she was a traveling lecturer for the Agricultural Institute in Onalaska.[6]

Catholic education began to expand when the Franciscan Sisters of Perpetual Adoration (FSPA) moved to La Crosse in 1871. Their primary mission was to teach. One of the early schools they staffed was St. Joseph Ridge Catholic School which began in 1873.

Higher education came to La Crosse County near the turn of the century. Until the establishment of professional schools for teacher training, called normal schools, teachers often had no more than a high school education and some were just sixteen-year-old girls. The Franciscan Sisters of Perpetual Adoration established St. Rose Normal Training School in 1890 to train its own members to become teachers. The La Crosse Normal School opened its doors in 1909.

Rural School Teachers

Rural school teachers were very much on their own.[7] The county superintendent of schools and the county supervising teacher made just three or four visits to each school each year. They checked for cleanliness, teaching ability, discipline, and general order, including recordkeeping for attendance and grades. The county superintendent issued final exams for all eighth graders who received their final grades in mid-May. The mark of a good teacher was to have her or his eighth graders pass the exam.

Minnie Christofferson was one of those early rural school teachers. After graduating from Onalaska High School in 1910, she took the one-year course at La Crosse Normal School which entitled her to teach in rural schools in the state of Wisconsin. She taught two years in Bohemian Valley and two years at St. Joseph Ridge public school before marrying Howard Kinney in 1915 and becoming a farmwife.

Eleanor Kinney Robinson followed in her mother's footsteps and attended what had become La Crosse State Teachers College. After graduating from the two-year elementary education course in 1936, she taught at the one-room Walker School in the Town of Hamilton for two years. "The school was just plugged with kids," Eleanor said about the thirty-five children in grades one through eight. Rather than teaching the students by age or grade, she grouped them by ability so each student could advance appropriately. Like other rural school teachers, Eleanor arrived at school early enough to start the fire to heat the building; to pump the water; to put lessons on the blackboard, often wearing gloves to try to warm her hands; and to dust the desks and window sills. In 1938, she was named principal of Elm Grove, a new state-graded school, which meant it had two classrooms, one for grades one through four and the other for grades five through eight, and two teachers, one of whom also was the principal. At the age of twenty-two Eleanor was doing triple duty: teaching, administering, and also supervising student teachers from the teachers college elementary department. When Eleanor married Ellsworth M. Robinson in 1939, she did not entirely give up teaching. During the summers, she was the demonstration teacher in the rural room of La Crosse State Teachers College. For three hours each morning, college students observed her while she taught twenty-five students from the Elm Grove school district in the Town of Shelby. The advisors for this model rural school were Alice Drake and Mauree Applegate. "We were on the leading edge of progressive education because Alice had just come back from Columbia University in New York," Eleanor said. Many of the students who were doing the observing already had teaching experience. They were coming back to school in the summers to extend their own education and to earn new certification.[8]

Mildred Lee was both a rural school student and teacher.[9] She attended Gills Coulee School in the Town of Hamilton and took the two-year course at La Crosse State from 1950 to 1952. In college, Mildred belonged to the Country Life Club, a group of rural teachers in training who met to discuss teaching and education. Immediately after college, she found a job at White School, so named because at one time it was the only school in the Town of Burns that was painted white. "There wasn't much competition for area [rural] teaching jobs. Mostly women were applying, and, occasionally, someone asked you to teach without applying," she recalled. During the years she taught, 1952 to 1955, her wages were $235 a month. Although many of the kerosene lanterns had been replaced with electricity two decades earlier, most rural schools still did not have central heating or indoor plumbing. Mildred's extra duties included getting the water from the pump, keeping the school clean, and firing up the stove for heat.

County Superintendent of Schools

When La Crosse County rural schools were at their peak enrollment, in 1937, Hazel Brown Leicht was elected county superintendent of schools, a position she held for twenty-five years. Her twentieth century predecessors were Emily Stromstad (1926-37), Blanche Chamberlain (1918-26), Anna Jenkins (1918), and Bernard F. Oltman (1903-18). Irene Meyer Schieche, who attended the rural Grandview School in the Town of Greenfield in the 1920s, recalled, "There were no men in the schools. The teachers were women and the county superintendent was a woman."

Hazel, mother of three, devoted her entire career to education. After graduating from West Salem High School in 1913 and La Crosse Normal School in 1915, she taught in New Lisbon and then in West Salem. As the first coach of the West Salem girls' basketball team, she traveled by train to games in Westby, Onalaska and Cashton. She was clerk of the West Salem school district when her minister convinced her to run against the incumbent superintendent. "At first I was mortified that my mother was running for office, but soon I was helping her campaign," recalled Jane Leicht Kaiser. "My mother was the first 'women's libber' I knew."[10] Hazel's son, Bob, enjoyed that first campaign. "I was fourteen and had my driver's permit so I drove all over the county delivering handbills for her," he recalled.[11] Hazel went on to win that election plus six more. "She tried to retire early once," said Jane, "but she was re-elected with write-in votes."

Her main responsibilities as county superintendent were to visit every school in the county's seventy-five districts, to conduct an institute for teachers in the fall before school started for the approximately 100 rural school teachers, and to organize a convention in the spring for the school boards — each district had a board of three members. She also served as secretary of the county committees on health, agriculture, and schools and was a member of the County Library Board and the Handicapped Children's Board. Hazel was proud that during her years of service the county schools hired the first speech correctionist and opened a room for the mentally handicapped. As she visited schools, it became apparent to her that many students needed special help: some for correcting their speech, others because they were unable to do the regular school work. She devised a plan to share a speech correctionist with the city of La Crosse schools. Next she worked with the state Department for Handicapped Children to offer instruction to mentally handicapped children of the county. Emily Gregg, a

First grade teacher Florence Whiting led her students from Washington Elementary (which was closing) to the new Emerson Elementary School on the other side of the university campus in La Crosse, January 27, 1956.

Florence Olson Whiting

rural school teacher who attended summer school for additional preparation, taught twelve students in that first group in a room at Fauver Hill School.[12]

In 1938, La Crosse County's rural school districts sponsored fifty-nine one-room schools, six state-graded schools, and four high schools.[13] By the time Hazel retired in 1962, she had worked herself out of a job by implementing the state mandate to consolidate all rural schools into districts with high schools: Bangor, Holmen, La Crosse, Melrose-Mindoro, Onalaska, and West Salem. She supported the consolidation but cited the school closures as the most difficult time of her career. She attended countless meetings to devise plans, present them to the small school districts, and listen to people's concerns. Citizens voiced their opposition at meetings that lasted far into the night. One veteran town officer pleaded, with tears in his eyes, for the continuance of the rural school because he believed that the annual meeting in a rural school is "the only true democracy left in America."[14] Hazel understood the pride each rural neighborhood felt for its school, which had long served as a social center. She also understood that parents did not want their children traveling longer distances to school. However, the Wisconsin Department of Education had decreed that by July 1, 1962, all rural school districts must be in a high school district. Hazel resigned January 1, 1962, when the administration of La Crosse County rural schools was put under the direction of W. Earl Zepplin of Monroe County. In 1965, the office of county superintendent was discontinued in the state of Wisconsin.

After Hazel retired she served on the West Salem School Board for nine years. On her ninetieth birthday, Wisconsin Governor Lee Dreyfus issued a proclamation for her contribution to education. In addition to her devotion to family, education, and community, she loved playing bridge and the piano, and listening to ballgames on the radio. She preferred the Milwaukee Braves to the Brewers and could recite batting averages and other statistics.[15]

City Teachers

"Suitcase teacher" was an apt description for many in-town teachers in the early part of this century. Generally, a teacher boarded with a family near the school and, depending on the distance, might visit her own family on weekends and for holidays. Teachers were supposed to be models of morality. They were not supposed to smoke, drink, swear, go out with men, or be associated with anything that might be considered controversial. Shortly after Florence Olson Whiting began teaching at Jefferson Elementary in La Crosse in the mid-1920s, she became involved in politics by supporting a candidate for the senate. The school superintendent reacted swiftly and sent her a letter saying she should "lay off" politics.[16]

Many La Crosse Central High School graduates benefited from Anna Mashek's principled life and devotion to teaching. However, her own formal education might have ended after eighth grade if she had not received encouragement from summer neighbors near her parents' farm in Bohemian Valley. She boarded in La Crosse to attend high school and did so well that these same advocates encouraged her to go on to the University of Wisconsin where she majored in English literature and was elected to Phi Beta Kappa.

She returned to La Crosse in 1908 to teach English at Central High School where she made a strong impression on her students. Charles Gelatt, who graduated in 1934, claimed she was "the best teacher I ever had. She was very demanding. Her daily motto was 'Wring all the juice out of the orange.'"[17] During her twenty-seven years at Central, her foremost desire was to help underprivileged students reach their highest potential. As a testament to "her intellectual endowment, her sensitivity to the needs of all students, and her response to the challenges of the community," Bookfellows, a study group of the American Association of University Women, suggested the new Central High School of the mid-1960s be named in her honor.[18]

Ruth Fruit's lasting contribution to public schools was the school milk program.[19] Born in La Crosse in 1886, she initiated the idea of serving milk to school children while teaching at Webster School from 1918 until her death in 1936. At first she bought the milk for her own students. As the idea spread to other classrooms and to other schools, she gave one month's salary toward expenses for a city-wide program. Her unassuming kindness touched and benefited many. For years she made it possible for disadvantaged children to participate in the YMCA and to attend scout camp by paying memberships, fees, and camp costs. She also was a charter member and loyal worker in the La Crosse Teachers Club.

"There are people who work and teach for a living, while others do that plus give a living bonus to their trade or profession,"[20] said school board member Joseph Liskovec upon Josephine Hintgen's retirement from the La Crosse public schools in 1957. In her four-decade career she served as teacher, counselor, director of guidance and curriculum, and assistant superintendent of schools. Josephine, a 1911 La Crosse Central High School graduate, recalled receiving valuable advice from one of her teachers, Anna Mashek: "I always talked over problems, plans, and everyday affairs with her. It was she who continually urged me to go to the University of Wisconsin. She gave me confidence because she had faith in me."[21]

Josephine Hintgen graduated from La Crosse Normal School in 1913, taught for a few years and then earned a bachelor's degree from the University of Wisconsin at Madison in 1920. That same year she became supervisor of attendance and vocational guidance for students in public, parochial, and vocational schools in La Crosse. Aware that changing industrial and social conditions were placing new responsibilities on the schools, she began presenting occupational information to eighth graders each week. This "forward-looking individual who kept the goals of the city school system at the highest possible standards"[22] did not always have the support of the La Crosse school board. Some members failed to see the value of the guidance program she developed for the schools. However, when R. W. Bardwell was asked about the importance of guidance during his interview for superintendent in 1942, he exclaimed, "She is one of the best guidance workers in the state, where her good program is well known."[23]

She also initiated career days, home visits to encourage students to remain in school, and cumulative record folders for each student. She spent much of her time and effort instilling a realistic perception of the world in her students. She also encouraged continuing education for all and set an example for others. In 1924, she earned a master's degree in guidance and education from Harvard University. She also attended numerous summer sessions at universities throughout the nation to explore English literature, applied psychology, international relations, U.S. history, mental hygiene, and supervision.

In her own words, Josephine Hintgen "always loved teaching and always liked to be trying new things."[24] Although active in many local, state and national organizations, her affiliation with the Business and Professional Women's Club turned her into a world traveler as she attended international meetings and participated in Good Will Tours. "These tours taught me much about living with other people and developing a sense of humor, business management, and the ideas of professional women of other countries," she said.

Special Education Teachers

One of the specialized educational programs that developed in La Crosse was instruction for deaf students. According to Joan Pitzner, who taught these students in La Crosse public schools from 1968 to 1988, instruction for the deaf began in the late 1800s when Judge Hugh Cameron persuaded the board of education to start a program to teach his son.[25] It is not known if such a program operated continuously from that day to this. However, La Crosse was ahead of most school districts in this respect when the Bureau for Handicapped Children was established in the state Department of Public Instruction in 1940 to ensure educational opportunity in the public schools for the handicapped.[26] Nida Saunders came to teach in La Crosse in 1946 and gave form and shape to the public school program for the deaf. The Kickapoo Valley native had taught in day schools for the deaf from West Virginia to Idaho since 1915. She chose this specialty, which was a rare one in those days, because her brother was deaf.[27] She was so strong in her convictions that deaf children should learn to speak that she did not include sign language in the curriculum. Instead, youngsters were taught lip-reading so they could adjust to the hearing world rather than expect the world to adjust to them.

In the late 1960s, La Crosse was one of just five districts in the state to offer specialized education for deaf students. The program had its greatest number of students when Joan Pitzner joined the staff in 1968. "Almost all of the students were deaf because their mothers had been exposed to rubella during pregnancy," Joan said. She began teaching finger spelling to the students, and Nida, who retired in 1961 but continued to serve as a consultant to the program, did not object.

Employment Issues

Until the 1940s and 1950s, whether by policy or by practice, school boards did not hire married women. Mary Bagley taught just one term in the La Crosse public school in the spring of 1853. Her marriage to Norton Roswell Smith that summer ended any possibility of continuing to teach.[28] Nearly a century later, Elvern Ericksen Nyseth's teaching career was almost curtailed by that same attitude.[29] With her three-year degree from La Crosse Teachers College in hand, Elvern began teaching forty fourth graders in Viroqua in the fall of 1947. When the time came to sign her contract for the 1951-52 school year, Elvern told the superintendent she was to be married in June. He took back the contract and, at her request, wrote the reason for not renewing it. "I can still see his healthy-sized script written across my contract: 'Miss Ericksen is going to be married this summer,'" Elvern recalled. In Viroqua, as in most school districts, being married disqualified even excellent teachers. The West Salem School District, however, was willing to hire married women. From 1951 to 1988, Elvern taught nearly 1,000 third and fourth graders in West Salem. The community honored her as a "kind, helpful, understanding and witty" teacher in 1990.[30] A few years after Elvern left Viroqua that school board changed its policy and began hiring married women because unmarried teachers were in short supply.

During World War II, the La Crosse School Board did make an exception to its unmarried-women-only employment policy, but only if the woman's husband was serving in the military. The wording, which was adopted unanimously on June 2, 1942, stated that the "resolution shall terminate at the close of the present war or at such time as the Board of Education determines."[31] The amended policy did terminate at war's end. Marge Schaller, who was interested in teaching in La Crosse schools when she graduated in 1948, recalled, "they wouldn't hire married women then."[32] So Marge, who credited her mother, who also was her sixth grade teacher, with inspiring her to become a teacher, began her thirty-four year career in her hometown, Bangor. Eventually she did teach in La Crosse when that hiring practice changed.

Another issue that affected female teachers was the pay differential between men and women. In Onalaska, in the 1940s, when teacher salaries were in the $1,000 to $2,000 range, men received an additional four hundred dollars each year for being the head of a household.[33] In the 1960s, La Crosse public schools were still paying an annual "head of household" stipend of a few hundred dollars to all male teachers in addition to their salaries, whether or not they had additional family members to support.[34] Women did not receive this even if they were the sole supporters of their households. Some unmarried women were supporting parents, brothers, and sisters as well as themselves.

Geneva Ragland had been retired from teaching for eight years when she became a member of the La Crosse School Board in 1960. During her second year of four years on the board, Geneva said, "You know, this isn't right that the men teachers should get bigger pay than the women."[35] According to Geneva, one of the men on the board came up with a plan to even out the salaries but then denied that the board had adopted it after he was confronted by several male teachers. Geneva asked for the minutes which proved that the board had decided to eliminate the salary discrimination against women. That policy finally ended in 1967.

Geneva also had an interest in the teachers' retirement fund. On March 14, 1957, she and twenty other retired teachers met at the La Crosse County Library to form an organization devoted to keeping the state retirement and pension fund secure. She became the first president of the La Crosse Area Retired Teachers Association (LARTA) and served as the first chairman of its legislative committee which monitored bills concerning retirees and lobbied legislators. A brief history of LARTA included proof that Geneva took the lobbying responsibility to heart: "Even on her 103rd birthday, in 1990, Mrs. Ragland told the local [LARTA] president to make our viewpoints known to the legislators at Madison."[36]

Florence Whiting, who also served LARTA as president, recalled the trips she and Geneva made to Madison.

We would try so hard to speak to senators so they could see the need....Wisconsin was one of the first states to really have a teachers pension, which was very fine, but they really didn't keep up with it enough for the older teacher.... In the earlier days, a teacher would probably teach their entire lifetime and many never married....They would get something like forty dollars for retirement per month.[37]

When asked about the results of their lobbying, Florence replied, "we never got very much out of it ... a little over the years ... we always said 'it will buy a few more postage stamps.'"

In 1942, fourteen area educators formed the Theta Chapter of Delta Kappa Gamma. This national honorary society of women teachers worked to improve the status of their profession, promoted education, and informed members on current issues — economic, social, and political as well as educational — so that they would be knowledgeable world citizens.[38] Josephine Hintgen was among the charter members. So was Ethel Scheel who recalled that early programs helped foreign-born people of the community become better acquainted with American culture. In the beginning, members primarily were single women, perhaps because married women had been barred from teaching for so long. Younger members with families joined in the 1960s. Thinking ahead to retirement, the group established a welfare committee in 1958. Its first project was the publication of a brochure to help teachers plan for retirement. Thetas also worked for improvement in the teacher retirement law.

When the La Crosse Education Association (LEA) began in 1945, its members taught at the college, at the vocational school, and in the public schools. Among its presidents were Jessie Caldwell, Ruth Strozinsky, Irna Rideout, Marilyn Huff, and Barbara Schultz. The original purpose of the organization was to promote the interests of education, to foster professional spirit, good fellowship, and unity among the educators of La Crosse, and to support any community projects that the group believed vital to the welfare of the city. Until the 1960s, college administrators and school principals frequently led the organization which primarily sponsored social and community activities.[39] In the mid-1960s, the professional association and its state and national counterparts, the Wisconsin Education Association and the National Education Association, became more like a labor union. In 1965, members voted 216-11 to make LEA the bargaining agent for La Crosse public school teachers. When contract negotiations reached an impasse over salaries and insurance in 1971, the LEA went on strike for one day. Although there was outrage in the community, there was solidarity among teachers. "I was not personally happy [with the idea of striking]," said Marge Schaller, "but we [teachers] have to stick together to make good. I made phone calls and picket signs."[40]

In 1972, Phyllis Grams was among five teachers aged fifty-seven to sixty-four whose contracts were not renewed by the Melrose-Mindoro School District. In response, the teachers challenged the decision with a lawsuit. Phyllis, who had taught in that school system for nearly twenty years, said, "We sued on the basis of age and sex discrimination. And after consistently favorable decisions at every level up to the [State] Supreme Court, we finally were awarded compensation for lost wages on the basis of age discrimination."[41] The court dismissed the sex discrimination charges because "only two of the five positions were filled by men," Phyllis recalled. "Of course, you would never find a preponderance of males in a low-paying situation such as teaching was at that time."[42]

Vocational Education

Miss Keefe's School of Shorthand offered one of the earliest opportunities for vocational education in La Crosse. In an 1894 newspaper article, Rose Keefe was described as "engaged in shaping the future and guiding the minds of hundreds who have sought her advice and instructions. ... In reaching out after talent to fill her school she is doing a large amount of good which is appreciated but not fully." The school's curriculum emphasized shorthand but also embraced commercial law, forms and practices, and business ethics "essential to an accomplished man or woman in this busy world."[43]

La Crosse Vocational School
Western Wisconsin Technical College

When La Crosse's first public vocational school, La Crosse Vocational School, began in 1912, it gave both men and women an opportunity to make their way in society by learning skills or a trade such as woodworking, drafting, accounting, or typing.[44] The vocational school's programs and facilities grew dramatically under the directorship of John B. Coleman from

1916 to 1963. As he worked on his primary objective, to prepare students for a good job in the shortest possible time, Aileen Henry Pinker was at his right hand. The Viroqua native served as his secretary for forty-seven years and then worked for Director Arthur F. Jordan until her retirement in 1965. When Aileen graduated from a one-year business course at Keefe Business College in 1916, she accepted temporary employment for two weeks at La Crosse Vocational School where she earned five dollars each week. From that usual starting point for women, Aileen became secretary to the director. Her domain grew to include student registration, attendance records, job placement, invoices and payroll, issuing work permits, and administering civil service exams. She also collected rent from the students who roomed in the Hixon House in the late 1940s. According to long-time business office accountant, Dorothy Stromstad, "Mrs. Pinker was strict, efficient, and knew every nook and cranny of the school." Aileen also kept in touch with the community by volunteering for the Heart Fund, chairing the Christmas Seal Fund Drive for many years, and belonging to the business women's service club, Zonta. Her community contacts were instrumental in helping graduates of the vocational school's College of Commerce find jobs. For her work in job placement, Aileen received special recognition from the Wisconsin Bureau of Personnel Leaders in 1963.

In order to attend high school, Dorothy Stromstad left her family's farm near De Soto, Wisconsin, and worked for her room and board in the John B. Coleman home in La Crosse from 1930 to 1934. She then enrolled in the La Crosse Vocational School's newly-developed College of Commerce. Upon completion of the one-year business education course, she went to work at La Crosse Lutheran Hospital. She returned to the vocational school in 1944, this time as a member of the office staff. When she retired in 1977, she was the office manager. Office responsibilities included selling books for all classes; writing receipts for every item sold because there was no cash register; issuing child labor permits, at twenty-five cents each, for all underage city residents seeking employment; sorting mail for the expanding staff; and keeping track of the reference libraries in each area and shop. She also filled the sanitary napkin dispensing machines in the girls' restrooms.

During Marie Peterson's tenure at the La Crosse Adult and Vocational School, from 1935 to 1972, it was not unusual for her to supervise six faculty and 700 students in the Business Education Department while teaching classes of sixty students in accounting and fifty in typing. Teachers gladly took on all sorts of extracurricular tasks during the 1930s, because, according to Marie, "we were so happy just to have jobs during the Depression." Her extra responsibilities included arranging programs for the theater that served the community and planning student dances and faculty socials. Much of her instructional time involved helping handicapped people become proficient in business skills. Her method and manual for one-handed typing brought world-wide prominence to the school. Another commercial instructor, Lillian Bitzer, had started a "sight" system. Marie's idea, however, was the first "touch" system of one-handed typing ever invented. There had to be two approaches, one for a person who had the use of only the right hand, and another for the left. After the typing system was included in an article that appeared in *The Reader's Digest* in 1942, requests for information arrived from all over the country and the world.[45] Marie outlined the method and mimeographed copies of it to be sent to inquirers. Dedicated to her profession, Marie served as vice-president of business education for the Wisconsin Association of Vocational, Technical and Adult Education for five years.

The early 1940s were a busy time for the La Crosse Adult and Vocational School. The school offered many courses to help the community and the nation cope with wartime shortages of labor, commodities and resources. In March 1942, ten ambitious women put in thirty hours of study at night school to learn how to operate a telephone switchboard. The school instituted the class, which was the first public training school for switchboard operators in the United States, to meet the demand for skilled operators for Camp McCoy and various branches of the federal government. Margaret Werel, long distance supervisor in the La Crosse Telephone Company and the Wisconsin Bell Telephone Company System, taught students how to receive and place long distance calls, and praised them for their pleasant voices and interest in the problems of the callers.[46]

In response to the need for women welders in defense industries, the school offered a welding class as an experimental cooperative project with the National Youth Administration. For eight hours a day during the summer of 1942, eighteen young women practiced the basics of welding. When asked by the newspaper reporter if the mathematical part of the program was difficult, the students responded, "No." One added, "If you've had algebra or geometry, it's easy." Their instructor, Harold Hawkins, said the students showed more aptitude for the welding trade than men, especially when working with light metals and smaller pieces. Three students, Jeanne Hengel, Janet Schildman and Mardell Rude, composed new words to "Ta Ra Ra Boom De-ay" to display their patriotism while they worked:

We are the welding gals,
We're Uncle Sammy's pals,
We do our work each day,
For the good old U.S.A.
And when you hear our song,
We're welding right along,
We're happy as can be,
Welding for victory.[47]

Katherine Schultz, who supervised home economics at La Crosse Adult and Vocational School from 1930 to 1958, taught nutrition and health classes to local Red Cross volunteer workers during World War II. They, in turn, spread this knowledge throughout the community. After the war, veterans were eager students in her hotel and restaurant management classes. In 1975, she received the fourth "Trail Blazer" award presented by Western Wisconsin Technical Institute. She was honored for "forging new paths" in her field of vocational education, particularly nutrition. Long before others, she stressed the importance of learning about and serving a well-balanced diet.

Shirley Lotze's presence and hard work at Western Wisconsin Technical Institute from 1969 to 1988 prepared many students for food management careers.[48] When the technical school dedicated its 1981 yearbook to her, the tribute in *La Tech*, titled "Our Lady of Foods," read, "At first she comes on to them [her students] as stern and serious, highlighting her strong personality, her determination and her honesty ... it is then they come to respect her. Then, gradually a twinkling smile lights up her face, and out comes her sense of humor and imagination ... it is then they come to love her."

Shirley's students learned about planning, preparation, publicity, entertainment, service, clean-up, and evaluation when they participated in the gourmet Dinner DeGala and the ethnic food component of the Oktoberfest Heritage Night. When the *La Crosse Tribune* sponsored its cookbook contest in the late 1970s and early 1980s, Shirley was an integral part of the judging team. In 1978, retired Northern States Power home economist Doris Flick narrowed the field of more than 1,300 recipes to seventy-two. Shirley determined the nutritional value of these top contenders. On the morning of the judging, she supervised the food service program students as they prepared the recipes for the judges to consider.[49]

Shirley's students could count on her humor to urge them along and her strong support to get them through a tough time. One older student found Shirley's encouragement essential to her own success. When school proved to be difficult for this forty-three-year-old student, she consulted with a school counselor. His response, "You'll never make it, you're too old and too fat," convinced the student to drop out. When she stopped in to say good-bye and to explain why she was leaving, Shirley (a stout and older woman herself) became "absolutely livid." The teacher put her hand on the student's shoulder, looked her in the eye, and said, "If I could do it, you sure can." Then Shirley told her own story of divorce in 1957 when society looked upon a divorced woman as "inferior" and "having something wrong with her"; of how she supported herself and her three young children as a baker, a cook, and a restaurant manager; and of how she decided to pursue an education because it was "the only way to move from blue collar into middle class" even though her family and friends thought she was "crazy!" That changed the student's mind, and she not only graduated with honors but also was the first in the class to get full-time, satisfying employment.[50]

In response to the state's requirement for a balance of men and women to oversee the policies of the school, women made their first appearance on the governing board of Western Wisconsin Technical Institute in the late 1970s. Judith Radcliffe, Linda Carlson, Jan Keil, and Mary Beth Solverson were the precedent-setting members. The new gender-balanced board did not move ahead without some difficulties. When the time came to replace retiring director Charles Richardson, one male member of the board raised his concern that the four women did not have the knowledge to select the new director. The women did, however, participate in the selection process.

Higher Education

Viterbo College and the University of Wisconsin-La Crosse began as teacher preparation schools. The presence of these two schools in the community made it possible for many local women to enter the education profession.

St. Rose Convent
Viterbo College

In 1849, six young Bavarian women joined a group of German emigrants in response to a call for missionaries in the United States. Their intent was to teach, but they were sidetracked when the bishop of Milwaukee asked them to staff the St. Aemilian Orphanage for Boys and to serve as housekeepers for St. Francis de Sales Seminary. In 1860, the original founders of what would become the Franciscan Sisters of Perpetual Adoration (FSPA) left, frustrated that they had been turned into housekeepers instead of teachers, and returned to Bavaria. The American sisters who had joined the order stayed on and, led by Mother Antonia Leinfelder Herb, returned to their original mission: teaching. They spent the Civil War years in a rural setting near Jefferson, Wisconsin, and, in 1871, moved to the frontier diocese of La Crosse.[51] They acquired the block bounded by Ninth, Tenth, Market, and Winnebago streets and began construction of what became the motherhouse of the FSPA, St. Rose of Viterbo. By 1880, the FSPA were training their own to teach in the twenty-five elementary schools they staffed in Wisconsin and Illinois.

At the end of the nineteenth century the new Mother Superior, Ludovica Keller, focused on raising the standards of teacher training. She named Sister Seraphine Kraus as directress of the schools served by the FSPA. By 1890, Sister Seraphine had planned a sequence of courses to prepare elementary teachers. Using Sister Seraphine's plan, the convent high school, which had been established to complete the education of the postulants, became St. Rose Normal Institute. The normal institute extended the postulants' education and improved their training for teaching. When it became apparent that the prospective teachers needed educational materials, Sister Seraphine wrote them herself. The convent press printed the first handbook, *Manual and Graded Course of Study for Use in the Schools Conducted by the Franciscan Sisters of Perpetual Adoration*, in 1902. Five years later, Sister Verena Dauser and Sister Seraphine began a joint venture that produced several textbooks for use in Catholic grade schools. When a great demand developed for *A History of the United States for Catholic Schools*, the FSPA reached an agreement with Scott Foresman Company to publish it in 1923 as *The Cathedral History of the United States*.[52]

Becoming an Accredited College

During the 1930s, St. Rose Normal Institute evolved into St. Rose Junior College and, eventually, Viterbo College, an accredited four-year school that was authorized to award a degree in elementary education. Grace McDonald entered the religious community in 1933. She completed high school within the walls of St. Rose and became a novice. Her first year as a novice "was like a one-year retreat during which we learned about being a sister and developed our spiritual life," she said. As a second year novice, she was "missioned," i.e., assigned, to a Catholic grade school in Athens, Wisconsin.

"We had a very good mentoring process," Sister Grace recalled. "I learned how to teach from the sisters who had been there a long time."[53]

The sisters extended their own education during the summer breaks from teaching. Their goals were to be as well prepared as their public school counterparts and to meet the various state requirements. "Most of us got our degrees through summer school," said Sister Grace. "We all flocked home each summer. There were 400 or 500 of us." Virginia Marcotte Larkin described the nonstop activity she observed as a child in the convent's neighborhood: "I grew up in the Catholic system, and I remember seeing the sisters going to school all summer long. I didn't think about what that meant until I was an adult. Then I realized that they were some of the first women around here to have degrees in higher education."[54] On summer evenings, neighbors gathered to watch the sisters enjoy their free time. The outsiders climbed atop the six-foot wall surrounding the courtyard and watched the sisters, in full habit, playing softball or roller skating.[55]

Viterbo College took its first step toward autonomy when it moved from St. Rose Convent into the new Murphy Center in 1942. The next year, the first laywomen were admitted as students. In 1954, Viterbo received accreditation from the North Central Association of Colleges and Universities, the American Association for Teacher Education, and the National Association of Schools of Music.[56]

Reaching Out into the Community

The FSPA also began reaching out into the larger secular La Crosse community. For example, in 1948, to share its academic mission and cultural offerings, Viterbo sponsored the first Great Books Program held in La Crosse. Sister Charlotte Bonneville, chairperson of the English department, and Sister Theodine, president-dean, led the discussion program. Thirty-one people participated the first year. Viterbo's group continued until 1950 when it merged with another Great Books program which had been organized at the La Crosse Public Library.[57] During Sister Grace McDonald's tenure as the fourth president of Viterbo (1960-1970), she received encouragement from D. J. Petruccelli, manager of the Chamber of Commerce, to become more active in the community. In 1965, when La Crosse competed for "All America City," Sister Grace was part of the delegation to St. Louis. "He [Petruccelli] must have thought it would be unique to have a black-robed nun representing La Crosse," she mused.[58]

Working with a long range plan for the college, Sister Grace began acquiring property in order to construct more residential space for the

Sister Grace McDonald, center, on the construction site of Viterbo College's Fine Arts Center, 1969.

Viterbo College

growing lay student population and to erect an arts building. Taking advantage of a new program put forth by the Kennedy administration, she applied for urban renewal funds. Because no one else had applied for these funds, La Crosse had to establish a Redevelopment Authority to receive and review the application from Viterbo. Resistance from two aldermen and from the La Crosse Home Owners Union, Inc., put an end to Viterbo's bid. Although Viterbo did not benefit, the larger community gained a Redevelopment Authority.

Sister Francesca Zoeller, Viterbo's third president (1952-60), had begun plans for a fine arts building. Sister Grace learned that the state of Wisconsin had federal grant money to be distributed to colleges and universities. "We might have been the only one that applied because we received one million dollars for our arts center," Sister Grace said. Additional funds came from government loans, the mother house, and the school's very first fund drive. In addition to teaching music, art, dance, and theatre in the building which was dedicated in 1971, Viterbo opened it to the public as a fine arts performance and resource center.

In 1970, Sister Grace was elected president of the FSPA, Viterbo hired its first male president, and the whole college became a co-educational institution. Over the years, Viterbo reflected transformations in the church and in society. The drop in the number of women choosing the religious life as a vocation coincided with changes that occurred in the 1950s. "That was when the Pope asked us to modify our habits [clothing], when sisters were beginning to drive cars, when society was beginning to let up on some of its restrictions on women," Sister Grace recalled. Since "we're made up of whoever is in society, those ideas began to come into the [FSPA] community. Many of us went away to school. We became more highly educated and began thinking more independently. Even in our own community we were beginning to change rules, to make them less strict about enclosure." As the number of sisters began to decline, Viterbo began hiring lay faculty. However, even if the Franciscan sisters no longer serve as president nor fill all the seats on the board of directors nor all the teaching positions, their influence is strongly felt. According to Sister Grace, "Viterbo College is us because it came out of the high school and normal school the sisters established to train their own to become teachers."

La Crosse Normal School
University of Wisconsin-La Crosse

Because the St. Rose Normal Institute limited its enrollment to FSPA postulants, the general public did not have local access to teacher training until the La Crosse Normal School opened its doors in 1909. This public institution broadened opportunities for many — for educators seeking teaching positions, for young adults desiring to become trained teachers, for community youngsters to attend a school that practiced new educational methods.[59] Because this was a teacher training school, all instruction was geared to preparing young adults to become teachers. Most of the first students lived in town and walked or took the streetcar to the school which was on the edge of the city. Others commuted by train from nearby communities or rented rooms from townspeople. Students enrolled in one, two, or three year courses of preparation. Before going off to teach in rural and urban schools, they practiced teaching in the school on campus. The

Training School or Campus School was an elementary and junior high school within the normal school. Faculty members and student teachers who were supervised by the faculty taught children from the community. These children, who mingled with and became part of campus life, were taught by people who were paying special attention to the art and science of teaching.

Specialties in Rural School
and Physical Education Teaching

In 1927, La Crosse Normal School's mission of preparing teachers was reflected in its new name, La Crosse State Teachers College. The college continued to emphasize two specialized training programs, one for rural school teachers and one for physical education teachers. Alice Drake joined the faculty in 1931 and proceeded to train teachers for the next thirty-four years. During that time, she became director of the rural education department and then director of the elementary education department. Long after her students became teachers, they continued to draw upon what they had learned from her. Ida Rusedahl Hunter, who taught at Valley View School from 1938 to 1941, wrote, "Many times during my teaching days when confronted with a problem as to what to do, I would close my eyes for a few seconds and reflect, 'Now what would Alice Drake say or do in this situation?'"[60]

During the early World War II years, the summer sessions of the rural school department were the busiest because women were returning to college for recertification to fill positions that were vacated by male teachers who had joined the military. "One hundred ten people came to observe on one day," recalled one of the college instructors, Marian Hammes.[61] Because teaching in a rural school was so different from teaching in the city schools, Alice Drake invited Marian Hammes to develop a rural school demonstration room within the Campus School. The rural room, which was as much like a one-room school as possible, served student teachers and rural children from 1947 to 1958. Marian, who had been an outstanding rural teacher, became the teacher of hundreds of rural teachers.

La Crosse Normal School developed a specialty in training physical education teachers and eventually became the only Wisconsin normal school certified to do so. That specialty became the institution's first degree program. Through the years, women faculty of the physical education department were leaders among the college faculty and models for the students. Young women from the small towns and rural areas of Wisconsin were intrigued by Emma Lou Wilder's eastern accent. They also were in awe of the seemingly boundless energy of this woman who loved mountain climbing, field hockey and tennis. Because Emma Lou's teaching career at La Crosse (1921-56) coincided with the institution's status as the only school in Wisconsin authorized to train physical education teachers (1912-58), she influenced generations of physical education teachers. From 1926 to 1930, she served as president of the newly formed Wisconsin Physical Education Association. She also served on the college's Faculty Steering Committee which appointed other faculty committees and set the agenda for faculty meetings.[62]

Beatrice Baird was a member of the physical education faculty from 1946 to 1974. She had a great impact on physical education and sports for girls and women, said former student and colleague, Jean Foss. "Bea Baird was the motivating force in our School of Health, Physical Education, and Recreation,"[63] said Jean, who served as chairperson of the physical education department, affirmative action officer, assistant to the vice chancellor, and associate vice chancellor before she retired in 1989. "She believed there was a more rarified atmosphere in competitive sports than there was in intramurals or play days. She believed competition helped highly skilled people reach a peak and showed the lesser skilled what they could aim for," Jean added. Bea served on the college's Faculty Steering Committee and its successor, the Faculty Senate, and was among those who initiated and administered the first Wisconsin Track and Field Meet for high school girls and organized the Wisconsin Women's Interscholastic Athletic Conference.

Expanding Beyond Teacher Education

As La Crosse State Teachers College began expanding the curriculum beyond teacher training, several distinguished women joined the faculty. Marie Park Toland taught speech and theatre at La Crosse from 1937 to 1966. "Doc" Toland tirelessly stressed the importance of the arts in instruction, on campus, and in society. She had a regal bearing that kept students at a distance yet earned their affection and respect. Her performance as "Elizabeth the Queen" was unforgettable. During the 1960s space race between the United States and the Soviet Union, when U. S. society was increasingly more concerned with the sciences rather than the arts, Marie greeted her students at the beginning of the semester with "Today, the emphasis [in colleges] is upon science, rather than English, history, philosophy or the fine arts ... for they are not necessary to defense ... only to civilization."[64]

Enrollment at La Crosse State dropped significantly during World War II when all but a handful of men entered military service. Women generally filled in for the absent male students and faculty. They produced the school's newspaper and annual, played in the band, taught classes, and assumed administrative duties in the school. However, the reverse was true in the registrar's office. When Lora Greene joined the armed forces, Milford Cowley, professor of chemistry, filled in as registrar. After World War II, enrollment doubled. Returning soldiers took advantage of the G.I. Bill of Rights. Experienced teachers returned to pursue a B.E. (bachelors in education). The teachers, who often had two- or three-year teaching certificates and many years experience, needed a diploma to meet the state's new requirements. These teacher-students formed their own club and named it The Drakels, in honor of Alice Drake, director of the rural and the elementary education departments.[65]

Mauree Applegate Clack (education, 1944-66), and Margaret Chew (geography, 1945-79) were among the new faculty members of the post-war era. Mauree supervised elementary practice teachers, taught creative writing, published several books in the field of children's literature, and lectured and led workshops all over the country. She described herself as a collector of deep blue Wedgwood china and a writer of "poor verse." She also was known to many children for her radio program about writing. It is estimated that over 60,000 children listened to "Let's Write" in the twelve years it was broadcast from Madison. The Wednesday morning programs inspired many fourth through eighth graders throughout the state to put their thoughts on paper and send them to her. She read every word.[66]

Margaret "Peg" Chew, who was born the same year the La Crosse Normal School opened, doubled the size of the geography department when she arrived to teach summer school in 1945. "There were great big crowds of teachers" returning to earn their degrees that summer, she recalled.[67] Peg was asked to stay on for the 1945-46 school year as housemother for Grandview dorm and as a part-time teacher. The next year she became a full-time member of the faculty. Because housing was scarce, Peg lived at the YWCA for a year. "My room was downstairs next to the gym. It had a kitchenette and a bath, but the wall of the bathroom didn't go all the way up to separate it from the gym," she said.

Each summer from 1963 until 1980, Peg led credit-earning tours sponsored by the university. Olive Gershon joined several of those trips which covered geography, economic conditions, history, and culture. Because she wanted to earn some extra money, Olive returned to teaching in 1963 after being home with family for seventeen years. "I planned to teach just one year to earn money to go to England to visit relatives. But I got 'itchy foot,' so I taught fifteen more years so I could continue to travel," she said. "Our tours were a success and given preferential treatment for two reasons: first, we were a university study group; and, second, Peg is such a gracious person, such a good ambassador for us and for the school....We got to see and do extra things because of Peg's efforts to make it really something special. She gave us extra dignity that some tour groups didn't have. One time we had an audience with the prime minister of India, Indira Gandhi."[68]

In 1951, La Crosse State Teachers College was renamed La Crosse State College to reflect its newly received authority to grant degrees in the liberal arts. As the number of students rapidly increased in the post-war years, townspeople such as Mary Hebberd were recruited to meet the demand for more teachers. President Rexford Mitchell asked her to teach in the English department for the spring 1947 semester. Then he asked her to teach in the summer session. "After that I was a regular — no haggling, no contract, very little talk of tenure and some of the other problems which came up in the future," Mary recalled. After a few years of teaching, she became the first director of public relations and alumni affairs until 1964 when she was replaced by Patricia Muller. Mary returned to teaching and then retired in 1976.

With the exploding growth of students, faculty, staff and buildings, new services developed for students. Early in the school's history, there were few administrators and support staff. In addition to being the school's physician from 1918 until 1941, Sarah Garrett Bangsberg was dean of women from 1923 until 1941. In that capacity, she supervised the living arrangements (which were off-campus because the first residence hall was not built until 1951) as well as the academic and social life of women students. "Doc" Bangsberg was an early purveyor of sex education for coeds. Prescriptions such as "no sitting on laps" and "don't drink pineapple juice when going out on a date" were reported as her suggestions to reduce passion.

Edith Cartwright served as the sixth and last dean of women. When she arrived in 1941, it was a one-woman office and there were fewer than 700 students. A female student did not visit the dean's office unless properly attired in a skirt, recalled Patricia Mertens, a student in the 1950s. "Carty" oversaw the building of residence halls on campus and saw the coming of self-governance for female students. Because the legal age of majority was still twenty-one, *in loco parentis* was still in effect on campus. For example, the curfew for women students in 1967-68 was midnight on Sunday through Thursday and one a.m. for Friday and Saturday nights. The attitude that "if you take care of the women the men will stay out of trouble" was beginning to change.[69] When "Carty" retired in 1969, deans of students no longer were assigned to students by gender. Instead, the dean and the associate deans took responsibility for a growing variety of services to students. Norene A. Smith, who had come to campus as assistant dean of women in 1961, took on the task of developing and expanding student housing, counseling and testing, and placement. The first counseling rooms presented a problem of privacy because "the walls didn't go all the way to the floor or ceiling," she recalled.[70] Norene also initiated and chaired the graduate program in college student personnel.

The Feminist Revival of the 1970s

The world continued to change. Women, who had worked for civil rights for Blacks in the 1960s, turned their energies toward guaranteeing civil rights for themselves. Title IX, which became law in 1972, was one manifestation of that effort. It required any institution receiving federal funds to offer equal opportunities for women and for men. Decades prior to Title IX, physical education instructor Beatrice Baird met with mixed success when she promoted athletic competition for women. According to Jean Foss, Bea single-handedly developed a women's field hockey team that was so good it received invitations to play other club teams around the state and the country. However, Bea's colleagues did not share her interest in intercollegiate competition.[71] Carol Hettinga Bassuener, who became assistant director of residence life at the university, recalled a time when there was virtually no support for intercollegiate athletics for women. "While I was an undergrad here in the early 1960s, some girls were almost expelled from school because they competed in a basketball tournament. Even in a phy. ed. school, there wasn't support for competitive athletics for young women. That was the way it was."[72]

Jean Kessler, who graduated from Wisconsin State University-La Crosse in 1963, was one of those young women who loved to play basketball. She recalled, "In 1961-62, I was part of an informal group of phy. ed. students that went to Milwaukee to play in the Amateur Athletic Union's annual basketball tournament. We weren't representing the school; we were just playing for the fun of competing. We did so well that our names appeared in the newspaper."[73] Although Jean and her friends were not official representatives of WSU-La Crosse, the school's faculty and administration were not pleased that the students had played in the tournament. As Jean remembered, "We were lined up and told how awful we were. We had felt good about what we had done and had had a great time, so their reaction was devastating for all of us. As punishment, they banned us from all WRA [Women's Recreation Association] activities on campus for the rest of the year."

The desire for gender equality on campus was not limited to athletics. An interesting role-reversal occurred in 1968 when Jean Foss declined to be nominated for secretary of the Faculty Senate because it was the stereotypic office for women. As a result, Wayne Kaufman became the first man to serve in that position. In 1971, Paula Wade became the first woman to preside over the Faculty Senate. The following year she was appointed the first Affirmative Action Officer on the La Crosse campus.

A new program, to assist community women seeking new directions in employment, education and community life, was established on the university campus in 1974. Shirley Haas, an activist for women's issues, was named the coordinator of Women's Education Resources (WER). At the time she also was a member of the Governor's Commission on the Status of Women. On April 20, 1974, the UW-La Crosse campus hosted "Homemaking and the Family: Changing Values and Concerns," the first in a series of state-wide conferences sponsored by the Governor's Commission. Participant reaction to the conference ranged from not wanting to be involved in such a "militant program" to posting "The Worth of Wives" on the refrigerator door. Another important first-for-La Crosse program was "Assessing the Need for Change: A Conference on Women and Health Care," held February 26, 1977, and co-sponsored by WER.

As coordinator of Women's Education Resources, Shirley also advised women seeking assistance in decision-making and developed non-credit classes in assertiveness, life-work planning, and management skills. "A male colleague, who was skeptical about management seminars for women, later offered such programs himself through the College of Business Administration," Shirley recalled. Although there was not always strong support from the traditional faculty, ad hoc instructors from the community made major contributions to the WER program. "They didn't just teach a class or two each semester. They followed up with their students in many ways and helped us develop ideas, programs, even mailing lists," Shirley said. "I'm glad the interns and instructors, such as Karin Bast, Dorothy Fitzpatrick, Beverly Mach and Marilyn Ondell, plus staff member Jan Gallagher have gone on to bigger and better opportunities."[74]

Shirley did some joint programming with others such as Sue Mercier at the YWCA and Mary O'Sullivan of the Women's Opportunity Center at Western Wisconsin Technical Institute (WWTI). When Mary began teaching English at WWTI in 1975, she noticed the increasing numbers of re-entry students. Most of them were women looking for training to build skills and confidence to re-enter the job market. "They just didn't have as many resources to turn to as the men did," recalled Mary, "and they were getting slotted into traditional female occupations with low pay that made it difficult for them to become financially self-sufficient." She explored ways to fund a program specifically tailored to re-entry women and discovered there was money available from the state and from the Vocational, Technical, and Adult Education (VTAE) system. When she received no comment from WWTI administrators about what she had learned, she sent another memo to them that said, "Good news. I've applied for funds." The Women's Opportunity Center opened on the WWTI campus in 1978-79. Mary served as the first coordinator, on a half-time basis.[75]

During the first year, Mary learned two important things. First, the center needed a certified counselor to guide the many women coming in for help, and, second, she preferred to return to teaching. Thus, in 1979, Jeannie Potter became the first full-time coordinator of the Women's Opportunity Center which offered counseling services in addition to life-skill and job-skill classes. In the early 1980s, the VTAE removed "Women" from the name of all the opportunity centers on its campuses throughout the state rather than appear to be discriminating against men.

In the spring of 1975, a Women's Studies Committee of twelve University of Wisconsin-La Crosse faculty, staff, and students[76] concluded, "Women's Studies is basic to the educational mission of the university, both as a corrective and as a field of study in its own right. Women's Studies seeks not only to extend understandings of the female experience but also to examine ways in which interpretations of human history have been altered or distorted by the traditional tendency to focus almost exclusively on the accomplishments and perceptions of men."[77] Judith Green, a professor of English, became the first director of Women's Studies, a quarter-time position. In her first year she established a resource center which prompted the question, "Why do you need a Women's Studies Resource Center? There isn't a Men's Resource Center." Judith's standard response was, "Oh, yes there is, it's called Murphy Library."[78] Vivian Munson became the second director, with a half-time appointment in 1977. She and the Women's Studies Committee worked hard to develop credit courses, largely staffed by women volunteers and outside professionals, that eventually became part of the university mainstream. In the 1980s, the director's position grew to three-quarter and then to full-time, the newly formed Women's Studies Student Association revived efforts to establish a child care center on campus, and the program became a full-fledged academic department that offered a minor in Women's Studies.[79]

At a reminiscing session about the Organization for Campus Women of UW-La Crosse, Marilyn Wigdahl remarked there wasn't much need for women to organize in the early years when the school was small and the faculty and staff were in touch with one another. However, by the 1970s, the campus had grown so large that many people did not know one another. Judith Green credited French instructor Joyce Telzrow with being the "spark" of the campus women's group. As a way to acquaint people, "Joyce organized brown bag lunch sessions for faculty women in 1970 or 1971," said Judith. In the fall of 1971, Joyce and Beatrice Baird became the first co-coordinators of the Association for La Crosse Faculty Women. The following year the group invited staff and students to join, changed its name to WOMEN, sponsored the first Women's Awareness Week on campus, and brought in black author, attorney, and feminist Florynce Kennedy as the keynote speaker. "Women are the new kind of nigger. The interesting thing is that it took them so long to realize it," she said.[80] In 1975, the group changed its name to Organization for Campus Women (OCW). The following year it sponsored the first "Directions" conference to acquaint campus women with how the administration worked. Judith Green said, "The conference helped me become chair of the English department. There were topics that we didn't understand that had been keeping women from moving into administration. We weren't using the term 'glass ceiling' then. We learned things that people who ruled us knew so that we could rule, too, for example, developing a budget. There was a whole new vocabulary I learned that day."[81]

Members of OCW recalled another event of the mid-1970s which helped unite women — faculty and staff, university and community. UW-La Crosse hosted an International Conference on the Status of Women, April 9-12, 1975. The conference was inspired by but not connected with the United Nations International Women's Year Conference held in Mexico City a few months later. Delegates from nearly forty nations converged at La Crosse to discuss the significance of women throughout the world. Controversy accompanied the event from the early planning stages to the final evaluation.[82] One student said about the political science professor who proposed the idea for the conference: "He was not interested in the status of

women, but with women of status who wouldn't rock the boat."[83] Some
campus women were unhappy about being excluded from the formative
planning stages. Community women's groups were offended that they were
asked to host breakfasts and luncheons for conference participants when
only a very limited number of community women were invited to observe
but not participate in the conference.[84] In terms of impact, the conference
program was less significant than the bonds forged by women as they
worked together to solve the problems involved in planning and hosting the
conference.

OCW has since addressed women's issues such as day care, sexual
harassment, tenure and promotions, and, perhaps the most controversial
issue, salary equity. From the beginning of the history of La Crosse Normal
School/University of Wisconsin-La Crosse, male faculty were paid more than
female. In 1912, the monthly salary for men ranged from $150 to $220 while
women were paid between $100 and $120.[85] The gap still existed when a
1980 study indicated that fifty-three faculty women were being paid less
than their male colleagues who had similar training and experience.
University Services Coordinator Eileen Polizzotto and Affirmative Action
Officer Julie Sichler spearheaded the salary study. OCW brought in an
expert from California to review and explain the La Crosse situation. Judith
Green recalled, "I never saw Ruth Nixon [who taught Spanish from 1947 to
1984] so angry before or after as when she realized how unfair the salaries
were. When a plan to correct the inequity was presented to the Faculty
Senate, the men did not want to go along with it because they feared they
would have to share the pie, that the pot of money wouldn't be enlarged."[86]
Ruth was incensed about the long-term impact salary discrimination had
and would continue to have for women faculty during their careers and into
retirement if it was not corrected. Eileen, too, was impressed with Ruth's
stand: "That late in her career, Ruth really didn't have to do anything about
this, but she had professional and personal standards. A line was drawn,
and she crossed it with her head held high." Eileen also said that the role of
Vice Chancellor Carl Wimberly should not be underestimated, "He took an
incredible amount of flack on this issue. He believed the university had to
right the wrong."[87]

❖ ❖ ❖

In spite of policies and practices which had worked against them for so long, many women made teaching their life's work. Nancy Ellingson, a painter of abstract landscapes, a writer of poetry and short stories, and a teacher of art and English at Central High School in La Crosse said of her chosen vocation:

> *I love teaching. I think I'm a preacher at heart....Sometimes*
> *you are not aware that you are sharing anything important*
> *through your work until you see it reflected in a student you*
> *are teaching or a person who is reading what you have*
> *written or someone who is looking at what you have portrayed*
> *in a painting....The position of teacher is an important one in*
> *society. I am passing on something of value to the future.*[88]

At Work in Industry, Office and Retail

One of the early ways that many women used their skills to earn money was to provide domestic service. They did so without leaving their homes by taking in boarders, laundry, or sewing. Or they lived and worked as servants in other households. At the end of the nineteenth century, women started expanding the horizons of the workplace. Domestic servants who had been at the beck and call of a household were attracted to the increased pay, regular hours, defined duties, and social companionship of factory, office, and retail work.[1]

Industry

La Crosse County industries offered a variety of jobs to women who worked in breweries, sorted pearl buttons, stripped tobacco, packed cosmetics, sewed clothing, assembled gauges, inspected ammunition, canned vegetables, and made lefse. Women also were instrumental in developing and running enterprises which manufactured beer, cosmetics, clothing, and food.

Early Industry in La Crosse

Brewing

German settlers established breweries in the area in the 1850s. Amelia Knecht and Johanna Heileman both became involved, through marriage, in the brewing industry in the last half of the nineteenth century. When she was widowed, Amelia carried on the business of the Onalaska brewery her husband had started in the 1850s.[2] She added on to the original building and opened a brewery bar, restaurant, and hotel. The hotel was particularly popular with farmers who traveled long distances to trade in town. The brewery building eventually became the Onalaska Pickle Factory.

Johanna Bandle emigrated from Germany to the United States with her brothers in 1852. She lived in New York City and then Milwaukee where she met her future husband, Gottlieb Heileman. They married in 1858 and settled in La Crosse where he successfully gained entry into the brewing industry. As their family grew to include eight children, Johanna supervised the construction of a brick mansion at 925 South Third Street. It was from this house that Johanna served noontime meals to the brewery's single employees. Presumably, she believed the married employees should go home for a meal prepared by their wives. Johanna continued the business that carried her husband's name after he died in 1878. When the G. Heileman Brewing Company was incorporated in 1890, she became one of the first women presidents of a corporation within the state of Wisconsin and the United States.[3] She held that position until her own death in 1917, just three years before Prohibition.

Unlike most other brewers, Johanna employed women. Throughout the industry, women were taboo because of an old myth that women might spread yeast infections. No brewer wanted to jeopardize the fermentation process by allowing women inside the operation. Although Johanna did hire women to work in the brewery, she did not allow them to work in the brewing and fermentation areas.

Pearl Button Manufacturing

Pearl buttons were made from clam shells harvested from the Mississippi River. Clam diggers often established their camps as soon as the ice went out. During the summer months, their families joined them. Wives and children cooked meals and sorted the clams, thus giving the men more time to gather the shells.

The Wisconsin Pearl Button Company operated at 730 North Third Street in La Crosse from 1890 to 1930.[4] The company "put out" some work. That is, in 1910, it paid approximately 150 women and children to sew buttons onto cards at home.[5] In the factory, men performed most of the button making operations, while women always worked in the button sorting department. According to a La Crosse County Historical Society article by Loretta Tennesen, once the buttons had been cut and polished, women sorted them into nine classifications or grades. However, sisters Angie Wiltinger and Alberta Fuchs, who worked at the button company as teenagers in 1920,

The Wisconsin Pearl Button Company, 730 North Third Street, La Crosse, counted on women to sort the buttons into various grades, c. 1920.

La Crosse County Historical Society

recalled their job was to sort buttons into one of four grades. "The first grade buttons were just beautiful but only two or three buttons out of ten would make that grade," said Angie.[6] The upper grades sold for the highest prices. If buttons were sorted improperly, the company could lose a lot of money. Inspectors examined the work of each sorter. If she had done her work carelessly, she was required to go over it again until every button was properly classified. Since she was paid by the piece rather than for her time, she lost pay for sloppy work that had to be redone.[7]

Cigar Manufacturing

Mary Longway was seventeen when she moved to La Crosse from rural Bangor in 1925. "My uncle got me and my sister a job stripping tobacco at Lorillard's tobacco warehouse. He always laughed at us when we screwed up our faces at the steam and the smell of the hot tobacco when it was dumped on the table in front of us," she recalled.[8] At first Mary boarded with the Roy Fredrickson family on Caledonia Street but moved to French Island in the 1930s. During the Depression, she found better paying work at the Moto Meter Gauge Company (previously called National Gauge and later known as Auto-Lite). Her jobs included cleaning glass for headlights, riveting brackets onto gauges, and soldering springs into sockets. Workers were laid off frequently due to fluctuations in production. "During those layoffs, I would go back to stripping tobacco," she said. During World War II, Mary, who had accrued seniority, worked fairly steadily at Auto-Lite which was producing oil and temperature gauges, speedometers, and blackout lights for lighting up instrument panels for B-17 bombers and jeeps.

Cosmetics

Ruth Johnson Maurer parlayed a beauty cream she concocted in the basement of her home into a successful business venture and a major cosmetics concern.[9] In 1903, her husband, Dr. Albert A. Maurer, handed her $300 and said, "Take this and throw it away on your fool idea — then drop it." Two years later, with $100,000 in capital, she incorporated the Marinello Company. As she reinvested profits and the business steadily grew, it moved from her basement to the 200 block of South Fifth Avenue and then to a new three-story factory at 225 South Sixth Street in La Crosse.

The Marinello Company employed approximately 150 people, most of them women. The men performed the chemist kind of jobs — mixing the powders and the rouges, the creams, and the lotions. The women packaged all of these products into small containers and gift sets. Men also worked in the shipping department. Ruth had some progressive ideas about employee relations. She provided a clubhouse for employees just north of the Sixth Street factory. Also, there was a company policy that any employee in need of a physical examination or medical care could receive treatment, at company expense, from her physician husband.

To expand her business, Ruth established her own printing plant, employed a crew of salesmen, and developed beauty training schools. The printing and lithographing plant, one block north of the factory, produced thousands of pieces of literature promoting Marinello products. Salesmen traveled the country selling products with names like *Blue Ameryl* and *Lettuce Cream* to drug and department stores. Annual sales reached three million dollars. By 1920, the Marinello Company was selling products throughout the United States, Canada, Mexico, South America, Europe, Russia, South Africa, Australia, China, and Japan. The beauty schools,

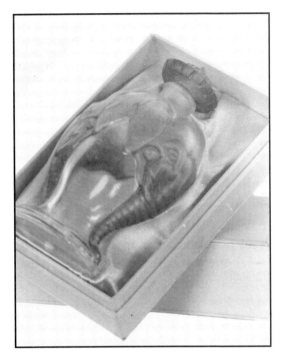

Products of the Marinello Company, a successful cosmetics manufacturing company started by Ruth Johnson Maurer, c. 1920.

Special Collections, Murphy Library,
University of Wisconsin-La Crosse

located in Chicago, Denver, Detroit, Los Angeles, New York, and Pittsburgh, taught proper use of the products and entitled beauticians to use the Marinello name in their business. Helen Nigro opened the first Marinello Beauty Shop in La Crosse on the third floor of the Rivoli Building in 1928.

In 1926, Ruth was persuaded to move the Marinello operation to New York City, a decision which put many La Crosse people out of work. It turned out to be a bad move for her, too. Shortly thereafter, she found herself without a business and just $30,000 to show for her years of effort.

Florence Oldenburg Munson was a Marinello employee. About fifteen years after her sister left the family farm for domestic work in La Crosse, Florence followed suit.[10] She worked as a dishwasher and a maid before going into factory work. Like other young women at the end of World War I, Florence was eager to leave domestic work for a job with better pay and fewer hours. At the Marinello Company, Florence filled, packaged, and labeled small cream samples and rouge boxes. She did that from 8 a.m. to 6 p.m., Monday through Friday, and from 8 a.m. to 5 p.m. on Saturday. Her pay was about $12 a week. With that money, she paid room and board to her sister and brother-in-law and shopped for clothing in downtown La Crosse on Saturday nights. At noon she often went to the YWCA on the second and third floors of a building at 420 Main Street. In the rest room (or lounge) there, she could supplement the lunch she had packed with soup and coffee for ten or fifteen cents. If she wanted to buy a complete meal, the cost was thirty-five cents. Instead of spending a nickel a ride for the streetcar, she walked everywhere.

Florence recounted that work schedules were clearly defined, but the Marinello piecework pay rate was not. One time she and other members of her department got together to plan to demand that they be told what that rate was. When the plant superintendent, Harriet Chamberlain, got wind of what they were planning, she called each member of the department into her office separately and then ordered each of them to go back to work and not to mention this again. On the next payday, Florence compared her pay envelope with someone else's in the department; hers contained two dollars less. When she asked the forelady in creams and rouges, Ella E. Beardsley, about the difference, Florence found the response unsatisfactory, took the afternoon off and found a new job at National Gauge.

Clothing

The "Leona" an ingenious undergarment that combined a camisole, underpants and slip, was patented in 1905 by a thirty-three year old La Crosse seamstress and designer, Leona Foerster Linker.[11] She formed the Leona Garment Company to manufacture this three-in-one combination until 1920 when it lost popularity because of the changing styles of the flapper era. Leona's early sewing talent led to an apprenticeship with a seamstress at the age of twelve. By 1895, at the age of twenty-three, she had developed her needlework skills, design talents, and self-confidence to the point of opening her own dressmaking shop in La Crosse. She and her sister, Kathryn, created fashionable dresses and ballgowns and the undergarments to go with them. Leona purchased fabrics and laces for their creations in Chicago. During one of those buying trips she must have shown samples of her work to the Gosshard Corset Company because it hired her as a designer and foreign agent in 1900. In that capacity, Leona traveled to Europe at least once each year. While there she attended the theater, opera, and other

The Leona, a three-in-one
undergarment created by
Leona Foerster Linker.
*La Crosse County
Historical Society*

...THE...

Leona Garment Co.

MAIN STREET   LA CROSSE, WIS.

Producers and Originators of Unique and Select

ARTICLES OF
FINE LINGERIE.

THE LEONA
THREE
PIECE
GARMENT,

Patented and Trade-
Marked, is the dain-
tiest, most satis-
factory and most
desirable garment
that has ever been
introduced. It is
so cut that the
THREE articles
are in ONE, and
yet take the place
of the three separ-

ate garments for-
merly worn, which
always produced
that clumsy effect
about the waist line.
It is, in fact, the
ideal garment of the
age, and is the con-
centrated form of
comfort, beauty
and practical use-
fulness, needing but
one trial to strike
conviction to the
heart of every
woman, who is
interested in fine
lingerie.

cultural and artistic events to observe what people were wearing. In her Paris office, she designed a new line and set to work with seamstresses, using lace she purchased in Zurich, to fashion design samples to show to retailers. After the last of the buyers placed their orders, she returned to her La Crosse business, upstairs at 221 Main Street, until it was time to travel for the next season. Her marriage to Charles Linker in 1907 did not slow down her business activity. She continued her responsibilities as proprietress of the Leona Garment Company until 1920 and as representative of the Gosshard Corset Company into the 1930s.

In 1920 and 1921, young women like Emma Raymond Fellows, who was in her late teens, could earn twenty dollars a week "making dresses for Sears and Roebuck" at the La Crosse Garment Company. It was located at Second and Market streets and paid employees, who worked eight hours a day including Saturdays, by the piece.[12] In the late 1920s, Mary Brown Sneath worked at the garment company to support her six children. "One day she came home crying because she hadn't made her quota for the day," recalled her daughter, Mary Lou Brown Rudolph. "She eventually worked her way up to be an inspector of other people's work."[13]

In the midst of the Depression, Jenny Ames, who was not quite eighteen,

Women worked six days a week at the La Crosse Garment Company at 1000 South Front Street, n.d.
Special Collections, Murphy Library, University of Wisconsin-La Crosse

went to work at the garment company, which then was paying workers 12-1/2 cents an hour. "My mother wanted me to go to business school after I graduated from high school in 1934, but I was more interested in working and getting married," Jenny said. In 1937, she married and went to work at Auto-Lite, which paid sixteen cents per hour — a twenty-eight percent increase in pay.[14]

Heavy Industry

After leaving the Marinello Company, Florence Munson worked at National Gauge for two years in the early 1920s.[15] Her schedule was 7 a.m. to 5 p.m, Monday through Friday, and 7 a.m. to noon on Saturday. Men and women worked side by side doing the same jobs but were paid at different rates: thirty cents an hour for the women; thirty-five cents for the men. "That was the way it was and it was just accepted," said Florence. The gauge company paid straight time rather than piecework. Because her production rate was higher than some of the other workers', she requested a raise. Her foreman laughed at her request. A couple of weeks later, when she unexpectedly ran into the manager, she again requested a raise. He also chuckled at her request. However, her next paycheck was figured at 32-1/2 cents an hour. According to Florence, workers at the gauge company had lunch hours but no coffee breaks, no paid sick leave, no hospitalization insurance. "It was unbelievable," she said. "I don't think anyone ever thought of those things until after they began organizing [unions] in the 1930s."

Because she generally worked faster and produced more than her co-workers, Florence decided to try piecework again, this time with a company that defined its expectations and pay rate. At the La Crosse Rubber Mills, Florence could make five to ten dollars more per week than at the gauge company. Each day she received a piece rate ticket which indicated the amount of work she was expected to do. As soon as she reached her quota, she could leave for the day.

The number of women in industrial jobs increased during World War II. They were doing their patriotic duty, like others across the nation, to fill spots vacated by men when they joined the service or new jobs created to meet the increased demand for production. Some worked at Outers Laboratories in Onalaska, packing gun cleaning kits that were distributed to U.S. forces throughout the world.[16] Others found work at La Crosse Rubber Mills, Moto Meter Gauge and Northern Engraving. Their jobs were not always steady and secure because of the limited supply of raw materials and the fluctuating demand for finished products. On May 20, 1942, the Moto Meter Gauge and Equipment Corporation laid off 140 employees because of government prohibitions on the use of copper and steel for private contract work. The following day, La Crosse Rubber Mills closed down for two weeks because it had exhausted its allotment of crude rubber for May.[17]

In 1942, Betty Lamb Dell Hyde inspected shells at Northern Engraving in downtown La Crosse. While her husband was in the service, Betty worked the 4 p.m. to midnight shift looking for any distortion in shape or size of the shells as they passed in front of her on a conveyor belt. Some concessions were made so the women could get home safely at the end of their shift. "They allowed us to leave ten minutes early so we could run to the Doerflinger's corner of Fourth and Main streets to catch the last bus," she recalled. Betty was pregnant with her first child but did not tell anyone because she knew she would not be allowed to continue working. This factory work was "one of the most desirable jobs women could have during the war because the pay was very good, so I worked until I was about seven months

Dorothy Clark, left, and Evelyn Lee packed gun cleaning kits at Outers Laboratories in Onalaska, 1943.

Evelyn Hougom Lee Collette

pregnant. The job required me to stand most of the time and my back was starting to bother me. I had three months leave from the job but decided not to go back to work because I had no one to take care of the baby," she said.[18]

In addition to final inspection, women at Northern Engraving performed a large portion of the machine operations needed to meet the defense contracts for cartridge cases. In the process of turning round brass slugs into shell casings, Helen Linehart fed the slugs into a punch press, Gladys Sokolik sent partially completed casings through a press to the next step which was trimming, and Ellen Young used a drill press to bore primer attachment holes in the base of shell casings.[19]

Florence Munson, who left the workplace when she married in 1926, returned to the Rubber Mills in 1943 because her family needed the money.[20] During the seventeen-year interim, the shoemaking department had been mechanized. Instead of working separately, all workers grouped around a moving belt and each performed one specific operation in assembling the shoes. Because the factory was filling government orders, guards were present and all workers were required to wear identification tags.

Lucille Wilkins supervised men making coolers for airplanes at Trane Plant 6 for one year during World War II.[21] During one period, she worked seven days a week for four weeks in a row. When the war ended, she returned to her role as housewife. However, when her husband would not let her spend money for new drapes for the living and dining rooms, she decided to earn it herself. "I went to see Auto-Lite's personnel manager, Roy Fritz. They were crying for help to produce all the gauges in demand for the post-war car production boom," Lucille recalled. "Mr. Fritz told me I could

Auto-Lite employees picketed the factory's Gillette Street entrance during a strike, January 1956.
Donna Steele Lemke

start that very day, but I said I needed a week to convince my husband to let me work. I planned to work just long enough to pay for new drapes." Her short-term intentions stretched into thirteen years. It was only when the plant closed in 1959 that she left her desk clerk job where she had recorded everyone's piecework and kept track of time slips.

Because Donna Steele Lemke's parents did not encourage her interest in attending college to become a teacher, she applied for factory work when she graduated from high school in June 1947. That work turned out to be "right up my alley," Donna said.[22] At the Rubber Mills she worked within an assembly group painting rubber cement onto pieces for shoes and overshoes. Although she was paid an hourly wage, the group had a production quota to meet. During a lay-off from the Rubber Mills in early May 1948, she joined Auto-Lite's speedometer department where "150 people were making gauges for Chrysler automobiles and Ford trucks." Many Auto-Lite employees had worked there since the 1920s and 1930s so new employees hired in the 1940s never gained seniority before the plant closed permanently. "Because I would always be low in seniority, I did not have a permanent assignment nor could I successfully bid on one," Donna recalled. "Instead I was a 'miscellaneous worker' and learned every job within the department. Each morning I reported to the desk to see what my assignment would be within the department. I liked the repair table best. Any equipment that did not pass the calibration tests went back to the factory worker to fix on her or his own time because they were paid by the piece, not for their time. If the gauge still did not work properly after their attention, it ended up on the repair table along with scratched gauges. I took them apart and salvaged and organized the parts."

Working conditions were less than ideal. "During the winter, the frost built up along the east wall," Donna remembered. "It was so cold that I worked in my overshoes with my feet in a cardboard box to keep warm." She also experienced frequent layoffs due to fluctuations in production. At those times, she worked in commercial laundries.

Donna was an active union member. When the union struck in the winter of 1955-56, she did picket duty with other striking employees. "Because it was so cold, picket duty shifts were just two hours," she said. Donna also belonged to the union's education committee and attended the School for Workers at Western Wisconsin Technical Institute where "labor representatives from throughout the community came to learn about labor laws such as the Taft-Hartley Act."

The La Crosse area suffered a recession when Auto-Lite, the city's second largest employer which employed 2,000 at its peak, closed in 1959. Some of the laid-off workers, like Lucille Wilkins, Mary Longway and Jenny Ames, retired. Younger workers, however, sought other jobs. Marilyn Stluka became a cross-country bus driver for Hiawatha Bus Lines and then a school bus driver for Holmen.[23] Donna Lemke went to work at the food service company at Wisconsin State University-La Crosse, but "I was not invited back after I tried to organize a union for food service workers," she recalled. Before retiring permanently, Donna served as a street crossing guard for school children at Twenty-first and Main streets in La Crosse for twenty years.[24] Marion Zumach Hopkins found work as the first meat wrapper at the A & P grocery store in downtown La Crosse. Her job led to joining the Amalgamated Butchers and Meat Cutters union so she was on the line when the group picketed the Boulevard grocery store on Losey Boulevard. During the strike, "La Crosse Mayor Milo Knutson crossed the picket line, bought a steak and stuck it in the faces of the picketers," she recalled. "But the people who lived in the house on the corner gave us coffee and let us come in their house to get warm."[25]

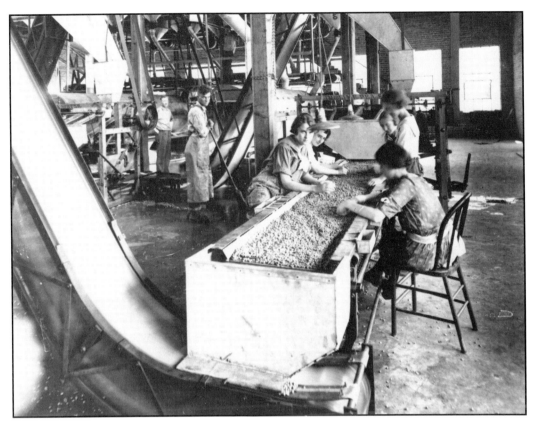

Women worked at the incline pea sorter at the Onalaska Pickle Factory, n.d.
Special Collections, Murphy Library, University of Wisconsin-La Crosse

Seasonal Industry

Canning Factories

Women and men alike found work when crops needed to be harvested, vegetables sorted, and cans packed. The canning factory in Onalaska was called the pickle factory. Bangor's canning factory began as the Hussa Brewery but was converted to can tomatoes, sweet corn, peas, and pickles during Prohibition.

The Holmen Canning Company, organized and incorporated in 1913, built its three-story plant with a viner shed in back in 1914, and planted and processed 300 acres of peas in the first year. In the 1920s, many young women and men worked there to earn money for college at twenty-five cents an hour seven days a week. They knew better than to take Sundays off during canning season. "If we took off work, we would never get work there again," Lillian Holter recalled.[26] The factory operated around the clock. "When I worked third shift, I walked home alone from the factory at 3 a.m. I certainly would never do that now," she added. Women used long wooden forks to pick up twenty-five empty cans at a time and put them on conveyors to carry them to other floors. Men tended the machines that sealed the cans. The cans were crated, boiled, drained, and put on a track to the warehouse. Women transferred the cans from the crates to boxes. "The warehouse was the best place to work because of the kidding, laughing, and joking, but it was harder work and we put in more hours," she recalled.

To compensate for the labor shortage during World War II, German prisoners of war helped pick and process peas. The prisoners were housed in the area, bused to the plants, and always supervised by a guard. The locals and the prisoners were able to communicate through an interpreter, and, despite the circumstances, each group discovered how nice the other was.

The Holmen Canning Company expanded over the years. A 1945 addition included modern equipment for whole kernel sweet corn production. In 1954, the plant enlarged so it could can wax and green string beans. Acreage increased from 300 to 3,000 or 4,000. "When corn and bean canning was added, there were many more people to be hired. They added a floor lady to manage the women workers," Mrs. Holter remembered.

Lefse Making

It was in the early 1930s that Bendika Holley of Holmen took the suggestion of a holiday guest and began mass-producing lefse on her wood-burning range. Although her son, James, ran into skeptical storekeepers in La Crosse, he found Norwegian families willing to pay sixty-five cents per dozen lefse. Eventually some stores began to carry a small amount of the Norwegian tortilla-like bread, made of potatoes, flour, and a little salt. Meanwhile, James' house-to-house business prospered and Bendika remodeled the basement into a lefse bakery to handle the orders. She paid neighbor women seventy-five cents a day to help her peel potatoes, roll out the dough, and bake the lefse. She had the job of mixing just the right amount of flour into the dough so that it would hang together yet not get too dry.

In 1951, the Holleys built a separate building on their Sweeden Coulee farm exclusively for baking lefse. After her death in 1953, the Holley family tried to honor Bendika's wish that they continue the business. However, managing a lefse factory in addition to the farm proved to be too much. For a period of time, they rented the lefse enterprise to Ernest Holley and then to

Myles and Leona McCurdy. In the mid-1960s, Leona McCurdy employed seven women, including Bendika Holley's daughter-in-law, Ethel. Even though they turned out sixty dozen lefse each day during their six-day week, the business was unable to fill all the orders. Eventually Ethel and her husband, Horace, took back the business his mother had started. Ethel would rise at four in the morning to cook and rice the potatoes and to mix the dough so it was just right. Six other women arrived at 8:00 a.m. to help her roll out, bake, cool, and package the lefse. At 4:30 p.m., their day was done. They repeated this process throughout the deep winter months of lefse-making season and sold the product to grocery stores and the Consumer's Bakery in La Crosse as well as to individual families. The Sweeden Coulee Lefse factory closed down when the Holleys retired from farming and moved into Holmen.[27]

Office

Eleanor Roellig Meinert entered the workforce at a time when a growing number of women were replacing men as office workers. She graduated from La Crosse Central High School in 1909 and went to work as a secretary for V. Tausche Hardware. Eleanor was the only woman in the office; the rest of the stenographers and clerks were men.[28] Between 1870 and 1920, the percentage of employed women who worked as clerks, cashiers, typists, and stenographers rose from less than one to twenty-five.[29] One factor which contributed to that growth was the general acceptance and use of the typewriting machine in the 1890s. The machine required nimble fingers — presumably a feminine attribute — but no initiative because typewriting was seen as simply a form of copying. Another factor was the labor shortage during World War I. When men went to war, women filled their places at work on the homefront. Eleanor continued to work after marriage and giving birth to twins in September 1918. Her husband, who was serving in World War I, did not learn that he had two sons until December of that year. A third son was born, in 1930, and Eleanor continued working until the mid-1930s. While she kept the hardware company books and interviewed salesmen, an older unmarried sister (referred to as a maiden aunt) took care of the three boys.

Violet M. Niedercorn attended high school in the late 1920s and took the business course which included typing, shorthand, and bookkeeping.[30] After graduating from Central High School in 1930, she became secretary to Edgar Gundlach at the Woven Cotton Padding Mills in La Crosse. Violet made the transition from employee to employer when she married John C. Evans in 1936. He owned Evans Cartage Company which began as a freight hauling business between La Crosse and Milwaukee. Her responsibility in the business partnership was to serve as receptionist and bookkeeper. Later they changed the business to moving and storage and became an agent for Allied Van Lines with vans traveling nationwide. After John died in 1963, Violet continued the business with the help of her brother-in-law, Robert F. Strehl, who assisted in management and sales. In 1966, she married Elmer J. Berg, an administrator for Gundersen Clinic. Even after he retired in the early 1970s, he left the running of Evans Cartage to Violet. She continued to go into the office each day until 1985 when, at the age of seventy-three, she sold the business to Piepho Moving and Storage and sold the building (under the Cass Street Bridge) to Russell Cleary.

When Mildred Anderson graduated from high school in 1922, the only office job she found paid eight dollars a week.[31] Mildred recalled her father's reaction: "If that's all the money you can make, then you should go on to school." She attended Eau Claire Normal School long enough to figure out she had "no desire to become a teacher." Instead, Mildred, who had taken typing and shorthand in high school, found work with Eau Claire Book and Stationery. At first she did a variety of odd jobs in the office but then was asked to take care of customer complaints. Mildred was "delighted" to take on the work of correcting the mistakes in shipments and in billing because she found it interesting to trace the problems. Her pay was twelve dollars per week. A couple of years later she went to work as "the only girl in the office" of A. Larson Construction Company in Eau Claire. She did all the office work except for bookkeeping. She earned thirty-five dollars every two weeks and "thought I was Mrs. Morgenthau." Marriage to George Nelson in 1924 did not prevent her from continuing to work, but pregnancy did. Before her pregnancy showed, Mildred informed her boss that she was quitting. Pregnancy was considered a delicate topic that should be avoided. Therefore, when he asked why she was quitting, she responded, "We're going to raise chickens." Mildred stayed at home for nearly twenty years raising Joan, who was born in 1925, and Marilyn, born in 1934, while George earned the family income.

She went back to work when George lost his job as a salesman for Drummond Meat Packing of Eau Claire because the company cut back its sales force. She found a job with G. E. Supply Company, a subsidiary of General Electric, at 222 Pearl Street in downtown La Crosse. There were just six people in the district office. She was the only one doing the perpetual inventory, that is, she kept track of the costs, selling prices, and identification numbers of the thousands of items that electrical contractors needed to wire a building. "They had never hired a woman before. After they hired me, they decided that it was possible for women to do things that men could do," Mildred said.

Because housing was scarce during that time, the Nelsons felt lucky to find a two room apartment in the Milner Hotel across the alley from G. E. Supply. Mildred discovered that when she stood by the elevator shaft at work, she could hear her ten-year-old daughter reading upstairs in their hotel rooms. Marilyn read out loud to keep herself company. Several times a day, Mildred stepped into the elevator to check on her daughter. "She had a loud voice. As long as I could hear her reading, I knew Marilyn was OK," she recalled.

When George found steady work as a school custodian, Mildred could have stopped working and returned to the home. However, she liked her work well enough to make plans to stay with G. E. Supply until she turned fifty-five in 1959. At that age she would be entitled to a pension of $100 a month. Instead, the company, which was based in St. Paul, Minnesota, laid her off during cutbacks in 1958 which reduced her pension to $16.50 per month.

In 1959, the W.A. Roosevelt Company asked her to handle its perpetual inventory of electrical and refrigeration supplies, which she did until she retired in 1972 at the age of 68. She had enjoyed retirement "for about two weeks" when she heard a radio advertisement encouraging people to go to H & R Block to learn how to prepare tax returns. She thought, "Why not go to school for the heck of doing something different?" Mildred looked at it as educational and had no plans to work. However, Margo Scott, "a large woman with a very deep voice and a generous heart," asked her to stay on as the receptionist which Mildred did until she had a heart attack in 1978. While Mildred was recovering, Margo left H & R Block and, with Eloyce Bell, formed Best Business Service. They asked Mildred to come to work for their bookkeeping and tax business. She worked half-days as the receptionist until she turned eighty and retired for good. As she looked back, Mildred said, "You know, it's strange but when I went to school I never wanted any math classes because I didn't think I could get it through my head, but then I ended up working with numbers at a tax office."

In the early 1940s, while preparing for a career in office work, Lorraine Jandt Fiet of Bangor held multiple jobs to pay for her education and expenses. To complement her first year of course work at La Crosse Adult and Vocational School, Lorraine worked half-days at the Bureau of Fisheries in Riverside Park under the supervision of Irene Ristow Happel. During her second year, Lorraine held three jobs at once. First thing each morning, she reported to the Belmont Cafe near the Rivoli Theater. "The owner dictated the menu for the day. I typed it and ran it off on a tiny mimeograph," she recalled. "And I was paid with one meal a day."[32] During lunch hours and on Friday nights, she worked at Woolworth's lunch counter. On Saturday afternoons, she served customers at the soda fountain in the basement of Doerflinger's Department Store. Lorraine began full-time office work in 1942. From then until she retired in 1989, she had just one employer at a time: Spence McCord Drug Company, Sears credit department, bill collector Walter Gundlach, First Presbyterian Church, and University of Wisconsin-La Crosse audiovisual services.

Like Mother, Like Daughter

Bernice Koblitz' strong work ethic set an important example for her daughter, Marilyn Koblitz Wigdahl. "She was never late to work, she was never sick, work came first for her," Marilyn said about her mother.[33] Bernice married right after high school and had three children. At the age of thirty-two, "She brushed up on her typing and shorthand and moved from the role of housewife to the world of academia. She probably earned eighty dollars a month working in the main office of La Crosse State Teachers College," her daughter recalled. At that time, about 1941, the campus consisted of Main Hall, Wittich Hall, and the Campus School. There were fewer than eight hundred students and about fifty-five faculty. Bernice's responsibilities included sorting the mail, answering and placing all telephone calls at the school's switchboard, and serving as secretary to the president. In 1965, Bernice became assistant to the registrar, Lora Greene, and Marilyn started her own career at the university. In the registrar's office, Bernice examined student records, reviewed student eligibility, and compiled the course catalogue. However, she continued to receive a secretarial salary until she retired at the age of sixty-three.

Marilyn started working just as the campus was beginning to explode in size. Like her mother, she, too, started in the main office sorting the mail and working the switchboard. By that time, Lorna Dux Vafeas was President Rexford Mitchell's secretary. Lorna filled that position in 1944 and served four more presidents and chancellors until she retired in 1982. Marilyn recalled that, in 1965, no one on campus had individual phones although each academic department had one telephone. Large departments had or shared a secretary. Smaller ones turned to Marilyn for help with typing and duplicating tests on the ditto machine. In the winter of 1966-67, Marilyn moved to Cartwright Center with the new ten-line switchboard. She took every incoming call and connected it to the appropriate office. She placed every long-distance call going out. Marilyn recalled how she handled bomb threats which increased in frequency during final exams: "When the switchboard lit up at ten minutes to eight on the morning of the Biology 100 exam, I knew it would be a bomb threat. In order to trace the call, I had to listen long enough to get the time and location of the alleged bomb and then throw a switch to lock in the call before the caller hung up."

From Secretary to President

Anita Froegel grew up in a family of industrious women. In particular, she observed three aunts develop full careers.[34] Aunt Frieda was the "backbone" of the photography business she and her husband George Haberman owned and operated from the 1920s into the 1960s. Aunt Till (Mathilda Lund), who "loved fun as much as flowers," owned Lund's Flowers in downtown La Crosse. Aunt Mahry (Marie Guentner) was secretary to the president of Trane Company. Anita learned a great deal from her about the importance of common sense, a strong work ethic, and loyalty in the workplace. "Because of Aunt Mahry's attitude toward work, I always looked up to her and thought of secretarial work as an honorable profession," Anita said.

The day after her graduation from Aquinas High School in 1955, Anita went to work as the secretary/bookkeeper for Jim McLoone of McLoone Advertising Specialties, Inc. Her interview had occurred early on a Saturday morning on the fourth floor of the Batavian Bank Building. As she waited in the dark hallway, a very large man, Jim McLoone, came walking toward her, followed by a slim man who turned out to be McLoone's accountant, David Baptie. The two of them interviewed her and hired her on the spot. "I was pleased because I sure didn't want to go through the interviewing process again," she recalled. That turned out to be her one and only interview because Anita has spent her entire career working at the growing firm that developed into McLoone Metal Graphics.

When she started, there were salespeople in the field, but she and Jim were the only people in the office. Over the next twenty-five years, she married, had four sons, and took on more job responsibilities as order department manager, office manager, credit manager, and corporate secretary. As Anita grew in her job, she counted on advice from Aunt Mahry who also expressed pride in Anita's progress. Jim used her as a sounding board for his ideas and decisions. By listening and interpreting and watching him in action, "I learned a lot about thinking creatively and how to use available resources," Anita said. When Jim died suddenly in February 1980, his wife, Helen, served as acting president for a few months until she sold the company to JSJ Corporation of Grand Haven, Michigan. Anita asked to become president of the company she had seen develop from a small advertising specialty sales operation to a manufacturing concern that employed more than 150. Martin Johnson, president of JSJ named her president in September 1981. The acquisition of McLoone by JSJ could have been a scary process because of the unknown; but it was not because there was "lots of trust and communication." Anita was especially proud that no employees lost their jobs at McLoone as a result of the acquisition.

She integrated the best of what she saw in her aunts and in her boss to form her own successful management style and to fulfill her own need to work. "I have really enjoyed going to work," Anita said. "I might have lost something of myself if I hadn't worked. I needed to have my mind challenged. My only regret is that Aunt Mahry did not live long enough to see me become president."

Retail

Another way women earned money was by selling everything from clothing to household goods to decorative items. Although sales clerks earned less than factory workers, some women found the cleaner workplace and possibility of advancement in retail more desirable than production work.[35]

Some women worked in retail part-time. For example, in 1943, during her college student days, Mitzi Mitchell Carroll sold women's clothing at Barron's Department Store in La Crosse on Saturdays. She recalled that her pay was 23-1/2 cents an hour and that Barron's had a very liberal return policy, even accepting garments people returned a week after purchasing them when "it was obvious to me that the dress had been worn in between."[36] The following summer, she found more lucrative work at the Camp McCoy Post Exchange which paid forty cents an hour and provided round trip bus transportation from town to the camp.

For other women, some form of the retail business was their livelihood.

Quillin's La Crosse Street Market's first employee, Marge Parker, was behind the cash register as a Mrs. Johnson paid for her order. AliceWang and Vince Riley were in the aisle at the left. Dorothy Hall and Esther Gates were in the aisle at the right. 1946.

Quillin's, Inc

Grocery Stores

As recently as 1945, La Crosse had 116 grocery stores.[37] Remnants of these numerous mom and pop groceries as well as variety stores are still in evidence. A few have taken on another retail identity; others have been converted to homes or torn down to make way for new buildings. The Quillin's grocery chain got its start when Ed and Greta Quillin purchased the Rennebohm Grocery at 1103 La Crosse Street in September of 1945 from Alvina Rennebohm who was retiring after forty-two years in the business.[38] In the early days, Mr. and Mrs. A. W. Rennebohm managed the store together. They opened at 4 a.m. in order to buy vegetables from gardeners. They often stayed open until 11 p.m. They bought butter in bulk from creameries in 400 and 500 pound lots. They sold syrup, sugar, crackers, and pretzels from barrels. They also sold all kinds of horse feed, including baled straw and hay by the ton. Alvina continued to own and operate the store for another thirty-two years after her husband's death in 1913.

Miss Potter's millinery shop in West Salem was owned by Ida Backhouse Potter Krohn, dressed in white.
One of the employees was Marie Krickman; the other is unidentified. c. 1910.
Estella Krohn Bryhn

Millinery Shops

When hats were an essential item in a woman's wardrobe, millinery was a common occupation. Hatmaking was a way for women to use their creative skills to produce some income without leaving their homes. They could turn their parlors or sunporches into small but productive hat factories with display and sales areas. Lillian Wittenberg had such a business in her home at the corner of Clinton and Avon streets in La Crosse from 1932 to 1970. One of her regular customers was Doris Gutzke, wife of the pastor of the Immanuel Evangelical Lutheran Church down the street. "Even a poor German Lutheran minister's wife needed a new hat for certain occasions," recalled Doris' daughter, Rachel Gutzke Gundersen.

Some women opened millinery shops in business districts and employed others to assist them in making and selling the hats. Early in the twentieth century, Ida Backhouse Potter took over the millinery business her mother

Aletta Werel, in polka dot dress and glasses, was surrounded by customers at a three dollar hat sale at Aletta's Hat Shop, Fifth and Market streets, La Crosse, 1950.

Judie Weber Strauss

had started in her West Salem home.[39] Even after she married Louis Krohn, Ida called her business Miss Potter's. Ida's artistic flair and business skill developed into a store-front business. She employed other women to help her shape each hat from buckram and adorn it with silk and velvet flowers and bows. Plumed bridal hats were one of her specialties. Miss Potter's was located in the first building north of the railroad tracks on Leonard Street. Thus, it was the first to succumb to the fire of 1911, which destroyed much of West Salem's business district. Fortunately, her sewing machine survived because someone had carried it up the street to Johnson's Drug Store. Because she had fire insurance money and her sewing machine, Ida was able to reopen her business.

Just before her forty-sixth birthday in 1945, Aletta Werel opened her millinery business, Aletta's Hat Shop, in a small shop across the street from her home at Ninth and Mississippi streets in La Crosse.[40] She had studied the craft of hatmaking and trimming at La Crosse Vocational School when she was nineteen years old but did not work in the business for another twelve years. During those years she married and started a family. Aletta's gumption and cleverness were instrumental in getting and keeping her first job. The manager of the Wyle Hat Shop hired Aletta in 1930 when she claimed to have sales experience even though she had none. Within three weeks she was promoted from clerk to assistant manager of the "first $1.88 hat store in La Crosse."[41] After Wyle's closed she worked at the Dotty Dunn Hat Shop, the Sanford Hat Box, and the Empress Hat Shop, all in downtown La Crosse. When the Empress went out of business, the outgoing manager encouraged her to take the furnishings and equipment at no charge. She did and stored the items in her garage until 1945 when she used the equipment to furnish her own business. She catered to working women as well as mothers by keeping the shop open from 1 p.m. to 9 p.m., and, in 1951, she moved her business to the corner of Fifth and Market streets.

In 1954, Aletta said, "I don't think you're dressed up unless you have a hat and pair of gloves on with your outfit." With that philosophy and a great deal of patience, she took pride in creating one-of-a-kind hats to complete clients' ensembles. In the 1950s, Aletta's Hat Shop provided fashionable hats for many style shows at women's luncheons held at restaurants like the Cerise or at the Mary E. Sawyer Auditorium, which was the site for the city-wide style shows. By the time Aletta retired in 1970, hats no longer were a crucial part of a woman's wardrobe. The patrons had aged and dwindled to a small number. After closing the shop, she occasionally fixed or remade hats for former customers. Always sewing by hand, she removed or added veils, flowers, and other finishing touches for hats for an aging clientele.

Dress Shops

Lottie's Dress Shoppe was a fixture in downtown La Crosse for half a century. As a girl, Lottie Klandrud, born in Onalaska in 1890, hired out to do domestic work to augment her family's income. As an adult, she worked at the telephone company and then the Standard Oil Company. As a sideline, she sold blouses to women in the oil company office. After five years, the blouse sales were doing so well that she quit clerical work and started her own business in 1923. At first she sold only sweaters and blouses, but business was so good she quickly expanded into an adjoining room and added dresses, suits, and coats. Customers climbed the old stairway to find garments jammed together hanging from racks in her second-floor shop which overlooked the downtown intersection of Fourth and Main streets. Her clientele did not mind the cramped quarters with peeling ceiling paint. They were looking for stylish clothing sold well below the prices charged in fashion centers. Lottie's question, "Do you know how much this would cost in New York?" was a familiar one to her customers.

Lottie, who dressed rather plainly herself, had a good sense of fashion and what suited her clientele. For instance, after a buying trip to New York City in 1954, she reported that New York women were following French designers and wearing skirts to the knee. Lottie knew that most La Crosse women preferred a becoming length of thirteen inches from the floor rather than following the dictates of the designers, and she returned with dresses to please her clients. On those buying trips, she usually kept certain customers in mind and purchased lovely things especially for them. Lottie employed Alice Aaness to handle sales and to make all the alterations. Miriam Scheppke was in charge of the junior department for many years.[42]

Department Stores

Marie Rupp Mielke spent the first half of her life taking care of others and the second half clerking. She was born in La Crosse in 1893, married Waldemar Mielke in 1916, and had a daughter, Betty, in 1921. Waldemar died three years later. When Marie became a widow, she and her daughter moved in with her parents and older brother, Herman, a veteran who returned from World War I paralyzed from the waist down. After their parents died, Marie continued to take care of her brother until he entered the veterans' hospital in Milwaukee in the 1930s. For a while, in order to support herself and her daughter, she took care of ill and physically-limited people in their homes.[43]

Sometime during the mid to late 1930s, Marie decided to try something different. She contacted Doerflinger's Department Store and was informed of a three-week opening as a clerk in the corset department. "But I don't know anything about corsets," she protested. "Don't worry, Mrs. Mielke, in three weeks you'll know everything about corsets," was the response from William Dunn, the department's manager. Her daughter recalled that Marie came home at the end of one day and said with a laugh, "Boy, am I tired. I have stuffed everyone who has had surgery or is having a baby into a corset." Marie's work performance in corsets led to an offer of a permanent position in the gift department. For several years, she sold pens, stationery, cards, sterling silver, and small gift items. This department was especially busy during World War II. Business was brisk because soldiers from Camp McCoy were buying writing materials to correspond with families and sweethearts.

Marie's base pay at Doerflinger's increased from $12.50 to $15.00 to $18.00 a week. It was possible to earn more than that from commissions, and she did. "My mother loved being busy and she loved having a little money," said Betty Mielke. Eventually Marie left Doerflinger's and went to work half days at a dress shop, then at Aletta's Hat Shop, and finally at Art's ice cream and gift shop on the corner of West Avenue and State Street. She retired in 1973, at the age of eighty.

About the same time Marie Mielke was starting her career as a sales clerk, Viola Doerflinger Fellows was coming into her own as the leader of Doerflinger's Department Store, founded by her father in 1881. Early in her life, Vi Fellows pursued a dream of becoming a concert pianist. She majored in music and art at Clarke College in Dubuque, Iowa, and studied concert piano in Chicago before marrying Sam Fellows in 1915 and settling into married life in La Crosse. Upon Sam's sudden death in 1929, she took stock of the situation and, with the good advice of an attorney friend, decided to use her controlling shares in Doerflinger's to go into the business herself.[44] Her younger sister, Leona Locke, had filled in for her own husband as advertising manager while he served in World War I. Now Viola stepped in to take her husband's place as the manager and buyer for the ready-to-wear and lingerie departments. Later she became vice-president, another position her husband held at the time of his death. She learned the trade on her own, relying on advice from good friends in merchandising in New York. When she became vice-president and then president of the company in the mid-1930s, she used the following motto as her guiding principle of management:

> *Think things over and talk them through carefully and thoroughly. When you're convinced in your mind that you are right go ahead, and don't let anybody stop you, but always remember "keep both feet on the ground."*[45]

Based on what she saw on her five or six buying trips to New York each year, she embarked on a ten-year plan to modernize the physical and merchandising aspects of Doerflinger's. What may have seemed to be an unwise expenditure during the Depression really was a wise business decision. She knew what the stores in the east were doing and believed that made sense for La Crosse, too. Under her direction, Doerflinger's maintained its position as the leading department store in the community.

Vi Fellows was a tall, handsome woman who enjoyed wearing the hats she purchased at Mr. John's during each of her trips to New York. "The secret to her success was her good taste," said her son, Sam Jr. "Her good taste extended to the store which always stocked as high a quality of merchandise as La Crosse could afford to buy."

Although Viola did not become a concert pianist, she did pursue her interest in music. She was an active member and officer of the La Crosse Music Study Club and a strong supporter of the La Crosse Symphony Orchestra, serving as president of the board at the time of her death at age sixty-seven in 1954. She pursued her gardening hobby on the grounds about her home at 1619 King Street and in her membership in the La Crosse Garden Club.[46]

For many local women, memories of Doerflinger's prompted memories of Winnebago women selling baskets. These women, from Brice's Prairie and Black River Falls, displayed their baskets on blankets which they spread out on the sidewalk along the Fourth Street side of the department store. Based on an extensive oral history interview with Mountain Wolf Woman in 1958 and her own understanding of the Winnebago culture, Nancy Oestreich Lurie wrote that basket selling was an important source of income for Winnebago women and their families.[47]

Floral Shops

Till Lund owned and operated Lund's Flowers at 533 Main Street, La Crosse, from 1945 to 1962. As a young adult, Till worked as a florist in a shop at Fifth and Main streets which later became Renner's Flower Shop. During World War II, she worked at MacDonald's Flower Shop. When Helen MacDonald retired, Till bought the business and renamed it Lund's Flowers.[48] She employed four or five people to serve customers at a time when people bought flowers frequently to decorate their homes, to give as gifts, and to send to hospitalized friends and acquaintances. Her niece, Anita Froegel, who helped in the shop from time to time, described a rose bowl, a single rose floating in a glass bowl of water, as a very common gift to send to even a casual friend in the hospital.

According to Till's daughter, Ruth Dadonna, Till delighted in arranging flowers in ever-changing, new, and bold designs. She attended conventions where she could learn the latest in styles from the nation's top designers. Her independent thinking and impatience with outworn convention often put her ahead of her time. She felt that flowers should be a part of life, that they could turn routine times into experiences to be treasured.

Gift Shops

Marion Whiteway owned and operated The Hired Hand gift shop from 1967 to 1985. All her employees, about fifty of them through the years, were women.[49] The shop was housed in a barn on the property she and her husband owned on the ridge overlooking La Crosse and the Mississippi River. "I loved the barn. It had such wonderful proportions," said Marion who appreciated such things. She had studied at the Art Institute in Chicago and worked as a commercial artist in that city before moving to La Crosse with her husband and children in 1962.

Customers often brought their houseguests to see the unique items and to enjoy the beautiful drive and view. "The Hired Hand's merchandise and setting were different from anything else in La Crosse," Marion recalled. "I worked hard to find the sources of artwork I sold." She generally bought from gift shows and handcraft shows. Her shop also provided an outlet for local artists.

"I loved the buying trips. I even liked the tax work," she said. "But when people came into the shop and said, 'I've always thought it would be fun to open my own shop,' I'd make sure they understood that it was work, too."

Services and Professions

From the earliest settler days of the 1840s, when Augusta and John Levy built the "first frame building erected between Prairie du Chien and Red Wing" to serve as a hotel and restaurant business as well as their living quarters, La Crosse County has counted on the services of women to contribute to the economy and well-being of the community. These included services provided predominantly by women, by wives in partnership with husbands, and by women as well as men. As years went by, opportunities for women expanded in fields traditionally dominated by men. A few entrepreneurs became involved in endeavors that were atypical for women.

Services Traditionally Provided by Women

Telephone

In addition to teaching and nursing, women have been predominant in certain professions and services. For example, when all telephone calls needed to be assisted by a person, women usually were the "manpower" behind the connection. Verna Hom McNeill began her forty-two year career as a telephone operator at the age of eleven. When she started working

Verna Hom McNeill worked at the Onalaska Telephone Exchange from 1908 to 1946. She started her career at the age of eleven.
Special Collections, Murphy Library
University of Wisconsin-La Crosse

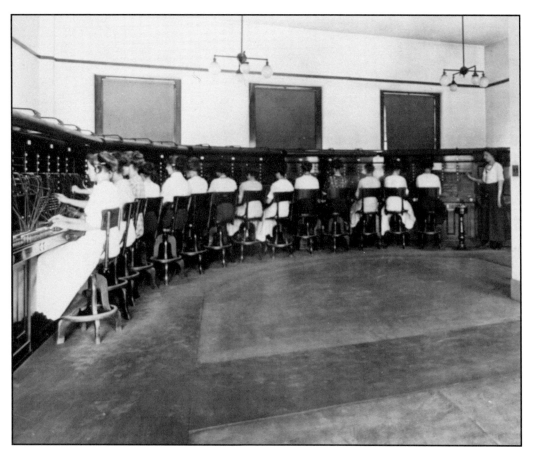

Telephone operators connected one caller to another at the switchboard of the La Crosse Telephone Company, n.d.

La Crosse County Historical Society

for the Onalaska Telephone Exchange in 1908, there were seventy local phones and three farm lines that extended into Green Coulee, Sand Lake Coulee, and Brice's Prairie. After Verna married Rex McNeill in 1916, they lived above Peterson's Grocery Store in Onalaska where another upstairs room housed the switchboard. When the McNeills moved in 1924, the switchboard moved with them. As the chief operator, Verna was often on call twenty-four hours a day to connect one phone customer with another. Verna transferred to La Crosse in 1946 and retired four years later when the phone company installed the dial system, which did not require the services of an operator for local calls.[1]

Hairstyling

According to Art Soell Jr., his grandmother, Louise Simon Soell, opened the first beauty shop in La Crosse in 1880.[2] Her "Hair Bazaar" at 327 Main Street was listed in the 1884-85 city directory. When Louise died in 1915, at the age of sixty, her daughter-in-law, Lelia B. Soell, took over the business, moved it up the street and renamed it Soell's Beauty Shop. For a while, the Soell family operated two businesses at 509 Main: the beauty shop in the back and a drug store in front. Lelia specialized in dying hair because her "eye for blending dyes made the coloring look natural," recalled her son, Art, who followed in the footsteps of his mother and grandmother by becoming a beautician before he became a liquor store owner.

Wilma Peters moved to La Crosse in 1939 and went to work for Pearl Harding who owned Pearl's Deluxe Beauty Salon and a beauty school.[3] Wilma was the school's licensed instructor. In 1952, she went into business for herself when she bought the Vanity Beauty Salon in the Newburg Building. She renamed it Wilma's and maintained that business for forty-one years until she retired at the age of eighty-three. Wilma's downtown location was convenient for dimestore clerks. "They would come in for a wash and set over their lunch hour. They returned to work with a scarf or hairnet covering their pincurls. When their hair had dried, they came back for a comb-out," she recalled.

Wilma joined the Coulee Region Hairdressers Association in 1952 and served three terms as president. "What fun we had at those meetings. Hairdressers liked to dress up fit-to-kill. We'd have a drink, conduct a little business, then enjoy dinner and a good time," she said. For several years, Wilma spent a few weeks each fall in Duluth, Minnesota, working with a national styles director who demonstrated new styles and techniques. "Just like clothing fashions, hairstyles were updated each year," she said.

Enthusiastic about the possibility of helping others, Wilma went out into the community and taught personal hygiene and good grooming to Brownie Scouts, Y-Teens, and grandmothers. For a few years, she was part of a group of hairdressers who volunteered their time at the asylum in West Salem. "After our day's work, we hauled all our equipment and supplies to the Insane Asylum to do hair for the patients," she recalled. "When our volunteer work was mentioned in the *Congressional Record*, the state government realized how beneficial the haircare was for the asylum residents and hired a regular hairdresser for them."

A number of beauticians had shops in their own homes. Sally Oswalt started out working for others in La Crosse but often did not return home until after her children got out of school. When she suggested to her son that he might be wearing out his welcome at the neighbors' house where he went after school each day, he replied, "I don't like being in the house when it's empty." That is when Sally decided to open a shop in her own home. She established Coiffures by Sally at 2116 Pine Street in 1959.[4]

Lessons in the Social Graces

Giving lessons in the arts and social graces was a socially acceptable way for women to earn money in the first half of the twentieth century. It also was a way for a woman to convey her passion for music or dance or painting. In the late 1890s, Grace Pettingill (who later married Gysbert Van Steenwyk) taught social dance classes.

> *After I got out of boarding school I didn't have anything I wanted to do, so I had a dancing class with 150 children.... I used to have this dance studio over Hoeschler's store and we had a little room in the back with a fireplace, and I always had a maid and she would take the children's coats and things. They [the boys] could never come into the room until they bowed to me and girls would curtsy.... All the boys in our crowd would come to the parties and they would bring big bunches of carnations, roses and things like that; all for favors. You would pick one of these up and give it to the person you wanted to dance with. That was the way it was.[5]*

Women could express their creativity and add a touch of elegance to their homes by painting china. From the early 1920s into the 1930s, Eva Frasier taught china painting at La Crosse Vocational School. This was a way to earn an income after her husband died. Her designs followed the shape of the Bavarian china she painted. A sugar and creamer, which she decorated with a rose motif as a wedding gift for a nephew, still remains in the family.[6]

Most piano teachers gave lessons in their own homes. Crystal Baebler Rounds, however, traveled to rural Bangor one day a week so that children in Burns Valley could learn about music. For five years in the early 1930s, Leona and Mildred Halderson received free weekly lessons because their parents, John and Bertha, provided their living room and piano for the teacher and her students. "My mother met Mrs. Rounds's bus at the intersection of Highways 16 and 162 near the cemetery going into Burns Valley and brought her to our house. At the end of the lessons, mother took her to Bangor to catch a bus back to La Crosse," Mildred recalled. Every thirty minutes a different pupil took his or her place at the piano to demonstrate progress since the last lesson and to receive more instruction. "We weren't ever going to be great pianists, but we did learn some music from this really nice lady and very knowledgeable teacher," Mildred said.[7]

In the last half of the twentieth century, the Marilyn School of Dance trained thousands of young people. Marilyn Wood, owner and director of the school, began her own dance training at the age of eight, became an assistant teacher at fourteen, and opened her first dance school in Sparta at age nineteen. Since 1951, the Marilyn School of Dance in La Crosse has graduated dancers that have gone on to perform professionally and to teach throughout the country. In addition to operating her business, Marilyn choreographed several musicals for the La Crosse Community Theatre and, with Frank and Lenore Italiano, helped found the Great River Festival of the Arts dance workshop.[8]

Prostitution

One of the oldest services, prostitution, has been a part of the La Crosse scene since the early lumbering days. Anna Bennett was neither the first nor the last, but she has remained the best known proprietor of a house of prostitution in La Crosse. She operated her business at the European Hotel, 216 North Second Street, from 1925 until 1946. Ma Bennett had a reputation for classy service. The exterior of the building did not look like much, but the public rooms inside were plushly decorated with chandeliers, carpets, and wall tapestries.

Experience, employment practices, and the right connections all contributed to her business success. Prior to 1925, she and her husband operated road houses just east of La Crosse and in Fargo, North Dakota, that featured moonshine, gambling, and "girls in the back room." During her years as a sole-proprietor, she employed attractive young women between the ages of eighteen and twenty-five and saw to it that they were well-dressed and healthy. Ma arranged regular medical examinations in Dr. James Heraty's office in the Rivoli Building and house calls when needed.

While the going rate for a visit to a sporting house was two dollars, one for the prostitute and one for the madam, customers could expect to pay five dollars at Ma Bennett's. However, her income was not limited to these fees. A former bootlegger sold beer to her in 24-bottle cases for three dollars. She turned a profit by selling the beer for one dollar a bottle. Even when Prohibition ended and prices dropped, she continued to charge the same. It is believed that this enterprising woman with a Scandinavian accent lost $150,000 to $200,000 when a local bank went out of business during the Depression. Yet she shared her wealth with others in the community. Several Depression-era families benefited from her concern and generosity. When "Compliments of a Friend" advertisements appeared in high school yearbooks or community programs, the reader often could attribute those to her. The YWCA could count on her to order twelve dozen doughnuts during its annual fundraiser. She retired to California in 1946 shortly after the last of approximately twenty raids on her business resulted in a sentence of $200 and four months in jail and shortly before paying the fine or serving the time.[9]

Home Economics

In 1926, Mary Dvorak Lamb started the Home Service Department of Wisconsin-Minnesota Light and Power Company. She demonstrated how to use the new kitchen appliances sold by the company that eventually became Northern States Power (NSP).[10] Mary joined the relatively new professional field of home economics when she graduated from St. Mary's at Notre Dame, Indiana, in 1909. She returned to La Crosse to teach domestic science skills in the schools. According to her daughter, Mary was the first trained home economist in La Crosse and in Wisconsin. As was the custom of the day, when she wed John Lamb she left teaching to take care of the home and family. When he died in 1925, leaving three young children for her to support, she taught evening classes in sewing and cooking for adults and worked at the south branch of the La Crosse Public Library.

The following year, she left the library and started demonstrating new household appliances — stoves, refrigerators, water heaters, washing machines, waffle irons, irons, mangle irons, electric fans, and clocks — in the power company offices at 122 North Fifth, La Crosse. Twice a month, on Wednesday afternoons, in a well-equipped kitchen, she dispensed helpful household advice while preparing foods. While teaching, she often wore

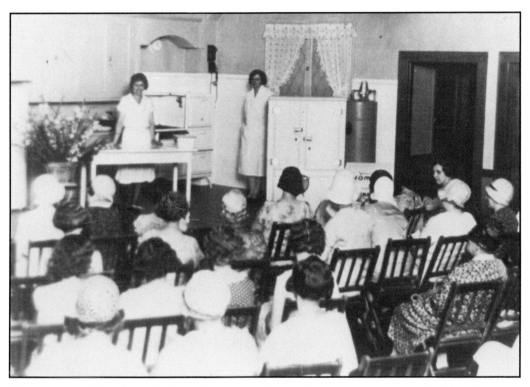

Home economist Mary Lamb, by the refrigerator, watched while a guest speaker shared advice with community women who attended classes in the modern kitchen at the Northern States Power Company office in La Crosse, 1937.

Betty Lamb Dell Hyde

---

earrings which depicted Reddy Kilowatt, the advertising symbol for electricity. Mary's daughter, Betty, cleaned up the kitchen after the demonstrations. "A friend usually helped me. We made good money, considering we were high school girls. We were awed by the makeup and hair of some in the audience because Ma Bennett was one of the best customers and she brought her 'girls' to the cooking demonstrations," Betty recalled. Mary also took the cooking schools on the road to clubs, churches, schools, and public halls in Hokah, La Crescent, Sparta, and Tomah. Members of the audience received prizes such as canned goods from local stores, NSP potholders and measuring cups and spoons, and the food Mary prepared during the demonstration.

She promoted improved cooking methods until her retirement in 1950 and, for most of that time, published a weekly recipe in the *La Crosse Tribune*. The recipes ranged from meatless Lenten meals (broiled salmon rounds and fish potato puff) to casseroles, and from budget balancers to desserts (mocha cake and lemon milk sherbet).

Libraries

Women were a strong force behind the development of library systems in La Crosse County. They recognized the need to provide libraries for city and rural families, worked to organize and improve the libraries, and provided important financial resources.[11]

La Crosse Public Library

For thirty years, Annie E. Hanscome was La Crosse's only librarian, first with the private Young Men's Library Association from 1874 to 1888 and then as first head librarian for the La Crosse Public Library when it opened in 1888. Her starting salary of $720 a year grew to $1,040 by the time she resigned in 1904. She believed the time had come for someone more qualified to direct the library.[12]

Mary Alice Smith was the city's first professionally-trained librarian. Her first task, cataloging the books, reflected that training. During her tenure (1904 to 1915), she developed a children's room, opened the North Branch Library in Brakke's Drug Store at 1353 Caledonia Street, and oversaw the 1909 addition to the main library building, which was made possible by several contributions including $5,000 from Mrs. Lucius (Geneva) Colman.

Before 1905, children under the age of fourteen were not allowed to borrow books from the library. That changed when financial donations from Elsie Gile Scott, Mrs. James (Agnes L.) Vincent, Mrs. R. E. (Louise) Osborne, and the La Crosse Chapter of Daughters of the American Revolution funded a room just for children. Mrs. A. W. (Cordelia) Pettibone's $5,000 donation was used to purchase children's books. The children's librarian, Mary MacDonald, visited all the schools in La Crosse to invite students to visit the new room. The response was overwhelming. Instead of the one hundred children anticipated, one thousand visited the children's room on opening day, March 4th.

Dedication was a hallmark of many women who served on the library staff. Anna Pedersen served for sixty-five years (1907 to 1972), all but four of them at the North Branch Library. She made that place a delight to visit when she hosted holiday parties and hobby shows. La Crosse native Lilly M. E. Borreson was head city librarian from 1915 to 1947. She saw the establishment of the South Branch Library in a World War I barracks and the dedication of the North Branch's very own building at 1552 Kane Street in 1942. Geneva Colman made another large gift to the library when she established a $10,000 endowment fund to honor her deceased husband in 1927.

Muriel Fuller grew up near West Salem, became head librarian in La Crosse in 1947, and oversaw the construction and 1952 dedication of a new building for the South Branch at 1307 South Sixteenth Street. Nellie MacDonald, who worked for twenty-eight years in the barracks, which was hot in summer and cold in winter, declared that the new building was "a dream come true." Muriel also chaired the statewide library service committee of the Wisconsin Free Library Commission, which lobbied for improved community library service. In 1949, one-fourth of the state's population had no free public library service, and three-fourths of the counties had no free service for rural residents.[13] Muriel left La Crosse in 1953 to work and teach at the university level, first in Michigan and then in Wisconsin.[14] During the 1960s, she took responsibility for the development of a bill to provide money for developing public library systems. The bill became law in 1971. As a tribute to her leadership and work, which emphasized and benefited community libraries, the Wisconsin Library Association established The Muriel Fuller Award. In its desire to recognize her as a mentor and inspiration, the association gives the award to practicing librarians for their focus on improving services within their library organization rather than for service at the regional, state, or national level.

When the La Crosse Public Library opened in 1888, the public was not allowed to go into the stacks without special permission from the librarian. Mary Alice Smith changed that policy sometime between 1904 and 1915 and made patrons feel more welcome. It was under Gertrude Thurow's direction, however, that the La Crosse Public Library became a lively community learning center. When she became head librarian in 1953, she applied her philosophy that "a library is a continuing education. Libraries are the greatest gift a democracy can bestow."[15] Recognizing the need for a larger facility, she began a vigorous campaign for the construction of a new library. To create community support for the building project, she created Friends of the La Crosse Public Library.

She thought of the library as a place where people could seek help as well as information. One hot summer day, a man staggered into the building. When she approached him, he asked if he could trust her. When she replied, "Yes," he said, "I'm drunk. Would you call Alcoholics Anonymous for me?" She did, and later she said, "Isn't it wonderful that he knew the library was a place where he could get help? So many people still don't know that."[16]

Women continued to make large financial gifts to the library during Gertrude's tenure. Mrs. Reuben (Helen H.) Trane memorialized her deceased husband with annual gifts of $5,000 from 1954 to 1960. Dr. Edyth and Susan Swarthout of West Salem decided to name the library and the La Crosse County Historical Society as two major beneficiaries in their wills.

By the time she retired in 1976, Miss Thurow had developed library systems for six surrounding counties, was named Wisconsin Librarian of the Year in 1959, and served as president of the Wisconsin Library Association. In 1975, she received a Special Services Award from the Wisconsin Library Association, which had been granted to only seven recipients before her. Longtime library volunteer Jean Wulling said of Gertrude, "Her placid exterior belied the many progressive ideas inside."

La Crosse County Library

In an attempt to circulate books and information to families in the rural areas of the county, women established libraries in their homes, formed study groups, and created traveling libraries. These efforts eventually merged to form the La Crosse County Library.[17]

Mrs. Frank (Emily) Tiffany was the inspirational and organizational force behind the 1898 creation of the Traveling Library System. She donated the first five books which were housed in the Town of Campbell home of Mrs. W. J. Dawson and served on the board with Carrie Bloomingdale, Emma Salzer, and Elsie Gile Scott.

In 1904, a group of progressive women asked the La Crosse County Board of Supervisors to establish a county traveling library in accordance with the Wisconsin state law of 1901. The county board complied, and the early library stations were located in homes, stores, post offices, a cheese factory, and, later, in schools. The small collections rotated from station to station. The head librarian of the La Crosse Public Library, Lilly Borreson, also served as supervising librarian of the La Crosse County Traveling Library. She campaigned hard to improve the services to county residents and helped bring about change in the Wisconsin Traveling Library Law. She advocated that county branch libraries be located on the main street and "be just as easy of access as the pool room."[18] Lilly also proposed, but did not secure, an "auto truck" to carry books to the homes of rural families. Her plea on behalf of county branch libraries was "to give the boys and girls, the men and women of La Crosse County what to me seems one of the greatest of God's blessings, an equal opportunity with the people of the city to get as many books and magazines as they want to read."[19]

During the years the traveling library served La Crosse County's rural communities, rats destroyed the books at one station and the Bangor depot fire destroyed others. Despite low circulation and difficulty in acquiring books and supplies during World War I, Lilly Borreson persevered. She saw the traveling library that had been conceived by a small group of women in 1898 become the La Crosse County Library in 1923.

A Cheerful Librarian

West Salem's first library began in 1927 in the home of Alice Jostad. Before long it found a home in the village hall.[20] In 1940, Dorothy Dudley, the daughter of a West Salem pioneer family, began her thirty-nine year tenure as librarian. She had an educational background in theology and tremendous knowledge of the Bible. She also was devoted to the library, had a keen interest in local history, and cared a great deal about the youth in the community. When asked why she was always so cheerful, she replied, "It doesn't bother me — the smiling process. It isn't difficult."[21]

A "Renaissance" Librarian

Although she was not a trained librarian, friends and library colleagues thought of Helen Leide as a "mother" and a "Renaissance Woman."[22] People recognized, respected, and valued her caring nature, intelligence, love of knowledge, and wealth of local information. In the 1950s, she led an adult study group at the North Branch Library. It was a pilot study of "The American Heritage Program," which pioneered the use of libraries for adult education in five U.S. cities. In the late 1950s and early 1960s, she worked for the La Crosse Public Library, spending most of her time at the South Branch but also substituting at the main library in the evenings. Carol Lee, who works in the public library circulation department and in collection development, took her children to story hour at the South Branch in the mid and late 1950s. She and a friend took other children as well as their own. "We would load up our cars with eight, nine or ten children. Some of them had mothers who were working and could not take them to the library, so we did and had a good time." Now and then, Helen substituted for Clara Laux who held a marvelous story hour for pre-schoolers. "She filled in wherever needed," Carol said about Helen who also had a passion for bridge, bird watching, and the environment.

Madeline Anderson, collection development coordinator of the La Crosse Public Library, met Helen when Madeline began her own library career as an aide at the public library in June 1962. "We were called 'pages' then," she recalled. When Madeline entered Wisconsin State University at La Crosse two years later, she felt very comfortable at the university library because Helen Leide had started working there. "Helen always took students under her wing," Madeline said. If a student came to her with a headache, Helen worked around the school policy which prohibited her from dispensing aspirin. Madeline recalled, "She would say, 'There is a bottle sitting on the desk. If something happens while I have my back turned, I can't really do anything about it.'" She also mothered faculty, gently reminding them of overdue books and offering to send someone to pick them up.

Husband-Wife Business Partnerships

Women did their share of the work in business partnerships with their husbands. Some kept the family enterprise going while the men were gone for periods of time. Others earned an income at another job in order to support the family and a developing business.

In the mid-1930s, when she was nearly fifty years old, Emma Krause asked her husband, Charlie, to "start something I can help you with or I will eat you bankrupt."[23] He was a traveling salesman for fourteen years. For the last three, she did the driving and sat waiting and eating while he made his calls. When Charlie responded, "Well, we will have to go into debt," Emma countered with, "If we do and lose it, we will go South and pick beans and nobody will find out what happened." The Krauses invested in a grocery store, a gasoline station, and a motel on the northeast corner of Losey Boulevard and Highway 33. They named their establishment Krause's Kabin Kourt. Later on, when they acquired a gasoline station at the corner of Losey Boulevard and La Crosse Street, Emma served as the roadrunner between the two locations. Because there still were very few houses along Losey at that time, Charlie cautioned her to drive into and through town rather than along the sparsely populated edge.

Lucy Lonkoski and her husband, Ray, owned Ray and Lucy's tavern on Eleventh and Adams streets in La Crosse, 1950.

Lucy Lonkoski

Taverns and Restaurants

While men tended to be the proprietors of downtown bars, most neighborhood taverns were the joint venture of a husband and wife. Lucy and Ray Lonkowski operated Ray and Lucy's, a neighborhood tavern at Eleventh and Adams streets in La Crosse, from the time they married in 1936 until 1950.[24] "There wasn't a lot of profit on nickel beers, so in the early days Ray worked on the AlCan Highway and the Great Lakes ore boats. He'd be gone for months at a time and would send money home," Lucy recalled. Although they had a liquor license, the tavern did not have a kitchen or a license to sell food. Instead, Lucy prepared food at home and served it free of charge. She fried catfish and baked raccoon and muskrat for parties for the softball team they sponsored. She also served ring bologna and liver sausage on crackers as a free lunch on Saturdays. "Schubert's Meat Market delivered and I paid one dollar for the meat," she remembered. By the time the United States entered World War II, Lucy and Ray had two young sons. "A tavern was not considered essential work. We knew Ray would be drafted into the

Nellie Westerhouse served breakfast, lunch, and supper six days a week at Nellie's Eat Shop in Onalaska in the 1940s.

Nancy Westerhouse Tolvstad

service, so he decided to enlist in the Navy," she said. Once again, Lucy managed the tavern, which was open from 8 a.m. to 1 a.m. every day. During the two years Ray was in service, Lucy worked hard and counted on friends and relatives to help her keep the business and the family going.

Nellie Dahlby Westerhouse loved to cook. She employed her talent to earn money and to support worthy causes. Nellie, her husband, Howard, and their daughters, Barbara and Nancy, lived on Onalaska's Second Street just north of Main Street. Other homeowners in their neighborhood rented rooms, often to single female teachers who were required to live in the community where they taught. These renters, looking for a place to eat, found that Nellie provided delicious home-cooked meals for fifteen to twenty people in her dining room. The price was seventy-five cents. She took pride in the variety of meals she prepared and kept track of menus in order to avoid frequent repetition.[25] In 1942, at the age of thirty-eight, she started Nellie's Eat Shop on Main Street. Howard opened the restaurant in the morning before catching the bus to work in La Crosse. Every Monday through Saturday for five years, Nellie served breakfast, lunch and supper to her customers, taking only an afternoon break in her twelve-hour day. She did not do much cooking at home because she moved the stove and refrigerator to the restaurant. Her daughter, Nancy, recalled, "We always went out for dinner on Sunday, her day off."

Nellie, who had "a knack for telling people to do things without sounding bossy," also had a keen interest in youth. In the 1940s she and Howard sponsored parties for Onalaska teenagers at the old Woodman Hall. She also served as a 4-H volunteer and as president of the YWCA from 1952 to 1953.

Real Estate and Insurance

Ben Sias may have been the elected leader of Onalaska (he served as mayor from 1946 until his death in 1950) but his wife, Floyde Johnson Sias, was the "grande dame" of the community. She stood nearly six feet tall, wore large jewelry, enjoyed telling stories, and loved to laugh.[26] Floyde began her career in teaching but later became a licensed real estate agent and continued the Sias Real Estate and Insurance Agency when her husband died. In 1959, she was the first woman to be president of the La Crosse Board of Realtors. She was a charter member of the Multiple Listings Service of La Crosse and served as president in 1963.

It was through the business that Floyde helped so many families. If she knew a client was having financial difficulties and might not be able to pay an insurance premium, she took care of it until the client could pay her back. "Many families had Thanksgiving dinners because of her generosity," remembered Marce Mehren who became acquainted with Floyde through the realtors association. "She also provided Christmas gifts for children of needy families. She was especially keen about providing shoes and eyeglasses."[27]

Floyde played the organ and directed the choir at Onalaska United Methodist Church for years. She was very active in the Republican Party and served on the La Crosse County Library Board for many years. In 1978, the Onalaska Common Council named the city's library building after her. She donated children's books to the library and established a trust fund in memory of her husband to continue providing good reading material for youngsters.[28]

Funeral Homes

Husbands and wives worked as teams operating funeral homes in the area. Onalaska has had three such partnerships: first, A. E. and M. J. Smith; next Sylvia (Casberg) and Clifford Fossum Sr.; and third, Elaine (Gilster) and Clifford Fossum Jr. Both Sylvia and Clifford Sr. were funeral directors when they married in 1928. They operated funeral homes in partnership with others in Coon Valley, La Crosse, and Onalaska before going into business for themselves in 1934. When they first moved to Onalaska, they rented a house for five dollars a month and used part of it for a funeral home. Eventually they expanded the business by opening funeral homes in Bangor (1945) and in Galesville (1947). Sylvia worked as a licensed and certified mortician for forty years. She was a member of the state and national funeral directors associations and, at the time of her death in 1967, she was secretary-treasurer of the Western Wisconsin Funeral Directors Association.[29]

The Dickinson Funeral Homes business got its start when Don and Hazel Dickinson bought the Sletten McKee funeral home location on the north side of La Crosse in 1955. Don was a licensed funeral director. Hazel was not, but she was indispensable to the partnership. Because they did not know if the business would be successful, Hazel went to work at Manke's Hardware store on the northeast corner of Clinton and Caledonia streets. She earned not more than one dollar an hour working as a clerk, and that was the family's steady income for a few years. Her paycheck fed the family and paid the debt the Dickinsons incurred when purchasing the funeral home. "A dollar doesn't seem like much, but you could buy a big bag of groceries for five dollars," Hazel recalled. Her regular hours were 9 a.m. to 4 p.m., thus she finished work just about the time their two sons were returning from school. Within a couple of years, the Dickinsons had enough loyal customers to give them confidence about the future of their business. Hazel returned full-time to their home above the funeral home at 1339 Caledonia. She answered the business phone and the door and did the book work. "That was before computers so I wrote checks, sent out bills, and wrote receipts in longhand," she said. Hazel also fixed the hair and cosmetics of the deceased women. "About ninety-nine percent of the people we served were people we knew so I didn't have fear of touching a dead body," she said.[30]

Livelihoods for Women as well as Men

There were fields of employment that, even in the early part of the twentieth century, offered opportunities for women as well as men.

Photography

Women represented thirteen percent of the people engaged in photography in La Crosse between 1853 and 1930. A few were photographers while larger numbers were photo processors and retouchers. Ellen Myers was the first recorded female photographer in La Crosse. She specialized in enlarging. Her portrait work, among the best in the period (1875-1890s), was especially popular among local women. The longest-lasting photography business partnerships included women. For example, when Gussie Kopetsky joined James Norris to form the Norris and Kopetsky gallery in 1924, they embarked on a successful partnership spanning more than thirty years doing portraits and wedding photography.[31]

Helen Mae Hoeft, born in 1894, had a national reputation as the "queen of photofinishing." She began work as a photographer in 1915 for Millard E. Reynolds. The firm became Reynolds and Hoeft five years later and, in 1926, the name changed to Paramount Photo Shop. In 1924, she coaxed her partner into investing in nationwide advertising for a pioneering idea, mail-order photofinishing. The new business, which she named Ray's Photo Service because she thought customers would not want to deal with a woman, started slowly and depleted her $400 savings. The day after Helen moved to Chicago and took a job as a clerk, Reynolds wired her to hurry back. Mail from all over the nation had started to pour in. Twenty-five cents accompanied each roll of film. The business grew rapidly, at one time employing 150 working in three shifts. "It was nothing to take in about $1,500 in quarters in one day," recalled Helen in 1954.[32] She became sole owner of the business in 1941 and sold it in 1955.

Entertainment

In the 1920s, Onalaskans watched silent movies at the Crystal Theater while Floyde Johnson Sias or Betty Dolbier provided piano music to reflect the action on the screen. The audience always laughed when Floyde accompanied the Western chase scenes because she swayed so much with the rousing music everyone thought she would sway right off the piano stool.[33] Betty Dolbier, who graduated from Onalaska High School in 1926, also was a member of the Viking Accordian Band, transcribed music for the Zor Oriental Band, and entertained on piano.[34]

In La Crosse, Marian Widrick and Olive Hagen Plamadore added the musical dimension for silent-moviegoers. Because Marian played by ear, she was especially good at providing mood music for the movies.[35]

For a few years in the 1920s, Guy and Eloda Sitzer Beach made La Crosse the headquarters for their traveling theatre, the Beach Stock Company. They settled into the community between acting engagements on the road — living in the Spanish style house they built on the corner of State Street and Losey Boulevard. They gave benefit performances for the

Entertainer Eloda Sitzer Beach posed with a milk wagon and several children to promote a school-related campaign which encouraged children to drink more milk, c. 1922.

La Crosse County Historical Society

"sanatorium" in West Salem and a special matinee for the telephone operators who were deluged with phone calls when the Beaches performed in La Crosse. Eloda, also known as "the little redhead," performed at the Elks annual Christmas party for needy children. Like other prominent entertainment personalities around the country, she lent her name to good causes, in particular, a school-related campaign in La Crosse that encouraged children to drink more milk.[36]

Eventually making La Crosse their permanent home in the 1940s, Julie and Mae Obreicht were members of a traveling family entertainment troup led by their brother Christy Obreicht. Two other sisters performed in the group: Nell, who, with her husband Arthur Palmer, later established the Lowell Inn in Stillwater, Minnesota, and Sarah, married to Johnny Sullivan, who had been part of the show and then worked at local radio station WKBH. Julie and Mae played piano and violin for local gatherings for many years.

Social Work

During her tenure as county probation officer, Dorothy Waite fought and won the battle with the La Crosse County Board to place delinquent and neglected children in a home-like setting rather than in the county jail or local hospitals. On December 13, 1929, she admitted the first child to the La Crosse County Juvenile Detention Home on the second floor of a building at Fourth and Vine streets in La Crosse. During the first year, sixty-nine children lived in the home.[37]

Elizabeth Beesecker was the matron of the La Crosse County Juvenile Detention Home from the mid-1930s to the mid-1950s. The young residents called her "Ma B."[38] She supervised as many as twenty-two youngsters at a time. Some of her charges were boys who had stolen cars and teenage girls who hung around Camp McCoy. She also sheltered, on a moment's notice, neglected and abandoned children and infants, sometimes answering the door in the middle of the night to find the sheriff standing there with a child in his arms. She did all the cooking and baking and taught manners to the children as they sat around a large table for meals.

In 1942, an inspector from the state industrial commission called the quarters "cramped" and the frame building a "tinderbox." The matron already knew that. She "slept with one eye open" to be alert to emergencies such as the time one of the boys set a fire. The inspector's words finally jolted the county board into action, and it purchased a home at 718 State Street. Elizabeth Beesecker and county probation officer Minnette Sprain directed the move. Minnette, one of the leaders of the effort to replace the home, was delighted that the new location had a large yard for the children to play in, something lacking at the original site.[39] From 1933 to 1957, she watched out for youth in trouble and in troubled homes. She kept tabs on youthful offenders. Sometimes she found new homes or at least foster homes for children in need of a safe and stable place to live.[40]

From 1929 to 1956, Josephine Fletcher not only managed the private La Crosse Home for Children, she also made it a warm, caring place for children so that they also could grow up to be responsible and caring. Members of the board of directors had great respect and affection for this five foot tall, white-haired lady. So did the children. Recollections of a former resident described Miss Fletcher's unmatched ability to understand and meet the different needs of each individual child. One of the many improvements was convincing others that the girls should stay in the home beyond their fourteenth birthday.

> *She was aware of the special need at this vulnerable age for love and guidance, which was not always offered in foster homes. During these years she tried to find out what our interests and abilities were, and how we could become independent and productive members of society. She*

encouraged many children to continue their education and
helped to find means to accomplish this goal.[41]

Miss Fletcher used her child welfare training and experience to make the house on Eleventh and Ferry streets an inviting family home for the twenty to thirty children who resided there. Proof of that was the neighborhood children who were invited to stay for meals and later begged their parents to let them live at the home. The children helped plant gardens and gleefully took part in tomato fights once a year. Miss Fletcher taught table manners and etiquette and encouraged participation in Scouting, the YMCA and YWCA, and in music and dance lessons. She also taught basic skills and how to accept responsibility by assigning household tasks to each child. "Although we weren't convinced of it at the time," this was an important part of the training. The La Crosse Home for Children was a home full of love because Josephine Fletcher had "a full life, filled with love."[42]

Post Office

When Hilma Gjestvang ended her twelve years as West Salem postal clerk in the early 1930s, the post office was elevated to a second class station and three men were hired to replace her.[43] Alice McHugh served as Holmen's postmaster from 1944 to 1977. She was the first person appointed to that position strictly on a merit basis from within the U.S. Postal Service. When she became postmaster, it cost three cents to mail a first class letter. When she retired, it took thirteen cents to do the same.[44]

Laundries

Sending clothing to a commercial laundry was one way to avoid doing the chore at home. Some women, however, did double duty because they did laundry at home and at work. When dirty clothing and bedding was sent out to be laundered, someone like Thelma Orr Zumach Stokes, who worked at Modern Laundry in the 1950s, sorted the items into big mesh bags of whites, socks, and colors, and tagged the bags with the customer's name. Generally men switched the heavy wet laundry from the washing machines to the tumblers for drying. Then women removed and folded the dry items.

Springtime was always busier because that was the time for refreshing curtains and blankets. In 1963, Thelma went to work in the Lutheran Hospital laundry. "The men sorted the dirty laundry. The women folded it and the blankets, too. We pressed lab coats. You'd do the sleeves first, then the body all the way around, and the collar last. I would spend all day reaching up and pulling the ironer down to do the pressing. That's why I have arthritis in my shoulders," she said. The last few years before she retired in 1976 at the age of 65, Thelma supervised the women workers.[45]

Expanding Roles

Clergy

The Reverend Nellie Mann Opdale served as minister of St. Paul's Universalist Church in La Crosse from 1898 to 1902. Shortly after her husband's death in 1892, she went on the lecture circuit on behalf of woman suffrage. A Racine newspaper article of 1898 reported that, "While engaged in this work she appeared before the legislature twice, commanding close attention on both occasions."[46] Nellie also became licensed to preach by the Universalist convention and served a pastorate in Mukwonago before coming to La Crosse. The same newspaper article stated, "Last June she preached for the first time to the congregation of St. Paul's at La Crosse. So well was she received that she was induced to spend her vacation there last September. During this time she preached twice more and the result was the call which she just accepted."

Two women briefly served as associate ministers of the First Congregational Church of La Crosse in the 1930s. Eunice Trumbro was hired in August 1930 to direct the Christian education program, to be responsible for the Young People's Society and the Junior Church, and to serve as a member of the Sunday School Committee. Eunice resigned at the end of one year because she felt her training in the ministry had not prepared her to conduct a successful program for children. Josephine Teetor succeeded her in August 1931 and remained as director of Christian education until 1933 when the congregation could no longer pay her salary during the lean Depression years.[47]

Much later, one female minister to serve La Crosse was part of a husband-wife team. Jeanne and Bob Tyler became co-pastors of St. John's

Reformed Church on January 1, 1978. In their first professional roles, the Tylers shared one full-time position as equal partners in the ministry which allowed them time to devote to their two children. The husband-wife ministry team also gave parishioners a choice in style and gender when seeking help. "We balance each other out," Jeanne said. "We share some services, others we do independently. Bob's sermons are more analytical than mine. I think women speak differently than men because of different experiences."[48]

Dorothy Kuechmann graduated from Colgate-Rochester Divinity School in 1946 but delayed her ordination until 1978. In a seminary dominated by men, Dorothy was one of the "gentlemen" in the class and sang "tenor" in the choir. "At that point [1946] in my thinking, and in the conception of the average church member, a minister was a man, and if he had a wife, she was his helper," Dorothy said.[49] Thirty years later, a three-week tour sponsored by Church Women United to experience the problems of cities changed her thinking. Dorothy believed her efforts to serve the disadvantaged would be strengthened through ministry. "It's important for women to be ordained," she said. "I don't see any difference in our [men's and women's] abilities." She became a leading force in ministry to the elderly in the La Crosse area.

Law

Razy Kletecka Chojnacki was the first woman to practice law in La Crosse. One of her Aquinas High School classmates remembered her as "very intelligent and sophisticated about the world. She was a loner of sorts, probably because she was so far ahead of the rest of us." In 1943, Razy graduated from Marquette University in Milwaukee, was admitted to the State Bar, and joined the La Crosse law office of Frank E. Withrow. Three years later she married a law school classmate, Leonard Chojnacki, and they established the Chojnacki and Chojnacki law firm. Razy and Len were the first and, at that time, only husband-wife legal team in the city and one of just a few pairs in the country. "Razy was highly regarded as an 'office' lawyer," said Daniel Flaherty who was a young trial lawyer at the time.[50] She handled a lot of family practice cases such as divorce, child support, and adoption. "It was a pleasure to work on opposite sides of a case with her," said another contemporary, Robert Joanis.[51] "She represented her clients ably and sincerely," he said. The husband-wife legal team also served as legal counsel for the local AFL-CIO. Razy's legal career was cut short by her death the day before her thirtieth birthday in 1951 of complications following childbirth.[52]

Although Razy's contemporary, Olga Bennett, continued to practice law and eventually became a judge in neighboring Vernon County, La Crosse did not have another female attorney until 1975 when Maureen Kinney and Janet Jenkins started their careers here. The novelty of female lawyers was evident in the headline of a 1975 newspaper article, "Local Women Lawyers Skirt Feminist Causes."[53] When asked whether the rights of women would be a priority in their fledgling law practices, Maureen and Janet put that issue in perspective. "It is an area of interest, but women … have to practice in a wide spectrum, not just one area," Maureen said. Limiting her practice to women's issues "would be pretty stagnating in a community the size of La Crosse," Janet responded. Looking back to earlier women in law, Maureen added, "Probably they did not have an opportunity to practice women's rights. There weren't any."

The labor shortage during World War II provided opportunities for women to hold jobs previously held by men, ranging from taxicab driver to pilot to news photographer. Dell Sallander, Florence Guy, and Freda Miner drove taxicabs in La Crosse during World War II.[54] Although they were filling in for men, their working hours were limited because they were women. A city ordinance stipulated that they work no later than 6 p.m. Also because of their gender, their male passengers generally did not expect them to open doors or carry bags. All of them had to change tires at one time or another. Although male passengers may have offered to help, the women transferred their passengers to another cab whenever such an emergency occurred. When asked about maintaining the vehicle, Freda said, "I know where everything is and if I had to, I'd probably be able to fix it."

Armed Forces Auxiliaries

Several La Crosse women answered the call to join women's counterparts to the armed forces in order to "free a man" to fly in combat or fight at sea during World War II. In August 1942, four area women joined the Women's Auxiliary Army Corps (WAAC) and a fifth, teacher Ethel Krueger, was accepted into the Corps' officer training program. Helene

Mary Belle Ahlstrom Smith was a pilot in the Women's Air Ferry Service during World War II, 1943.

Mary Smith

Calendar, who had fourteen months of nurse's training at St. Francis School of Nursing, left her job as a maid in the A. P. Funk home in La Crosse to take an assignment in the service as an assistant in surgery. Dorothy Strehl, a widow who believed women needed to take the place of men, qualified as a switchboard operator after taking that training at La Crosse Adult and Vocational School. Esther Selke left her work as a clerk at Kresge's dime store to serve as a military chauffeur. Marion P. Olson traded her cash register at the Bodega Lunch Club for a typewriter in the WAAC.[55]

Mary Belle Ahlstrom Smith, while she was studying chemistry at the University of Wisconsin at Madison, decided that she wanted to learn to fly. "Back then, it was something that most girls didn't do. It sounded real interesting and exciting," she said.[56] She earned her pilot's license after obtaining the only spot for a woman in a training course for ten civilians offered in La Crosse. When she tried to enroll in a secondary training course in Madison, she ran into "the same old story." At first, "the instructor told me, 'We can't take any girls,' but then he called back to say, 'We have room for two girls,'" she recalled.

When the first call came for women pilots to join a flying group to serve the war effort, Mary did not have enough flying time under her belt. However, she was ready for the second call a few months later because she had been flying a small plane between Madison and La Crosse in order to accumulate hours. During her twenty-three months with the Women's Air Ferry Service (WAFS), she checked out as a pilot for fourteen different kinds of planes. "I ferried everything from little tiny planes to B-24s over forty-seven states and five Canadian provinces to deliver aircraft to training fields and points of embarkation," she recalled. Mary also served as a test

Photographer Frances Burgess, left, and Susan McCabe, who edited the women's page, worked together at the *La Crosse Tribune* to report on news and events of interest to women in the 1940s, 1950s, and 1960s.

La Crosse Tribune

pilot on advanced training planes and as an instrument instructor on LINK trainers, simulators for navigators, before she married another pilot, Leonard Smith, in January 1946.

Newspapers

Frances E. "Franny" Burgess began work as a proofreader at the *La Crosse Tribune* when her father, publisher Frank H. Burgess, offered her a part-time job in 1934, but it was World War II that gave her the break she really wanted. Because of the reduction in available manpower, women had to take over other jobs on the paper. Photography was one of them. Although Franny never had formal training in photography, her artistic bent and eye for composition produced prize-winning photographs over the years. She loved the arts and was a member of the La Crosse Sketch Club from its founding in the 1930s and of the La Crosse Music Study Club.[57]

In the same way that the role for women had been confined to the home, the news for and about women was confined to the women's page of the newspaper. Into the 1970s, the *La Crosse Tribune* had a page or section of the newspaper devoted to reporting events in women's lives. A typical women's page of the 1950s included meeting announcements for various clubs and organizations; brief articles about garden clubs and nursing alumnae; fashion features; recipes; engagement, marriage and birth announcements; and advertisements for laundry soaps, women's clothing, and beauty shops.[58] Even organizations like the League of Women Voters, whose members studied topics such as the United Nations or the quality of the water supply, were relegated to this section. Signe Schroeder, who was public relations chair of the League in La Crosse in the early 1960s, remembered futile meetings with the *Tribune* staff to request that news items appear in the news section rather than on the women's page of the newspaper.

Susan McCabe edited the women's page for forty years. She joined the *La Crosse Tribune* staff as a proofreader in 1920. Five years later she became editor of the women's page where she recorded a large segment of La Crosse's social and cultural history. Joining her was Franny Burgess who moved from the city desk to the women's department. They worked long hours in tandem for many years to cover news and events of interest to women; Susan with her notebook and Franny lugging around a large camera.

At the time of her retirement in 1965, Susan described four decades of changes in the community and the world as viewed through the women's page:

> *In 1925 social life was active and so were the women's clubs and patriotic organizations, many of the clubs still in their infancy. Wedding write-ups of the day missed nothing. Every sleeve "came to a point over the hand." ... [During the Depression] people who did have a party wouldn't let a newspaper publish it because they didn't want anyone to know it.... Charity balls at the old Pioneer hall were abandoned, the money annually raised for public aid in this way completely inadequate to the growing need.... clubwomen were more determined than ever in their desire to help in every situation, and so the organizations kept going.*
>
> *Then came the war clouds in Europe and Asia. Clubwomen were told "put away your bric-a-brac." They did — and plunged into war activities of every kind.... With opening of Camp McCoy, wedding news came in such a deluge that no newspaper could handle it. The* La Crosse Tribune *was*

rationed on paper like all other publications of the country.
[After the war,] Sunday home layouts and other feature stories
were introduced to relieve the monotony.... Most of the beautiful
homes in the city have been pictured in this way.[59]

The changes in the content of the women's page reflected the changes in women's lives. While Jan McLain was women's editor of the *La Crosse Tribune*, from 1969 to 1974, she used her position to increase community awareness of women's issues. In a regular column, she addressed topics such as the equal rights amendment (both U.S. and Wisconsin), how women could establish their own credit rating, the economic role of women, reasons women retained their birth name, and the lack of women's history in text books. In an attempt to correct the dearth of information, she proceeded to write a series of biographical articles about women who were significant in our nation's history.

Women were the mainstay of community weekly newspapers because they generally served as the correspondents who reported the happenings from their coulee or rural neighborhood. According to Estella Krohn Bryhn, the correspondents named "who had Sunday dinner with whom; who had ridden to the stockyards with her husband on Monday when he sold hogs (so Ole wouldn't spend all the money on those new fangled slot machines or in the saloon); and whose gall bladder had just been removed."[60] Estella was the *West Salem Journal*'s correspondent from Wet Coulee. When she graduated from West Salem High School in 1931, her plan to study journalism at Marquette University was thwarted by lack of money. She put aside her dream of newspaper work and attended the one-year rural teaching course at La Crosse Normal School. In the fall of 1934, a group of friends set up a quilting frame under the apple trees next to the Krohn family home and went to work stitching a green and lavender double wedding ring quilt as a gift for the March 1935 wedding of Estella and Milton Bryhn. The Bryhns began farming in Wet Coulee where they raised twin daughters and an adopted son brought to them by the county probation officer, Minnette Sprain.[61]

One Monday morning, when she dropped off her news from Wet Coulee, the *West Salem Journal* publisher, Don Griswold, asked, "Will you work for two weeks until I can get someone who knows something?" Those two weeks in September 1972 developed into a long stint as news editor, which meant she was responsible for the authenticity of all articles in the paper. Estella's lyrical writing style informed and entertained county residents for thirty years.

Each Wednesday the newspaper staff set the type, ran the flatbed press, folded, addressed, and bundled that week's edition of the paper. On Thursday, they tore down the forms, removed much of the West Salem news, and refilled the forms with news of Bangor provided by Kathryn Meier (1949-1965) and then Della Berg (1965-1971) who were the editors for the *Journal*'s sister publication, the *Bangor Independent*.

The Bangor newspaper office was a one-person operation. During her tenure, Della ran the business as well as the news side of the paper from her home.[62] In addition to editing the information supplied by the correspondents, writing news stories and her occasional column, "Lin-O-Type," and compiling items for the historical "Way Back When" feature, she also sold the advertising, did the billing, and kept the books.

In the late 1970s, Jan McLain was publisher/editor of a weekly newspaper in La Crosse, the *Coulee Gazette*. She put all of her energy into starting the *Gazette*, and, in January 1976, assembled the first issue on a dining room table.[63] As the paper evolved from a monthly to a bi-monthly to a weekly publication, the enterprise moved out of the home and into an office, and the staff grew to include twelve people. Jan appeared to be living and breathing the newspaper, "If you stop in to see the *Gazette*'s publisher and are told she is unavailable because she is asleep on her office floor, don't be shocked or feel you are being ignored. When one starts a workweek at midnight Sunday and lives with the *Gazette* until 6 p.m. Wednesday plus 8 to 12 hours a day on Thursday, Friday, and Saturday each week, one gets a few winks of sleep wherever and whenever the eyelids simply won't stay open any longer."[64] Jan resigned in the summer of 1979. Plagued by the lack of advertising support for a second newspaper in the community, the *Coulee Gazette* folded a few months later.

Radio

There were just three radio stations in La Crosse when Jean Gitz and Joe and Evelyn Rohrer moved to town as the new owners of WLCX in 1957. Jean's contact with radio began with music and programming and wound up on the business side of radio operations. One summer in the early 1940s, a station in Rockford, Illinois, opened a studio in Jean's hometown of Freeport. Jean performed live music on the piano for fifteen minutes out of the three hours that WROK broadcasted each day.[65] In 1944, Jean graduated from Carleton College with a major in music and headed for New York City, where she found work at the American Society of Composers, Authors, and Publishers (ASCAP). Two years later she headed west to join her mother in Colorado Springs. There Jean learned about a fellow who was starting a radio station. She became music librarian for the new station, thus beginning a long-time friendship and partnership with the Rohrers. As music librarian, Jean cataloged the music, selected what was to be played, and wrote "lots and lots of scripts for the announcers. They didn't ad lib in those days," she said. It was not long before Jean became the program director, which meant she was responsible for determining the eighteen hours of programming each day from 6 a.m. when the station went on the air until it signed off at midnight.

When WLCX came on the market in La Crosse in 1957, there were only about 700 radio stations in the country. "We bought it for a giveaway price," said Jean. Joe was president and manager; Evelyn was vice-president and traffic director. Jean began as program director and quickly added business manager to her responsibilities as a partner. "With a small staff of eight, I felt I needed to learn about every part of the operation. To gain some sales experience, I made calls on a few small accounts, like Aletta's Hat Shop and the Alpine Inn," she said.

One of the significant lessons Jean learned from Joe was the importance of a community-minded attitude in programming as well as participation in the community. As co-owner of the radio station and as an individual, Jean Gitz Bassett passed that lesson on to others by her own example. WLCX donated thousands and thousands of dollars worth of free time for community causes. Her own earliest community involvement was as a transportation volunteer for Social Services. She "toted people in need of rides" to medical appointments and to visit relatives at Oak Forest Sanatorium. Jean joined the board of the Salvation Army in 1961, chaired the Oktoberfest Ladies Day luncheon for several years, and got the La Crosse Public Education Foundation on its feet in the early 1980s. Her actions have manifested her belief that "you need to care and to do for your community."

Bill Hoel got to know Jean when he was hired as WLCX's news director in 1975. "Joe made the top money decisions but Jean really ran the daily operations of the radio station," Bill said. "WLCX was unquestionably the best place I've ever worked because I felt like I had all the power I needed to do my job."[66] Bill credited Joe and Jean with schooling him in the importance of being community minded. "Jean is infinitely patient, incredibly caring, willing to spend time, always friendly, and has always shown terrific caring for the community," he said. A person of few words, she nonetheless has "quietly broken ground." She was the first woman president of the La Crosse

Area Chamber of Commerce (1977) and the first woman to chair the United Way Campaign (1979). She also has served on councils and boards for the First Presbyterian Church of La Crosse, the presbytery, the synod, and the General Assembly of the Presbyterian Church. Judy Bouffleur, a long time community volunteer who has worked on several church committees with Jean, described her as "a giver and a risk-taker who is not afraid to step up and do what needs to be done. Yet she always does it in a gentle and inspiring way. When she asks others to do something, they say yes because they realize Jean is doing more than she's asking of them."[67]

Banking

When the sum total of services offered by banks was checking, savings, and loan services, women entered banking at entry level positions such as in the proof department or as typists. A few eventually worked their way up into more visible and responsible positions over the years. Alice Osterhout graduated from La Crosse Logan High School in 1959 and went to work in the proof department of the State Bank. "There were no female bank officers at that time. The proof department is where women generally started," Alice recalled. "I sorted checks to verify deposits. Because I liked changes, I volunteered for whatever came along. I stayed in the proof department for six months and then spent three months in the bookkeeping department. Those were the days before computers so we used posting machines."[68] Alice spent the next few years as a teller and then moved into loan processing. When State Bank opened its Shelby branch in 1972, Alice was one of two women assigned to work there. Although a male officer opened and closed the bank, Alice had worked in so many areas that she could handle all the bank services. She was named branch manager in 1984 and an assistant vice-president in 1990. "Although we don't see women bank presidents around here, it is not unusual to see women as vice-presidents," she said.

Lill Twining graduated from high school in 1967 and went to work at National Cash Register (NCR) producing microfilm. Three years later, during one of NCR's layoffs, she found work as a part-time typist at Union State Bank in West Salem. "I decided to stay because I found this was the work I really enjoyed: people and numbers. Through the years I've found it very satisfying to help give a young couple a new home, to help find the way out for someone in financial distress, to help plan for the future," Lill said.[69] The bank's assistant vice-president of lending served as Lill's mentor. "He kept challenging me and telling me 'you ought to try this job.' He taught me everything he knew about lending, and, when he left the bank in 1976, I got his job," she said.

Banking services began to change drastically about 1980. Prior to that time, "service and loyalty created the bond between bank and customer," said Natalie Hartigan. "However, when the banking industry expanded into student loans, credit cards, third party brokerage services, insurance programs, and retirement programs, the long-term relationships people had with their financial institutions began to change."[70] Because customers were starting to shop around for the best deals, banks started hiring marketing specialists. In 1981, First Bank in La Crosse hired Natalie as an officer, rather than at an entry-level position, to market its new offerings. Natalie had spent her early adult years as an elementary teacher, a homemaker, and a community volunteer. In the late 1970s, she returned to school to prepare to re-enter the workforce, enrolling in business courses that would complement the management and business skills she had developed as a volunteer. Ten years later, she opened the first licensed brokerage office in a La Crosse bank and in the First Bank system.

Atypical Enterprises for Women

Utilities

Susan Swarthout became involved in the utility business by helping her father, who owned Neshonoc Power and Light Company. During her summer vacations from teaching, she returned to the family home in Neshonoc and assisted her father by keeping the books and records and reading the meters. "One time when I was making a call to read a meter, the little boy who lived at the house shouted, 'O mamma, here comes that electrical woman!'" she recalled.[71] As the utility business grew and became more complex, so did Susan's involvement. In 1921, at the age of forty, she retired from teaching to manage the power plant plus the extensive rental properties owned by the Swarthout family. The plant, which pre-dated the Rural Electrical Association, supplied light and power for an immense area around Neshonoc. The dam that created Lake Neshonoc was built in 1939. One year later, 900 customers counted on the power company for electricity. In 1947, Susan sold the Neshonoc Light and Power Company to Northern States Power. During the quarter century she managed the plant, she also developed herds of purebred Holsteins on farms near West Salem. Upon her retirement, she devoted her time to community interests and to building a barn to showcase the prize-winning Holsteins.

General Contracting

Ethel Olberg Tausche was a spirited, enterprising woman who had a general contracting business in the 1920s and 1930s.[72] In 1914, at the age of twenty-five, Ethel Olberg married Archie Tausche of the Tausche Hardware Company. One of Ethel's early money-making endeavors was to prepare chop suey in her home and sell it to the Bodega. She drove while her older son, Robert, who was eleven at the time, delivered the chop suey to the downtown

Ethel Tausche was an avid golfer and an enterprising woman who built several homes in La Crosse between the first and second world wars.

Family of Ethel Olberg Tausche

La Crosse restaurant. A friend of Robert's accompanied them until the friend's mother objected that Ethel drove too fast. Ethel used the chop suey money to finance her passion for golf. She played even when very pregnant with her second son, Richard, who was born in 1920. In days when pregnant women often did not appear in public, Ethel just borrowed an old baggy shirt from the caddymaster so she would have something roomy to wear.[73] For three consecutive years, 1928 to 1930, she was Ladies Champion at the La Crosse Country Club.

In the years between the world wars, Ethel built and sold twenty-one homes representative of housing for middle class America. Most were stucco bungalows using one of four floor plans. She used only Kohler plumbing fixtures in the homes she built. At least that is what she told Governor Walter J. Kohler when she met him in 1930. Ethel could talk with governors and general laborers with equal ease. To help her laborers, she added a trailer and hitch to her car and hauled supplies so they did not have to wait for deliveries. She also stood firm in order to get what she needed. In 1936, she was building four homes in a row on Ferry Street between Twenty-third and Twenty-fourth streets. She told the manager of Northern States Power (NSP) that she needed gas lines extended to these properties. Because the houses were the only ones on the block, he said there were not enough customers in that area. She called his bluff by saying she would take the matter to the governor, who at that time was Phillip La Follette. The power company installed the gas lines, and, whenever the NSP manager saw Ethel, he kiddingly asked how she was getting along with the governor.

In 1939, she built one of her last houses, her "dream home" at 400 South Fifteenth Street. She stopped building when it became difficult to get construction materials because of wartime shortages. A brief walking tour reveals that concrete examples still exist of the work of a woman who also loved golf, music, cardplaying, and storytelling.[74]

Women have participated in the economic livelihood of La Crosse County since the early settler days of the 1840s. In the late nineteenth and early twentieth centuries, women's options broadened beyond domestic-related tasks to include photography, hairstyling, and library work. Manufacturers relied upon women for much of the detail work in their factories. Another avenue of employment developed when La Crosse Normal School opened in 1909. As a result, area women obtained economic independence by becoming teachers in city and rural schools. By 1920, La Crosse had four hospital schools of nursing, thus making it possible for more young women to enter that field. During the rural to urban population shift that followed World War I, many young women chose better-paying factory jobs or entered the mostly male bastion of office work.

During the Great Depression, there was social pressure for women, especially if they were married, not to work, because it might mean taking a job from a man. However, there were women who needed to support themselves and their families because their own husbands were out of work. It was a different situation in the early 1940s. When men joined the armed forces during World War II, women were vital to filling the jobs that had been left vacant. The necessity of entering a new field gave some women an opportunity to develop a lifelong career. Government-funded daycare centers were established to make it easier for women with children to join the war production effort.

At the end of the war, a national effort encouraged women to step aside so that returning veterans could reclaim their jobs. Although women were moved out of the higher-paying occupations, there were more opportunities for them in office work and teaching during the late 1940s and the 1950s. The rapid postwar growth of service industries called for numerous clerical and office workers. Increasing school enrollments, from kindergarten through college, opened more teaching positions for women and ended the policy of not hiring married women.

A pattern that had formed early in the century held true into the 1960s. A woman often worked for a few years after graduating from school and before marrying and raising a family. When the children were grown, she might return to a job, most likely as a sales clerk, secretary, nurse, or teacher. That pattern began to change in the 1970s because of the movement for equal rights for women and the growing need for more than one income to cover family expenses.

As educational and employment opportunities expanded, more women embarked on careers in fields that were just opening up to them. Older women who already had raised their families went back to school to prepare for the next stage in their lives. Their options had grown far beyond sales clerk and secretary to encompass the entire range of occupations in society. Younger women who already had availed themselves of the broader choices were less likely to interrupt their careers to start families. They continued to work during their childbearing years and relied on daycare services to help them manage the demands of family and job.

La Crosse County women have been significant participants in a wide range of income-producing activities. Some held jobs that were considered women's work, while others led the way into fields that, in the past, were dominated by men. At the end of the twentieth century, the majority of women spent most of their adult years engaged in the broad array of employment options in the workplace.

In the Community

Before the middle of the nineteenth century social custom placed a ban upon the participation of women in public affairs. The appearance of a woman on a public platform was regarded in those times as a disgraceful sight. But there arose the demand by militant leaders for 'women's rights.' The influence of women in the temperance and anti-slavery crusades and, finally, their patriotic work during the Civil War, helped to break the bonds of custom. Women began to enter more fully into the intellectual and civic life of the time through the formation of organizations that had a variety of purposes.

A History of La Crosse, Wisconsin, 1841-1900[1]

In their history of the city of La Crosse, which was published in 1951, Albert H. Sanford and H. J. Hirshheimer devoted one of the book's 250 pages to women's organizations. Brief mention was made of a reading club called the Coterie, the Ladies Art Class, the La Crosse Women's Club, the Fortnightly Club, the Daughters of the American Revolution, the Women's Christian Temperance Union, the Woman Suffrage Club, the Woman's Industrial Exchange, and a reading circle that became the Ibsen Club. They concluded the section with a comment on the "remarkable growth of women's clubs" during the 1890s. "Hardly a woman in the city is not a member. Even young girls were organizing themselves."[2]

Local women used domestic, nurturing, and organizational skills to improve circumstances for friends, neighbors, and others they would never meet. Some of the community work they did was paid, but the vast majority of it was carried out by volunteers. Once a group identified a cause, one of the major responsibilities of its members was to raise money for that purpose.

Church groups were one of the earliest ways women used their talents to help others. Women also invested in their communities. They recorded area history to provide a link from the past to the present and the future. They lobbied for civic improvements which resulted in improved health and better education. They prepared youth for the future through organizations which fostered good citizenship and leadership. They protected the environment so that future generations could enjoy the benefits of Mother Earth. Their cultural pursuits were instrumental in extending their own educations and in developing the community's appreciation for the arts. They campaigned long and hard for the right to vote and then used that acquired status to perform public service. Their commitment to social causes provided safer places for women and children to live, better working conditions and opportunities for women, better care for children, the elderly and the disabled, and choices in reproductive health care. The women of La Crosse County donated countless hours and raised incalculable sums of money for the common good.

𝒲𝑜𝑚𝑒𝑛 𝑎𝑛𝑑 𝒯𝒽𝑒𝒾𝓇 𝐹𝑎𝒾𝓉𝒽

As soon as the little white churches with their spires pointing heavenward began to dot the countryside where Norwegian immigrants had settled, the 'Kvindeforening' (ladies' aids) were organized.[1]

"When Bethel Lutheran Church was organized in 1885, the women played a vital part never expecting or receiving any recognition. The list of charter members contains only the names of the men."[2] Although the names of La Crosse County women generally do not appear on official historical documents, they did put their skills to work for their churches or synagogues. Within congregations, women organized themselves into Ladies' Aid Societies or Women's Leagues. They organized events that not only raised money but also provided fun for the whole congregation. The funds bought supplies, paid for building projects, and supported parochial schools and distant missions. Women often constituted the music program, directing the choirs and playing the organ. For some, church work was their only activity outside the home. "My mother wasn't one to join lots of organizations but, from 1900 to 1960, she was very active in her church, St. Paul's Lutheran, where she chaired the sewing circle," said Helen Hanson about Anna Benson Hanson.

Until the 1960s and 1970s, a typical member of a women's group was married with children, a "stay at home mom" who also might volunteer in schools and in the community. No one worried about the demands on working women who chose to participate in church work. In the 1860s and 1870s, single women teachers who attended sewing circles of the First Congregational Church of La Crosse were expected to contribute their share of cut-and-sewed rags for the rag carpets. No allowance was made for the probability that they had less time to do that preparatory work at home. The church organized its guilds to accommodate all women whether married or single, at home or in the workplace. Babysitting was provided while mothers attended meetings. During World Wars I and II, records show that many married women were employed outside the home in war-related industries;

consequently, the Congregational Church held nighttime meetings to accommodate the women working in factories.[3]

In order to broaden the impact of the work of their individual congregations, women connected with other churchwomen of their own faiths. Catholics formed the Catholic Women's League and the Catholic Daughters of the Americas. Lutherans established the La Crosse Circuit of the Women's Missionary Federation. Each organization benefited from the talents of the individual congregations that contributed to the larger group.

In 1942, representatives from all faiths began working together to promote peace and to understand each other's faith when they formed the La Crosse chapter of Church Women United.

Ladies' Aid Societies

La Crosse County was only sparsely inhabited when, in 1852, the Ladies' Sewing Circle of the First Congregational Church of La Crosse organized "to raise funds by the labor of our hands, and such other laudable methods as the society may deem expedient for the temporal, social and spiritual prosperity of the same."[4]

In the nineteenth century and the early years of the twentieth, ladies' aid meetings were held at least once a month in the members' homes. The Ladies' Aid of Our Savior's Lutheran Church of West Salem organized in 1883 to learn about missions and raise money for the missionaries.[5] The group met every three weeks. The hostess provided lunch for which everyone put ten cents into the treasury, all of which went to support the missionaries. Getting to meetings could be an adventure. "Conditions were different then," responded Our Savior's historian, Vernetta Romskog.

> *No hard surfaced roads, cars, telephones or home conveniences as we have now. One can imagine, though, the fun to watch the discomfort when eight or ten West Salem women would pile into a farmer's wagon, or sleigh in the winter, and ride out to the country meetings. Once a storm came up when a meeting was held at the Christian Hanson home in Scotch Coulee. All the people from any distance had to stay all night. A little girl left at home recalled the anxiety felt when her mother failed to return that night.*[6]

Members of the Ladies' Aid of Our Savior's Lutheran Church of West Salem returned from a meeting at the Carl Hauge home. They were identified as Selma Gudmundson, Mrs. Martin Johnson, Mrs. Sander Johnson, Hattie Indahl, George M. Johnson, Anne Indahl, and Mrs. George M. Johnson. May 1912.
Our Savior's Lutheran Church, West Salem

The Bethel Lutheran Ladies' Aid Society, which organized in 1886, met once a month from ten in the morning until late in the afternoon. They brought their babies and small children with them, often having to carry them as they walked long distances to the homes of the members. Dinner was furnished by the hostess and served at noon. The afternoon was spent sewing, knitting, or "tying" quilts and always included a Bible study. The meeting closed after the customary Scandinavian afternoon coffee.[7]

The main purpose of these societies was to raise money to support their church and its work. "Women knew how to make money and hold on to it, so, when the church needed money, the women were asked to raise it," said Helen Hanson.[8] They did this in a variety of ways that used their well-developed skills of cooking, baking, sewing, organizing, and entertaining.

They prepared and served food for church suppers and public gatherings like auctions and fairs. Trinity Lutheran Church of La Crosse was the first group to sell food at the Interstate Fair. In 1912, church volunteers boarded the streetcar at 6 a.m. with roasted meat, gravy, soup, and gasoline stoves. When they disembarked, they carried their load a half mile from the end of the car line to the fairgrounds, located between Campbell Road and La Crosse Street in La Crosse. They also carried every drop of water they used in tubs across the fairgrounds. Proceeds from the meals and lunches ranged from $300 the first year to more than $1,000 when gas, water, and electricity were finally installed at the fairgrounds.[9] During the 1920s and 1930s, the women of North Presbyterian Church prepared three church dinners a year. A typical menu was roast pork, mashed potatoes and gravy, mashed rutabagas, cabbage salad, apple sauce, sandwiches, pie, and coffee. The price was fifty cents, and the profit was seventy-five dollars.[10] About the same time, the women of Immanuel Lutheran, the German Lutheran church on La Crosse's north side, put on sauerkraut suppers.[11] During the 1930s, Our Savior's Lutheran Church of West Salem held Silver Teas and charged fifteen cents per person. The women of Our Savior's also sponsored an annual lutefisk and meatball supper which reflected their Norwegian heritage. All minutes of their meetings were written in Norwegian until 1919.[12] Women of La Crosse County churches raised money from pie, basket and ice cream socials, cookbook and bake sales. In more recent years, labor-free "no-bake" bake sales reflected the reduced amount of time women had for volunteer activities.

Women put their sewing skills to work to support their churches. In the nineteenth century, the Congregational Church women made shirts, quilts, and rag carpets and sold them in local stores. Church bazaars featured many items stitched by church women. Marie Hovind, a member of St. Paul's Lutheran Church, worked in the yard goods department of Doerflinger's Department Store and provided fabric remnants at a reasonable price for her church's sewing circle. Anna Hanson cut the pieces for aprons and dishtowels and distributed them at the circle meetings. The women assembled and embroidered them to be sold at the church bazaar.[13]

Women sorted clothing and household items they no longer used to be sold at rummage sales. Other fundraising activities of the distant and recent past included Dickens parties, where members of the Congregational Church dressed in costume and dramatized scenes from Dickens' novels, home tours, and sales of items ranging from house plants and greeting cards to nuts and candy.

They used this money, earned by their hard work in camaraderie with others, to fund church missions, to support their congregation's building, furnishings and operations, and to contribute to local and worldwide charities. The Congregational Church women supported missions at home and abroad. Their home missions, from the 1880s to the early 1900s, were Olivet and Bethany Chapel in La Crosse. In the early 1900s, they supported Beira Mission in southeast Africa.[14] In 1905, the original eight members of the Women's Missionary Society of the North Presbyterian Church of La Crosse decided their dues would be five cents each month with half the amount going to home missions and the other half to foreign missions.[15] In the late 1940s, Our Savior's Lutheran Church of La Crosse began a local mission to serve people on the growing south side of La Crosse. That mission became Our Redeemer Lutheran Church which organized its own Ladies' Aid in 1950 which in turn began raising money to support foreign mission work.[16]

Women helped build, furnish, and operate their churches, parsonages, and schools. In 1865, the Congregational Church women purchased two lots at Seventh and Main streets in La Crosse as a building site for the church which occupied that corner from 1870 to 1950.[17] Anna Wiesner Kohlwey literally helped construct the first Catholic church in Onalaska. Her father, August Wiesner, who had brought his family to America from Germany in 1882, donated the land. He helped with much of the building while Anna hauled the lumber from the mills to the site with a horse and wagon.[18] Members of the Holmen Lutheran Church Ladies' Aid, organized in 1899, made special efforts to raise funds when their congregation decided to build a church. With the fruit of their labor, they purchased church pews, the altar, the carpet, plush and fringe for the pulpit, and applied several hundred dollars to other expenses connected with building the church in 1907.[19] Bells Coulee Lutheran Church called upon its Ladies' Aid in 1902 to help pay the pastor's salary.[20] The bell that still beckons the congregation to worship at Our Savior's Lutheran Church of West Salem was purchased in 1891 by the Ladies' Aid. In 1907, the society helped the youth group purchase English hymnals for the congregation which at that time was singing hymns in English and in Norwegian.[21] When the Asbury United Methodist Church, which was established in 1946, had financial difficulties in its early years, the women came to the rescue. "A newly formed congregation and a new building had huge expenses. The women 'bailed them out' helping with the fuel bills, furnishing the parlor, kitchen supplies, office supplies, carpeting," all in addition to giving continued support to missions in this country and the world.[22] In the 1960s, the Altar Society of St. Patrick's Catholic Church in Onalaska raised money for furnishing a new school while the men raised money for the building. "We also volunteered in the school library and for playground supervision," recalled Irene Kreisel Schaller.[23]

Serving others who were less fortunate was another important aspect of the work of women's church groups. They served the needy in their own neighborhoods and around the world. More recently, local food pantries, Gerard Hall (for unwed mothers), Salvation Army, La Crosse County Social Services, and New Horizons (a shelter for victims of domestic abuse) have benefited from donations of cash, clothing, and layettes. Women have delivered Mobile Meals to the homebound and sent gifts and cards to shut-ins. Our Redeemer Lutheran Church women have shared Christian fellowship with residents of several nursing homes by providing snacks and crafts, weekly coffee hours, picnics in the park, Christmas gifts, and bingo. Another social and charitable activity was quiltmaking. The Dorcas Guild of Our Savior's Lutheran Church of West Salem, the women of Faith Lutheran Church, Bethel Lutheran Church and of Our Redeemer Lutheran Church have sewn and tied quilts for Lutheran World Relief, Salvation Army, New Horizons, and people suffering from house fires, floods, and serious illness.

Women also did their part for church maintenance. In addition to providing supplies for the sanctuary and sacristy, visiting the sick, making baptismal gowns, and sending books overseas, the Altar and Rosary Society of St. Joseph the Workman Cathedral (founded in 1863 and later called Cathedral Women's Organization) laundered altar linens.[24] Besides helping finance young men studying for the ministry, assembling school packets, and "adopting" a resident of Bethesda Lutheran Home in Watertown, Wisconsin, the women of Faith Lutheran Church also cleaned the church.[25]

As women's lives have changed, women's church groups have adapted to the changes. The emphasis on educational programs for women has grown while the involvement with labor and time-intensive service and projects has abated. As the numbers of members available for weekday activities and service decreased, "the challenge was and continues to be to provide opportunities for service for those women who are juggling career and family."[26] Meetings were scheduled less frequently, sometimes annually rather than monthly, and projects became less labor-intensive and more focused on education. The Holmen Lutheran Church organization "changed considerably from being an arm of the [congregation] to being involved with national and international concerns especially through Lutheran World Relief programs."[27] Bethel Lutheran Church women acknowledged that "lifestyles for women have changed and we do not seem to have as much time to satisfy the need for church affiliation. Therefore, women have found new ways and new ideas to practice their faith and Christian beliefs. They

One of the annual projects of (ALCW) American Lutheran Church Women of Our Redeemer Lutheran Church was "Operation Christmastime." From left, Mrs. Erwin (Ardys) Mikelson, Mrs. Gayle (Myrna) Grim, Mrs. William (Wanda) Cairns, and Mrs. James (Dorothy) McLaughlin wrapped gifts for needy children and residents of local nursing homes. November 1966.

La Crosse Tribune

have extended their interests and concerns into the community, the whole country, and even into foreign countries. Church women are uniting with other church women with one common goal — to bring help and hope to those in need."[28]

From Music and Sunday School
to the Church Council

The very existence of church music and Sunday school programs often depended on women. From 1901 to 1970, Bells Coulee Lutheran Church had ten pastors but only five organists. The women who filled the church with music were Amanda Lindstrom, Anna Olson, Olga Freng, Estella Bryhn, and Marcella Krueger.[29] Sylvia Houkom Tabbert was the organist at First Lutheran Church, Onalaska, for thirty years.[30] However, Altah Evenson Nelson probably set the record for longevity. She began playing the organ at Halfway Creek Lutheran Church in 1918, when she was sixteen years old. At that time it took two people to operate the pump organ. Her father, Peter Evenson, who was the church custodian, assisted her. For sixty years, she played for nearly every wedding, funeral, baptism, confirmation, and Sunday worship. When she first began, these events were held during the day, necessitated by limited lighting and horse-drawn transportation; a hitching rail was as much a church accessory as a parking lot is today. When Halfway Creek Lutheran Church celebrated "Altah's Day" on January 29, 1978, she reflected, "We were brought up with the idea that you had an obligation to take part in church work, not just participate whenever it was convenient."[31]

In groups and as individuals, women made religious education possible. The original purpose of the Holmen Ladies' Aid in 1899 was to provide funds to finance a local parochial school. The Ladies' Aid of Our Savior's Lutheran Church of West Salem raised money for the addition of a parish education unit in 1956. Women taught, organized, and supervised Sunday school and vacation Bible school. In the late nineteenth century, the First Presbyterian Church of La Crosse established a mission and Sunday school in La Crosse's "Goosetown" neighborhood. Grace Chapel was built at 416 North Sixteenth Street by the Presbyterian men and boys in 1892. Sunday worship services became popular because the Reverend Claude Shaver (1917-1925) preached in German. Anna Cronon, however, strictly directed the Sunday school in English.[32]

Before the 1960s, it was rare for women to hold formal positions of leadership in their churches. Members of the Ladies' Aid Society of St. John's Lutheran Church of rural La Crosse did not even serve as officers of their own group until 1950. They organized in 1902 to promote the spirit of Christian fellowship, further Christian knowledge, and aid the congregation in the work of the Lord. The pastor served as the general chairman of the Ladies' Aid for the first forty-eight years.[33]

"In the past, women were involved with the ladies' organization and altar duty and teaching Sunday School. Now they usher and are on the Church Council," said Neva Ritter who was president of the Olivet Lutheran Church Council in 1995.[34] Our Redeemer Lutheran Church elected Susan Thompson as the first female president of the congregation, in 1978.

When the Congregational Church organized in January 1852, half of the twelve persons casting votes of equal authority were women. However, "once the congregation was established and growing and the community changed from a rough frontier town into a city of polish and sophistication, the women adopted the genteel roles of Victorian society and did not pursue roles of church leadership until nearly a century later."[35] Although the women raised the greater share of the money during that time, the men controlled the finances and served on the committees and boards. In 1965, Rachel Meyer "was elected president of the Board of Deacons, the important governing board, but it was not until 1971 that the top lay position of leadership was held by a woman. In June of that year, Ruth Weigel was elected moderator of the congregation."[36]

A local exception to the rule was Lilly Heck. In 1935, she was ordained as the first woman elder of the North Presbyterian Church in La Crosse. Lilly went on to become the congregation's first woman commissioner to the General Assembly.

The Revival of a Church

The St. Elias Syrian Orthodox Society, originally formed in 1908, was practically non-existent from the 1920s until the mid-1970s. The few continuing members of the society relied on visiting Orthodox priests who came only for special occasions and services. The group, which welcomed Greek, Lebanese, Serbian, and Russian as well as Syrian Orthodox Christians, built a church at 716 Copeland Avenue in La Crosse and dedicated it in 1917. Nearly sixty years later, in 1976, a group of Greek and Syrian/Lebanese people initiated plans to re-establish the La Crosse Orthodox Community. Margaret Ablan Gillette and Nancy Batrouney headed a phone survey committee that found a strong desire for a new church. In late 1977, St. Elias Eastern Orthodox Church had a resident priest, regularly scheduled liturgies, and a Ladies' Society for fundraising. Shortly thereafter, artist and parish member Constance Mahairas began replacing the icons on the church's front wall, known as the Iconostasis, to reflect the Byzantine tradition of subject matter and color.[37]

Jewish Women's League

In 1913, Armand Tuteur noted two women's groups in his article "The History of the Jews of La Crosse."[38] A group of "humanitarians and unselfish God-fearing women" organized the Ladies' Benevolent Society of the Reform Hebrew Temple about the year 1873. Although the society's records were lost, it is known that the members aided the needy, poor, and distressed. "Many a refugee and his family from Russia, who, upon coming to this country and settling in La Crosse with hardly a penny in their possession, have been gladly assisted by this noble organization of women," wrote Tuteur. The first officers of the Benevolent Society were Mrs. Leopold Wachenheimer, president; Bertha Langstad, secretary; and Dora Hirshheimer, treasurer. Forty years later, the group was still meeting monthly in the homes of its members.

Eva Sabelwitz, whom Tuteur described as "a noblehearted and philanthropic woman of high character and good standing in the community," organized the Ladies' Aid Society of the Orthodox Synagogue in 1905. This group also raised money to relieve the poor and hungry. In addition to electing Eva president, the society chose Mrs. Moses Omerberg, vice-president; Mrs. E. Segel, secretary; and Mrs. M. Jacob, treasurer. The membership grew so quickly in its first five years that the society divided into two.

During the 1920s, women of the Jewish community connected with the synagogue at 414 North Eleventh Street in La Crosse prepared food for holiday observances. During social get-togethers in the 1930s, they decided they wanted a more formal organization. In 1937, Esther Levy, Ida Ebin, Rose Epstein, Mrs. Harry (Sarah) Goldstein, Mrs. Moses (Minnie) Omerberg, Mrs. Hyman (Anna) Goldstein, and Sarah Glickman founded the Jewish Women's League.[39] Its purposes were fundraising for the synagogue, performing community service, and serving as a social forum for the Jewish community. In the early years, League members cared for transients who were without funds. During World War II, they furnished kosher foods to

Jewish men stationed at Camp McCoy. After the war, each League member adopted a family overseas to whom they sent monthly packages of food and clothing.

In anticipation of the financial needs of a new synagogue, which was built in 1948, the Jewish Women's League embarked on almost weekly fundraising activities within the Jewish community. The League sponsored dinners at the YMCA, picnics, raffles, and bake sales. The members also hosted "home parties where people paid for the privilege of playing cards. The men played poker and the women played mahjong," Sally Levenstein recalled.[40] The profits completely equipped the new kitchen. The group also organized and funded the religious school and established a library within the synagogue.

Mrs. Louis (Ida) Ebin demonstrated how to make potato latkes for the Jewish Women's League.

La Crosse Tribune

Fundraising efforts during the 1950s paid off the $25,000 mortgage on the synagogue plus the mortgage for the rabbi's house. Since that time, funds raised by the Jewish Women's League have been used to beautify and refurbish the synagogue, enhance the quality of Jewish life in La Crosse, provide a congenial atmosphere for social activities, and participate in the community affairs of La Crosse.[41] For many years, in addition to fundraising, Dora Hirshheimer and Sally Levenstein tended to "the garden," their name for the Jewish Cemetery on Losey Boulevard, Ansche Chesed.[42]

Uniting Congregations
within a Faith

When enough like-minded people work together, they can have a more significant influence on whatever issue they address. In order to have a stronger and farther reaching impact, La Crosse County women banded together in larger same-faith organizations. These larger societies linked the women of each church body into one "thinking, praying, and giving" body of church women and extended their activities.[43] Women who participated in these larger groups exercised their skills as planners, educators, and leaders.

Catholic Women's League

Mrs. John F. Doherty, a member of a progressively-minded group from the Irish Catholic parish of St. Mary's in La Crosse, approached Bishop James Schwebach about the possibility of organizing the women of all the city parishes to work together for the benefit of the church and the community. With the bishop's approval, the first meeting of the Catholic Women's League (CWL) occurred on November 11, 1915, in St. Mary's School Hall. When the group's plan was explained to Bishop Schwebach, he commented, "No harm can be done — maybe some good will come of it." These words became one of the League's favorite quotations.[44]

The League's early goals involved civic and patriotic projects instigated in particular by Charlotte Kohn, historical ventures by Cora Desmond, the Gibbons Club through which Catherine Hayes involved young people in civic affairs, the Catholic Benevolent Society to which both Mary Devine and Eleanor Funk were dedicated, and Red Cross work led by Mrs. Edward (Sarah) Evans and Agnes Hayes. A major concern of CWL was to take care of the Catholic community in situations in which little or no other help was available. During World War I, the Ladies' Linen Club of the fledgling group devoted its efforts to aiding wartime chaplains. Nettie and Margaret Bott, Kathryn Kohn, Margaret Spettel, and Mary Devine prepared vestments, altar linens, mission boxes, and comforters for the chaplains. League members also established an employment bureau for girls and women, conducted a thrift shop at the Park Store in La Crosse, and supported efforts of the medical society and the Board of Health to establish a free dental clinic, to test for tuberculosis, and to weigh and measure parochial school children.

In 1934, in response to Pope Pius XI's call for "Catholic Action," members of the Catholic Women's League helped organize the Diocesan Council of Catholic Women (DCCW). This broader association connected local women with the National Council of Catholic Women and gave them opportunities to reach further and with greater strength into issues of human rights and social justice, international affairs, family concerns, and church relations. Locally, since the 1950s, the League has emphasized its annual scholarship tea to benefit young Catholic women from La Crosse high schools pursuing advanced education at Viterbo College.[45]

Women's Missionary Federation

On November 14, 1925, the Ladies' Aid of St. Paul's Lutheran Church of La Crosse hosted an organizational meeting of the Women's Missionary Federation (WMF). Seven ladies' aid societies from Norwegian Lutheran churches in La Crosse, Galesville, Whitehall, and Holmen met to establish the La Crosse Circuit of the WMF. They elected Helga Gundersen of Our Savior's in La Crosse, president; Mrs. L. S. Reque of Zion Church in Galesville, vice-president; and Mrs. H. T. Braa of St. Paul's in La Crosse, secretary. By 1959, the WMF included thirty-eight societies and had a membership of 4,000 local women.[46] In 1960, women's mission groups of the various branches of the Lutheran church began to consolidate into the current Women of the Evangelical Lutheran Church in America (W-ELCA).[47] These larger groups held synod gatherings and national meetings to determine a course of action that would make a difference for women. For example, discussions about the role of women in the Lutheran church led to ordination of women in 1970.

Catholic Daughters of the Americas

Five charter members with common spiritual, charitable, educational, and social goals instituted a local chapter of the Catholic Daughters of the Americas, Court La Crosse #1183, on June 14, 1931. They were Margaret Blaschke, Agnes Breene, Mary McGarty, Grace Schubert, and Beulah

From 1956 to 1978, the Catholic Daughters of the Americas operated a thrift center in La Crosse to provide used clothing at a low cost and to raise money for other charitable causes. Among the many volunteers were, from left, Bea Horschak, Ann Schmikla, Elsie Kotnour, Marie Hammes, and Clo Freking, November 1971.

La Crosse Tribune

Skemp. In accordance with its spiritual mission, the group supported the education of priests and distributed religious reading material in railroad and bus stations and to Civilian Conservation Corps camps, army camps, and missions. Court La Crosse also sponsored the first women's retreat in La Crosse, held at St. Francis Hospital in August 1932. Attendance was greater than anticipated. Members felt that the enthusiasm for spiritual renewal and enlightenment warranted plans for future retreats.[48]

From 1956 to 1978, this group sponsored and staffed the Catholic Thrift Center in La Crosse. Bea Horschak devoted her energy to directing the center. In the first five years, 395 volunteers provided 3,578 hours of service. The thrift center provided clothing and other supplies at no cost to needy families and individuals. During the flood of 1965, it aided 2,000 flood victims. The thrift center also sold items at low cost to the general public. Profits from these sales were given to other local charitable organizations such as United Fund, Christmas Fund for St. Francis Nursing Home, and Committee on Aging.[49]

The Catholic Daughters of the Americas' membership of teachers and other professionals, businesswomen, mothers, homemakers, and grand-mothers devoted a portion of each meeting to religion and current issues. It also sponsored speakers on timely topics for public meetings, an annual poetry contest in the local schools, and a television series that explained and demonstrated the parts of the Catholic Mass, performed by students from Aquinas High School.[50]

Uniting Women of All Faiths: Church Women United

Seeking strength and unity during the crisis of World War II, wives and mothers of U.S. servicemen met in Atlantic City, New Jersey, to form an interfaith group committed to peace. The La Crosse chapter of Church Women United (CWU) began the next year, 1942, when interested women met at the YWCA to plan the area's first World Day of Prayer service. Representatives from all denominations joined together in this interfaith group of women working for peace and justice in their own community and in the world. In the early years, members put together clothing "Parcels for Peace" and layettes for babies of refugee mothers. La Crosse was one of the first units to hold an annual Interfaith Tea to promote understanding of other faiths. Planning for the event rotated among Catholic, Protestant, and Jewish women. Sometimes the tea included a visit to the synagogue or a church for an introduction to that religion.[51]

In the 1960s, Betty Luxford, president of CWU, Ann Poehling, president of CWL, Patricia Sheehan, and Claire Theisen were instrumental in forming CWU's monthly dialogue group to discuss current issues of peace and justice. Wishing to put faith into action, this group became the nucleus of Fish, an organization of volunteer helpers. It provided household assistance, emergency babysitting, and rides to the doctor. Pat Sheehan recalled that each day the two volunteer drivers "started at 6 a.m. and didn't stop until 6 p.m."[52] In the early 1970s, "when the price of gasoline went way up during the oil embargo and there were fewer women with time to volunteer because so many were going to work, we realized we couldn't continue," she said. Members of Fish began meeting with local government officials to convince them to take over services such as transportation. Although Fish disbanded when government agencies began to supply these services, the dialogue group still exists. More recently, in its effort to fight the root causes of women's and children's poverty in the La Crosse area, Church Women United has supported scholarships for women in need, the New Horizons shelter for abused women, and emergency food pantries.

CWU took a stand on some national and international issues. For example, it supported passage of the Equal Rights Amendment. CWU also supported the boycott of Nestle products and encouraged others to show their opposition to the company's policy of promoting the use of infant formula rather than breast milk in Third World countries. That business practice had dire consequences for the babies. The formula needed to be mixed with sterile water. That was not available, and families were unlikely to use their precious fuel to boil the water. When the formula was not properly prepared, babies developed diarrhea and died.

In 1979, Mary Kisken, a leader in the local group who went on to become president of the state organization from 1980 to 1983, explained that sometimes the group did not take stands on controversial issues. In the case of nuclear power, for instance, CWU educated its members so they could make individual decisions. CWU did not even address the abortion issue because it was considered too controversial and would likely split the membership.[53]

Generally, Church Women United encouraged members to get their own congregations involved in working for social change. Sister Thea Bowman of the Franciscan Sisters of Perpetual Adoration presented a "Songs of Freedom" program to a packed and joyful auditorium at one of the group's meetings. Sister Thea's medium was music, and her message was peace and justice for all. Her involvement in civil rights had deepened after a visit to her hometown in Mississippi. Her commitment "had a deep impact, it inspired others," Dorothy Kuechmann said. Sister Thea's concluding message to the ecumenical gathering of women was, "Just keep on doing what you're doing. You're doing it right!"

Community Investment

Women from all walks of life and every part of the county have invested time and energy to improve life in this corner of Wisconsin. They have preserved the past, made civic improvements, prepared youth for the future, and protected the environment for all to enjoy.

Preserving the Past

Local women have preserved the history and heritage of the area through historical societies, monuments, art and architecture, and writing. The La Crosse County Historical Society (LCHS) dates back to 1898. Both men and women were active organizers, board members, and volunteers who discovered, collected, preserved, and published historic records and data relating to La Crosse County. Gloria Bailey Jackson, LCHS collections manager from 1983 to 1993, compiled files on women of local prominence and produced exhibits which highlighted their lives and contributions. Women also were major benefactors of the society's museum. In 1965, Mrs. Frank (Alice Green) Hixon gave the Hixon family home on North Seventh Street in La Crosse to the society. In 1973, Edyth and Susan Swarthout of West Salem willed $500,000 to the city of La Crosse for

Susan and Edyth Swarthout, utility company manager and physician, respectively, were community philanthropists, n.d.

La Crosse County Historical Society

the "construction of an addition to the Main Library ... for the use of the library and the La Crosse County Historical Society." A bequest from Wanda Stern, who wished to give the community a gift in memory of her German parents, funded the landscaping for the museum's courtyard, which was designed by local landscape architect Judith Johnson.[1]

Other citizens organized historical societies specific to their communities: West Salem in 1974, Onalaska in 1986, and Holmen in 1994. The seeds for Bangor's historical society were planted when Laura Wheldon, who died in the 1970s, bequeathed a cupboard of collectibles to be displayed in the village library. Because the library in the village hall did not have room for the cupboard, it was put in the clerk's office. While Della Berg, the village's clerk-treasurer, was sharing her office with this cupboard, she began thinking of the people who said, "We really ought to form a historical society." In 1981, she put notices in the newspaper inviting people interested in preserving Bangor's history to meet. Eventually the meetings rounded up enough people to organize the Bangor Area Historical Society in 1983. Della served as its first president.[2]

Smith Valley School Museum

When the Smith Valley School was closed in 1977, a group of women in the school's neighborhood set out to convert the 1887 part of the structure into a museum. They wanted it to depict a typical rural school of the 1920s. They scouted around to find desks, books, and supplies from that era. Those who did the work also bore most of the expense of the restoration. Joan Dolbier, Connie Kjos, and Kathy Brown negotiated with a school in Minnesota for wooden desks with wrought iron sides. Volunteers spent many hours scraping gray paint off the exterior brick and tearing off the newer blackboards to reveal the old slate underneath. The group of workers also included Marianne Loeffler, Carol Bassuener, Jan Keil, Carol Brown, Dorothy Oertel, and Virginia Werner who was one of five generations of her family to attend the school. When the museum opened on July 27, 1980, it contained a phonics chart, old texts and ancient books (many of which were used when the school opened), a 45-star and a 48-star United States flag, and a pot-bellied stove.[3]

Historic Sites

In 1914, the Twentieth Century Club erected a plaque in Myrick Park at the site of two effigy mounds of the Turtle Clan. The La Crosse Chapter of the Daughters of the American Revolution placed a granite boulder in Pettibone Park to mark the site of the city's first trading post. The group also attached a marker on the building on the northeast corner of State and Second streets in La Crosse to indicate the site of the first building in the city.[4]

In the early 1970s, Carroll Gundersen lobbied the La Crosse Common Council for a historic preservation program to recognize the city's traditions and heritage. When the council established the La Crosse Historic Sites Commission in 1973, she was one of five citizens appointed to it by Mayor Peter Gilbertson. Carroll chaired the site selection committee of the commission, and Mary Funk served as secretary. Mary Hebberd and Margaret Holley were members a few years later when Carroll became president of the commission in 1976.[5] Through the years, the commission has researched, identified, and attached plaques indicating the historical significance of buildings and sites. The group also worked with the common council to revise the original ordinance to provide for various degrees of protection from demolition and/or exterior modification.

In the late 1970s, Joan Rausch decided to leave nursing education and pursue a master's degree in art history with an emphasis in architectural history. She worked as a surveyor for the Wisconsin State Historical Society for one year before starting her own business, Architectural Researches. In 1983, the city of La Crosse hired her to conduct an intensive survey to identify resources of historical and architectural significance that might be eligible for nomination to the National Register of Historic Places. Joan's architectural survey and photography produced a 400-page report. "Although the report basically was shelved, it was worthwhile because it hadn't been done before and all the information was collected in one spot," Joan said. "Now [in 1996] we're starting to see results from that project, for example, the development of a historic district in downtown La Crosse."[6]

Marion Cape Biehn painted several historic landmarks before they were torn down. Among those she documented were the La Crosse National Bank, upper left, the Northwestern Railroad depot, upper right, and La Crosse's Front Street. February 1968.

La Crosse Tribune

Capturing History on Canvas and Paper

In efforts to preserve local history, women recorded it on canvas, in print, and in their personal writing. Artists Marion Cape Biehn and Chris Nudd painted and sketched local landmarks. In the 1960s, La Crosse businessman Tom Holstein commissioned Marion to save on canvas what was being destroyed by the wrecking ball. "Paint any building you think has historical value," he told her. "I'll give you $25 for it!" That began Marion's quest which included the 1904 La Crosse County Courthouse (demolished in 1965), the 1886 La Crosse Public Library (replaced in 1967), the La Crosse National Bank at Third and Main streets (built in 1881, destroyed by arson in 1979), and La Crosse's Front Street before urban renewal.[7]

In 1968 and 1969, the weekend issues of the *La Crosse Tribune* published a series of paintings and articles by Chris Nudd.[8] Ten by fourteen inch prints of her artwork of historic La Crosse could be purchased for $1.95 each. The accompanying text described the history of the building or scene and the people associated with it.

Local women also have preserved the county's history and their own by writing it down. According to a La Crosse County Historical Society article by Gloria Jackson, they did not always receive credit: "Almost the complete section on the history of La Crosse city in the 1881 *History of La Crosse County, Wisconsin* was taken from an account written by Fredericka Augusta Levy ... [however] her name is barely mentioned in the book and then only as Mrs. J. M. Levy in the biography of her husband."[9] During the 1930s, Ida Tilson wrote a regular column, "Old Timers," for the West Salem *Nonpareil Journal*. Estella Krohn Bryhn of West Salem published two collections of her newspaper articles and columns which described rural and small town life, *Around the Coulees* and *Early Schools of La Crosse County*. Several women researched and wrote articles about people, buildings, and cultural and social life for the La Crosse County Historical Society's newsletter, *Past, Present & Future*. In the mid-1980s, Marge Gollnik, Judy Rommel, and Mary Meehan-Strub interviewed early members of Extension Homemakers clubs. The taped and transcribed interviews provided descriptions of the clubs' activities as well as the lives of women in the 1920s, 1930s, 1940s, and 1950s.

When urban sprawl began encroaching on the rich farm land west of West Salem along Highway 16, Hazel Rahn Heider decided to record a history of the Waterloo area: "I felt a history of the settlers and local folks might be interesting.... I researched farm records, newspaper articles, plat books, and talked to elderly people."[10] The result was *Along the Waterloo Road*, published in 1981.

Shelley Goldbloom wrote for local newspapers in the 1970s and 1980s and for the pure joy of writing. She inspired others at Western Wisconsin Technical College and at the Harry J. Olson Senior Center in La Crosse to write down the stories of their lives. One of the writing groups published its collection of poems, letters, and essays in 1993. It was called *Shelley's Golden Blooms: 1090 Years of Wit and Wisdom*, referring to the cumulative age of the fifteen contributors.

Norwegian Heritage

In a 1976 article, *La Crosse Tribune* staff writer, Joan Lybarger, observed that "fierce loyalty to origins ... is as typically Norse as the fjords and forests of the Land of the Midnight Sun." She went on to write that this "pride of heritage created an immigrant cultural world ... as generations ... strive to preserve their Norskdom."[11] For decades Borghild "Borghy" Lindevig Olson has been an important force in preserving Norwegian culture and language among Norwegian Americans.[12] Born on a farm in the Westby/Coon Valley area in 1921, she developed an interest in genealogy in her teens when a high school assignment required her to interview her grandparents about Norway. Her avocation has included the difficult and rewarding task of reuniting descendants of Norwegian immigrants with their relatives in Norway. She has written letters in Norwegian to Norwegian newspapers, led tours to that country, and taught the language at Western Wisconsin Technical College and in connection with the Sons of Norway. In 1991, she received the St. Olaf Medal, bestowed on behalf of Norway, for her efforts in "furthering Norwegian culture and heritage, both here and abroad."

Civic Improvement

The desire to improve the condition of their communities was another reason women organized volunteer groups. Although men formed the associations to establish cemeteries, women formed the societies, such as the Green Mound Aid Society, to raise the money to take care of them. Groups like the Twentieth Century Club, the La Crosse County Community Council, and the Citizens Education Committee called for better lighting and zoning within the city, arranged for health care for needy children, taught illiterates to read, raised money for community causes, and campaigned for better schools.

Green Mound Aid Society

Women from New Amsterdam, Amsterdam Prairie, and Council Bay organized the Green Mound Aid Society in 1896 as an auxiliary to the men's Green Mound Cemetery Association. The purpose of the women's society was to raise additional money to pay for caretakers and for the general upkeep of the cemetery, located two-and-one-half miles north of Holmen. Early records show that men were paid one dollar and women were paid fifty cents for one day's work. The first officers were Minnie Crook, president; Mrs. James (Harriet) Dale, vice-president; Emma Westerhouse, secretary, and Siebe Chalsma, treasurer. The group of approximately twenty met every two weeks, usually in the home of a member who would serve a complete meal to those in attendance. Through the years, the society raised funds through food and apron sales, ice cream socials, silver teas, and a patched shirt project.

The society sponsored a clean-up day each spring. Participants brought rakes and other tools to prepare the grounds for the next growing season. Painting bees brought people out to rejuvenate the front fence, gates, and archways. On the eve of its seventieth anniversary, the society could look back with pride on installing a water pump, building and equipping a toolhouse, planting evergreens, and repairing and straightening monuments. It also had an unbroken tradition of contributing flowers for funerals when burial was at Green Mound.[13]

Twentieth Century Club

Members of the Twentieth Century Club of La Crosse generally were well-educated, married, leaders in their church and community, and not employed outside the home.[14] When this study club organized on April 29, 1901, it emphasized the arts and culture. Through the years, however, it put more emphasis on community affairs. In their pursuit of an improved life for La Crosse residents, members of the Twentieth Century Club lobbied against spitting on streetcars and smoking by motormen and by conductors. The members settled for "No Smoking" signs. The club also petitioned for lights in city parks (1909), asked the Health Department to have toilets in stores clean and sanitary (1913), and assisted in distributing cards to be carried on all delivery wagons to advertise the "Spring Drive Clean Up" of April 1917. The group promoted an improved zoning ordinance and asked the Common Council to appropriate one thousand dollars to hire a zoning expert to do the work. In November 1945, the club sent a resolution to the mayor and council that the city take the initiative to promote a suitable housing site for erection of homes for low-income families. When the elms that formed archways over many city streets began to succumb to Dutch elm disease in the 1970s, the Twentieth Century Club contributed to the purchase of new trees.

La Crosse County Community Council

During World War I, the Woman's Committee of the La Crosse County Council of Defense carried out a variety of patriotic work, fund drives, and surveys under the leadership of Grace Edwards.[15] Members of the committee represented every section of the county and put in full days, from eight in the morning until six in the evening, carrying out their responsibilites. Cora Olson was the representative, or captain, of the twenty-first ward in the city of La Crosse. She described the work of the committee in a speech she gave to the Webster School Homemakers Club.

> *We weighed and measured children under the age of sixteen. Also had their births properly registered and on file at the court house. We also assisted in the registration of alien enemies at the city hall. It was our opportunity to meet the German people and let them know that the ward workers were friendly and willing to help them. They didn't like the idea of being fingerprinted.... We had to go to the homes of some of these people and explain a lot of things before they would meet us half way.*[16]

Cora and her co-workers solicited their ward for many fund drives: thrift stamps, Liberty bonds, Near East relief, Red Cross, City Nurse, Soldiers and Sailors relief, and the unemployed.

When peace came in November 1918, the Woman's Committee was reluctant to disband because, in the words of the chairman, "If La Crosse County needed the services of women during the war, their service is needed in peacetime equally as much." On October 4, 1919, the committee reorganized as the La Crosse County Community Council. Between the world wars, it coordinated the work of forty-five women's groups[17] from throughout the county to make it a better place to live and rear children. For example, in cooperation with the La Crosse Medical Society, the four hospitals, the city's public health department, and the La Crosse Common Council, the Community Council conducted a Free Children's Clinic on Saturday afternoons. Between 1919 and 1929, over three thousand cases were treated

In 1950, Carroll Gundersen was named "Man of the Year" by the La Crosse Chamber of Commerce for her community leadership. Among her activities was observing sessions of the United Nations and then educating the community about the work of this new organization.

La Crosse Tribune

by the free clinic.[18] The Community Council procured from the U.S. Census Bureau a list of all the illiterates in La Crosse County. Thirty-six public school teachers and two club women volunteered to go into the homes and teach these people to read. This literacy program continued until fewer than one hundred remained, most of whom were seventy or older.[19] During the 1920s, a committee of the Community Council met weekly, while the Wisconsin legislature was in session, to study bills before the legislature pertaining to the welfare of women and children.[20]

During World War II, the Community Council's well-organized system of ward captains engaged in civilian defense. The captains and six hundred block workers assisted with bond drives, recruited for the Women's Army Corps, and ascertained the number of mothers of small children engaged in industry. By 1944, both men and women belonged to the La Crosse County Community Council, which had about fifty affiliated clubs and organizations as well as 300 individual members.[21]

Although women were instrumental volunteer workers in community organizations for years, it was not until the middle of the twentieth century that they became more visible and received public recognition. In February 1950, the La Crosse Chamber of Commerce named Carroll Gundersen as its "Man of the Year." Sixteen of the seventeen organizations which had a vote indicated she was their first choice because of her civic leadership. She devoted most of her time to Red Cross, Girl Scouts, and the League of Women Voters. Carroll was particularly effective at speaking and fundraising because she believed whole heartedly in her causes. Naming a woman as "Man of the Year" was such a novelty in 1950 that the story about Carroll went out over the Associated Press wire and appeared in newspapers across the country.[22]

Carroll's sister-in-law, Mary B. Gundersen, said that the best thing she ever did for the League of Women Voters was to recruit Carroll. However, Mary was a leading community activist herself. In 1962, she became the first woman to serve as president of Community Chest, the group that raised and disbursed money to charitable and welfare agencies. In her annual President's Report, Mary noted that one of the Chest agencies, the La Crosse Home for Children, had begun construction of a new building. She did not mention that she had served on the board of the children's home and had been instrumental in acquiring the land for the new building. However, she used that example as a way to remind the community that: "If La Crosse wishes to compete for the honor of being one of America's outstanding cities, it must not only provide adequate financial support for its charitable and welfare agencies, but seriously consider improvements in their programs and physical equipment." Mary specifically mentioned the Day Nursery, the YWCA, and the YMCA as needing attention because they were operating in facilities that were "old, run down and inadequate" and "out moded for programs of today."[23]

Citizens Education Committee

Support for public education in La Crosse became an urgent priority for some in the early 1960s. They believed funding for the school district budget was consistently and thoughtlessly cut by the La Crosse Common Council whose members and the mayor were more concerned with the mill rate for taxation than with the education of children. When the La Crosse Education Association called a public meeting, the citizens responded. The Citizens Education Committee (CEC) was formed in January 1961 with Margaret Fish as chair and Sally Levenstein as secretary. The group encouraged support for public education and planned a strategy to gain better funding for the schools. At the time, the board of education was appointed by the mayor and confirmed by the city council. The council, not the school board, voted on the allocation of money for schools within the city budget as recommended by the City Plan Commission. In order to gain first-hand knowledge about this process and to report what they learned to the CEC, members attended many governmental meetings. Marian Ramlow, Sally Levenstein, Ruth Anderson, and Margaret Fish observed the deliberations of the planning commission, city council, and school board. At one lengthy meeting held in the mayor's office, these women sat on a stack of city plan books all afternoon because no chairs had been provided for citizen observers. Vera Quisel, Mary Hebberd, and Robert Voight reviewed the voting records of council members on six key issues affecting schools. Their study showed that five incumbents up for re-election were "non-supportive." The CEC recruited candidates who would give more consistent support to the schools. As a result, four out of five of the incumbent council members were replaced.

Next, the CEC began to work to establish an independent school board with fiscal autonomy. The League of Women Voters helped prepare a petition and, with other groups, collected signatures to call for a referendum that would establish a directly-elected school board. Marian Ramlow and Sally

Levenstein delivered over 3,000 signatures to the city clerk. The referendum passed in 1966, and the first direct election of school board members took place on July 1, 1968. In the meantime, in 1965, the state of Wisconsin ordered that all school districts must be attached to a high school district. This gave impetus to the unified school district plan which the CEC promoted to gain fiscal independence for the public schools of La Crosse. However, the School District of La Crosse did not gain control over its own budget until the state abolished fiscal control boards in 1983. Over a period of ten years, members of the Citizens Education Committee, many of whom were women, spoke to school, church, and club groups in support of school building programs, adequate funding for schools, curriculum concerns, redistricting, a directly-elected school board, and the unified school district plan.[24]

Preparing Youth for the Future

Several women's groups encouraged education, good citizenship, service, and leadership in younger members of the community. In 1919, the Young Women's Christian Association organized the Girl Reserves "to train teenage girls for leadership through self-governing clubs, and to bring them so in touch with the YWCA that throughout their lives they will be its ardent supporters, the timber as it were, from which other associations shall be built."[25] The La Crosse Chapter of the Daughters of the American Revolution promoted dependability, service, leadership, and patriotism through its annual DAR Good Citizenship contest in La Crosse area high schools. Groups like Campus Dames (university faculty wives) and Catholic Women's League sponsored scholarships for young women who continued their education after high school.

To give high school-age girls an opportunity to experience the satisfaction of volunteer work, the Lutheran Hospital Senior Auxiliary formed the community's first Candy Striper program in 1965. ZeDona Christiansen initiated the service and then asked Gretchen Burns to direct it. From 1971 to 1979, Gretchen led the orientations, scheduled and supervised the young volunteers, organized the recognition teas, and even filled in to sort mail and deliver flowers if a volunteer did not show up. "One of the purposes of Candy Stripers was to show the girls the careers available to them in health care and medicine," she said. "It was very satisfying for me to see the girls go on.

Some of them are RNs and unit secretaries at Lutheran Hospital. I still get Christmas cards and family photos from all over the country."[26]

Through organizations like 4-H, Girl Scouts, Lutheran Girl Pioneers, Job's Daughters, Junior Red Cross, and Junior Golf, women instilled values in their young neighbors as well as in their own children.

4-H

Under the auspices of 4-H, several women helped rural girls and boys live up to the organization's oath:

> *I pledge my head to clearer thinking,*
> *my heart to greater loyalty,*
> *my hands to larger service,*
> *and my health to better living*
> *for my club, my community and my country.*

La Crosse County demonstration agent, Mrs. Lynn (Rachel) Gullickson, became director of girls' 4-H club work in 1926. The volunteers who led the girls' clubs were Doris Lee of Holmen, Palma Hanson of Onalaska, Alice Stenslien of Coon Valley, and Marian Markle, Emma Wick, and Helen Herman of La Crosse. The following year Rachel reported there were 208 members in nineteen active girls' clubs. She cited the outstanding work done by county girls. Mildred Pfaff, of Mindoro, made eight garments. Marian Markle, Mormon Coulee Club, canned 1,011 pints of fruits, preserves, and vegetables. Mary Margaret Hussa, Bangor, kept the neatest club record book, and Helen Herman, Smith Valley, was named best reporter. Alice Hauser and Mary Hartley, both of Fauver Hill, represented La Crosse County at the 1927 state fair and took second place with their breadmaking demonstration.

Young people gained leadership experience as officers within their own clubs. Violet Niedercorn, who was president of the Mormon Coulee Club at the age of fifteen in 1927, eventually ran a business with her husband and managed it on her own after his death. In 1929, a leadership club affiliated with 4-H was started in the Rural Course at La Crosse State Teachers College. Palma Hanson became the assistant leader. The purpose of the club was to give leadership training to future rural school teachers. During the first year of its existence, the leadership club emphasized how to conduct P.T.A. activities in rural communities.[27]

Josie Broadhead and Molly Sacia carried on the tradition of women helping youth grow and prepare for the future when they served as 4-H leaders in the last half of the twentieth century. They helped girls and boys learn about solving problems, making decisions, working together, and developing leadership skills in activities that ranged from drama, food and animal judging contests to nature studies. Josie, who loved to write, served as drama project leader and playwright for the Mormon Coulee Club for more than twenty years.

Molly became a leader in 1960 when her son joined the Union Mills 4-H club at the age of nine. "I remember my husband helping Greg get his pigs to the fair ... we would load at 4 a.m. as pigs do not stand the heat," she recalled. Molly helped other members of the club, too. "It was fun to wash, brush, and trim the calves to get them ready for the fair. We even used finger nail polish on their hooves to make them shine," she said.

As a project leader, Molly helped with insect, tree, flower, and conservation projects. She taught how to make nets and that the best time to catch moths is at night under artificial lights whereas the best time to catch butterflies is in the bright sunlight. She also stressed the proper way to kill and mount the insects. "Sometimes, when you look at the displays, many of the insects are still squirming," she said.

In her third decade of 4-H work, Molly found herself helping the next generation. When two of her grandaughters, Megan and Amy Sacia, and four members of the Walshak family planned a cowpie toss as part of the Farm Fun activities at 4-H camp in 1995, Molly made the cow pies. "We could not have real ones for the kiddies ... so I made seven of them out of papier mache, painted them brown, glued on some kernels of corn and grass. You should have seen their eyes when they were to toss them."[28]

Girl Scouts

Mrs. J. E. McConnel founded Girl Scouting in La Crosse when she started a troop in 1917, just five years after Juliette Low organized the first group of girls in the United States.[29] Bertha Shuman led the second troop in La Crosse and directed camp for the early scouts during the 1920s and 1930s. Her spirit, hard work, and love of the out-of-doors gave many girls a chance to experience camping. In 1926, a group of girls at Our Savior's Lutheran Church in La Crosse prevailed upon Mrs. M. B. Skundberg to start a troop. Marguerite Anderson joined it when she was ten years old. "My mother had died, and I was reaching out for a role model," she said. "I found Mrs. Skundberg, and I lived Girl Scouting." Eventually, Marguerite became an assistant leader and then a leader.

The troops formed a council in 1931 and elected Mrs. R. C. Whelpley as the first president. That same year, Mrs. R. G. McDonald and Dorothy Funke organized the first cookie sale. "They bought cookies, big sugar cookies, from Erickson Bakery," recalled Dorothy's niece, Nancy Hyde Gerrard. "We had to deliver them without breaking them," Marguerite added, "and that wasn't easy because they were as big as saucers." The scouts sold 4,834 dozen cookies priced at twenty cents a dozen. Thirty years later, scouts in the Riverland Council sold 48,619 boxes of cookies. "Camp Ehawee is the camp that cookies built," said Fran Skemp, because profits were used to develop the council's own camp. Land north of Holmen was purchased in 1951, and Marguerite's troop was the first to camp there, in the summer of 1952.

In its early years, scouting emphasized outdoor activities and homemaking skills. "Girl Scouting is where I got my feet wet in homemaking," Marguerite said. "For the hostess badge, we planned a tea for our parents. We did all the baking and all the serving. For the housekeeping badge, we had to clean the advisor's home — everything from scrubbing toilets to polishing silverware." Marguerite, who earned the highest scout award, the Golden Eaglet, in the 1930s, was awarded the highest recognition for adults, the "Thanks Badge," in 1962.

Fran Skemp, who was a Girl Scout in Chicago during the Depression and a leader in La Crosse from 1967 to 1977, said another important lesson in scouting was being kind to one another "because we are working with fifth and sixth grade girls who can be very unkind to each other." Fran received her "Thanks Badge" in 1977. "I had learned so much and scouting was so important to me that I wanted it for my daughters, too," said Fran, who raised seven daughters and felt like she had a hand in raising the ninety girls who had been members of the troop.

"What I remember from scouting was marching," said Nancy Hyde Gerrard, who tried it for just one year in the 1930s. "Our leader must have been a carry-over from World War I because she had us march to music from a wind-up Victrola." Nancy rejoined when her daughters joined Girl Scouts. A troop needed a leader for the dance badge, so Nancy, who had taken lessons from Rosalie Lyga at the Loreto Club, took that on. Next she became a Brownie leader. Eventually she served as a local board member and as a national volunteer with Girl Scouts U.S.A. Even though Nancy did not stay with scouting as a girl, she was committed as an adult and earned the "Thanks Badge" in 1979.

Lutheran Girl Pioneers

Concerned about values that might not be compatible with its teaching, the conservative Lutheran churches of the Wisconsin Synod did not allow its young female members to be Girl Scouts. However, Jean Masewicz of Mount Calvary Lutheran Church in La Crosse thought it important that these girls have an opportunity to enjoy the scouting experience within a religious context. Therefore, she and her pastor, Harold Backer, organized the Lutheran Girl Pioneers in 1954. Bernice Kohlmeyer, who became district counselor for the La Crosse area, southeastern Minnesota, and Iowa, recalled that the second caravan, or chapter, was chartered at her church, Grace Lutheran in La Crosse. Members learned skills in citizenship, leadership, homemaking, etiquette, first aid, camping, nature, baby-sitting, music, dramatics, and handicrafts. For each skill mastered, the girl received a charm to add to her Pioneer bracelet. Forty years after the inception of Lutheran Girl Pioneers, La Crosse was the headquarters for the national organization which served 6,000 girls throughout the country.[30]

Job's Daughters

From its beginning in 1940, Bethel #27 International Order of Job's Daughters influenced hundreds of young La Crosse women.[31] Leo Jenkins served as the group's first Associate Bethel Guardian. Mary Markos Coury was the first Bethel Guardian, the female adult advisor. She served from 1940 to 1943 and was succeeded by Maud Bond (1943-45), Evelyn Schultz (1945-67), Joyce Horlie (1967-72), Carol Wolover (1972-78), and Mary Callaway (from 1978). Patterned after the biblical story of Job, the young officers were called honored queen, senior princess, and junior princess. During World War II, local members joined national efforts of Job's Daughters to raise money for thirteen ambulances for the armed services, provide afghans for soldiers and hospital veterans, and purchase war bonds. The group's membership more than doubled during the time Evelyn Schultz served as Bethel Guardian. Approximately two-hundred and fifty girls between the ages of thirteen and twenty volunteered their time in nursing homes, participated in "Go To Church Sundays," and enjoyed social events including the annual father-daughter banquets. Eighty-nine attended the Jobie Slumber Party at "Mom Schultz's" cottage on French Island on August

31, 1963. Membership began declining later in that decade. Potential members were spending their time at jobs, sports, and other opportunities that had not been available to girls before then. As more women joined the workforce, fewer mothers had time to serve as members of the adult advisory Guardian Council. Also, the decline of membership in the male Masonic Lodge, both local and national, meant fewer girls had the Masonic relationship necessary to join Job's Daughters. In order to survive the changing times, Bethel #27 changed its meeting time to fit with other activity schedules, and, while maintaining the original principles, the Guardian Council adjusted to the way the lives of youth had changed since 1940.

Junior Red Cross

Local youth learned about the commitment to and satisfaction from serving others, at home and abroad, through the Junior Red Cross, sponsored by the Red Cross. La Crosse's Longfellow Junior High Junior Red Cross visited Hillview Nursing Home on weekends. Irna Rideout, the group's adult advisor, credited Mary Krum Munson for this adopt-a-grandparent program in the early 1960s. The students made favors for meal trays, played checkers and cards with the residents, and helped the women shampoo their hair.

The high school and junior high school age members learned about other parts of the world when they compiled large boxes of artwork and exchanged them with other countries. They also prepared smaller gift boxes to ship all over the world. Each container included items to be used at home and school, such as a comb, toothpaste and brush, paper and pencils, a small toy, and a wash cloth. Sometimes the recipients wrote letters. "It was good for the members to know they were helping others," Irna said.[32]

During high school, Mary, who eventually became a middle school teacher in La Crosse, was sponsored by the Junior Red Cross for a cultural exchange to Ecuador. As part of a team of high school students from all over the United States, she spent the summer of 1965 in Latin America. The first week, in Puerto Rico, taught the students cultural courtesies and what to expect. Mary spent the next two months living with families in Ecuador, visiting mental institutions, prisons and government offices, working in schools, and teaching basic health and nutrition. Before ever leaving home, though, she received some of the best preparation from her Spanish teacher at La Crosse Central High School. "Mrs. [Kathleen] Spence put me up in front of class every day to practice Spanish," Mary recalled.[33]

Some La Crosse youth developed a commitment to the Red Cross in another way, through their association with Eleanore Wollschlaeger when she was in charge of the Junior Golf program at the La Crosse Country Club. Pauline Weigel Connell, who began golfing at the age of twelve and was Junior Girls Champion in 1962, 1963 and 1964, described Eleanore as "one of the neatest ladies on earth."[34] She did not emphasize techniques, such as how to swing. Instead, she taught many young people the etiquette and the rules of the game. In a gentle way she encouraged them to keep trying and converted them from "just slapping the ball around to really enjoying the game," Pauline said. Don Iverson, who played on the professional circuit from 1971 to 1979, also benefited from Eleanore's approach to golf. "She taught us that the game should be played properly, according to the rules," Don said.[35] Eleanore instilled a dedication to community service as well. Pauline became involved in Red Cross because of her. "Before I was old enough to give blood, I started volunteering at the bloodmobile. And I'm not the only one affected this way. Eleanore got people to reach out, not because they felt they had to but because they wanted to in the same way she did," Pauline said.

Protecting Mother Earth

Irene Schieche taught her children to love and respect nature, telling them not to kill snakes or bats because they did much more good than harm, not to pick wildflowers, if there were only a few, and never to torment spiders or insects, who have a rightful place in nature. Irene, who raised her three sons and three daughters in the 1930s, 1940s, and 1950s, also taught them not to litter. "There was a time when people routinely dropped wastepaper on the sidewalk as they strolled along or threw it out the car window when out for a drive, but Barbara Frank's mother [Irene Schieche] never let her children do that," said Nancy Goode, an environmental activitist and friend of Barbara's.

"Women have always had a special affinity with nature," said Barbara, "perhaps because our menstrual cycles and childbearing roles remind us often and forcefully of our biological natures, rooting us firmly to the earth." As early as 1895, the public record showed that La Crosse women were concerned about the environment. In a special edition of the *La Crosse Sunday Press* produced entirely by fifty-one women under the direction of editor-in-chief for the day, Mrs. Angus (Mary Baker) Cameron, on February 17, 1895, the editorial page included "What the Women of La Crosse Want":

> We want to see the pump question settled and pure water in our
> homes.... We want to see the foot of State Street laid out in a
> little park where people may sit and gaze on the scenery of the
> Mississippi which is unsurpassed at this point.... We want to
> see our city made more beautiful with parks and clean streets.[36]

It was a woman who led the effort to save La Crosse's largest landmark. For many years Grandad Bluff, which towered above the city of La Crosse, was owned and shaped by quarrymen. When a new quarry company purchased the property in 1909 and began blasting on the south side, people feared that the bluff might be lost. A group of wealthy citizens formed a committee headed by Ellen Pennell Hixon, widow of Gideon Hixon, to save the bluff. She gave twelve thousand dollars to purchase portions of the bluff. An additional three thousand dollars, which came from twenty-two donors, was used to acquire the adjacent forest and land at the base of the bluff and to build roads and other improvements. An anonymous newspaper columnist of the time, the Gossipper, said, "Mrs. Hixon has thought far into the future of this good little town and ... planned to do something that will perpetually add to the happiness of all who hereafter may come to live within its steadily expanding boundaries."[37]

Garden Clubs

Garden clubs, often social in nature, reflected women's interest in nature and beauty. They offered programs on growing plants and landscaping. They usually had a conservation chair. The La Crosse Garden Club was organized in 1932 as an evening class at the Vocational School. The members were interested in learning about horticulture. One member, Katharine Martindale, was particularly interested in conservation. At the club's flower show in 1947, she showed pictures and a map of Midway Prairie. The club was trying, with the help of the University of Wisconsin, to preserve the prairie as a scientific area. In 1961, Katharine received the Conservation-Community Service award at the Wisconsin Federation of Women's Clubs convention for working "vigorously and effectively in many phases of conservation. Through her constant efforts she succeeded in having an area between Midway and Onalaska set aside as a preserve known as Midway Prairie Scientific Area" for the study of wild flowers.[38]

In addition to beautification, the Nathan Hill 76ers Garden Club was interested in historic preservation. Women in the Medary neighborhood organized the club in 1976. The group's first major project brought attention to Nathan Hill, a landmark along Highway 16. The members erected a large wooden marker and landscaped the spot to which black slaves Nathan and Sarah Smith fled in 1864. The group won a State Garden Club Award in 1981 for honoring and preserving this historic site.[39]

Pat Meir Shedesky, who published several articles on gardening, acquired her love for plants from her grandmother and aunt who lived next door along Highway 14. "I used to beg my dad to have a portion of the vegetable garden so I could plant gladiola bulbs," Pat remembered.[40] When Pat married Albert Shedesky in 1953, they settled on his family's farm property along Highway 33. There was plenty of room for vegetable and flower gardens and perennial beds. Pat joined Town and Country Garden Club in 1956 in order to meet more people who enjoyed gardening. The next year she published her first article in a national gardening magazine. Over the next twenty years, fifty of Pat's articles appeared in *Flower and Garden*, *Popular Gardening*, *Organic Gardening*, and *Horticulture*. In 1972, Ken Blanchard, the publisher of the *La Crosse Tribune*, asked her to write a regular column on gardening. For two years, in a Sunday column entitled "Let it Grow," she shared timely tips and wisdom gained from years of experience.

Mae and Alvin Peterson

Mae Rose Draeger, who was born in 1888, attended and taught in rural schools before she married another teacher, Alvin Peterson, in 1917. They bought a twenty-acre tract of land in Onalaska in 1920 and moved there permanently in 1923. There they raised their son and daughter, lived on the bounty of their garden and his writing, and devoted themselves to nature and writing.[41] They were self-taught naturalists and conservationists who acquired a tremendous knowledge of natural history. According to florist John Zoerb, Mae retained that knowledge until her death at the age of 102. Alvin and Mae turned their acreage into a wildlife sanctuary and followed conservation practices to attract and protect all forms of wildlife and encourage the growth of wild plants. When Alvin's hearing diminished, they began to spend more time with plants than birds. The La Crosse Chapter of the State Botanical Society is named the Alvin and Mae Peterson Chapter.

Alvin wrote nature-related books and articles. Mae, who wrote poetry about nature, also served as assistant county librarian in Onalaska from 1960 to 1968. The last page of one of her books of verse, *Pathways of Song*, described the author as "a former teacher, librarian, weaver of rugs (and dreams), housewife, great grandmother, and always a gardener and out-door friend."

Water Study by the League of Women Voters

In the late 1950s, the League of Women Voters, at its local, state and national levels, surveyed water resources and water conservation practices. Because this information was not readily available, La Crosse League members interviewed government officials, studied maps and census reports, and toured several rural dam projects. They learned about the water pollution problems of farm run-off and the lack of sewage treatment in some populated areas. The Minor Mississippi River Basin report compiled in 1959 by Margaret Fish, Clare Engelhard, Kathleen Munson, Audrey Uber, Avis Lewis, and Caecilia Davy covered Mississippi River tributaries from the Bad Axe River to La Crosse. This group identified flood control, control of siltation, and control of pollution as continuing problems which needed attention. The League of Women Voters of Wisconsin combined the information from La Crosse with reports from other areas of the state to compile a summary of water use and administration in Wisconsin. The League of Women Voters of the United States combined the Wisconsin profile with that of other states to make a report on the conditions of the nation's water supply to President Eisenhower. This national report promoted coordination and cooperation of federal, state, and local governments with private interests in the formulation and administration of water policies and programs, equitable financing, and regional or river basin planning. The League's action prompted regional water studies throughout the country. These studies were the early stage of discovering what was polluting the water supply and what preventive measures could be taken.[42]

Environmental Educators

At one time, La Crosse State University required all students training to become elementary school teachers to take a nature study course. Laura Schuh, who joined the university's biology department in 1957, taught that course from 1973 until she retired in 1983. Because Laura frequently took the students to the marsh, she wrote a guidebook for them in 1976. Two years later she revised the La Crosse River Marsh guide for use by the general public.[43] Malenna Smith illustrated the marsh guide. A gifted artist and writer, Malenna edited the Audubon Society newsletter. She also shared her knowledge about plants, as well as birds, when she led field trips on topics such as mosses and lichens.[44]

In the late 1970s, Deon Nontelle, a biology instructor at the University of Wisconsin-La Crosse, offered short courses on wildflower identification for the general public. The work she did for her master's thesis on the wildflowers of La Crosse County provided the basis for these classes: Buds and Blossoms of Spring, Fruits and Flowers of Summer, and Weeds and Seeds of Fall. Participants always were impressed by her knowledge, patience, good humor, and obvious love for the subject matter as they followed her on the trails of Myrick Marsh and Hixon Forest.[45]

Linda Malick came to La Crosse in 1980 to teach biology at Viterbo College. Fortunately she did not limit her teaching to textbooks nor the classroom. Linda helped other teachers develop environmental education programs in the local schools. She introduced young students to nature when she brought marsh water into their classrooms so they could see the micro-organisms living there. With college students, she continued a project initiated by Joseph Kawatski which tested mayflies for polychlorinated biphenyls (PCBs) as a way to measure the level of pollutants in the Mississippi River. In connection with the University of Toronto, she banded Monarch butterflies in order to study their migration patterns.[46]

Environmental Scientists

Rosalie Schnick, a research librarian turned technical information specialist in aquaculture, began working for the U.S. Fish and Wildlife Service (USFWS) in 1967.[47] Based at the fish laboratory on French Island, Rosalie served as a commissioner for the Onalaska Lake district, worked with the local Youth Conservation Corps (a public works program for young

Marian Havlik, an expert on the Higgins' Eye Pearly Mussel, formed her own business, Malacological Consultants, to do research on rivers for endangered freshwater mussel species.

Marian E. Havlik

adults based on the old Civilian Conservation Corps), and was a member of the executive committee of the Mississippi River Research Consortium. She took her knowledge and beliefs to the general public when she spoke to community organizations about recycling and when she taught at the first local celebration of Earth Day. The event called attention to the fragility of our planet and the limited supply of its resources. The idea for an Earth Day was initiated by Wisconsin's U.S. Senator Gaylord Nelson in 1970 and celebrated across the country. Rosalie also was the lead author and editor for a Fish and Wildlife Service 714-page handbook, *Mitigation and Enhancement Techniques for Upper Mississippi River Systems and other Large River Systems.*

Biologist Pam Thiel worked on the Illinois State Water Survey before completing a master's degree at UW-Madison and joining the Wisconsin Department of Natural Resources in 1978. She began as a temporary employee and became Mississippi River Fisheries Supervisor and then a project leader for the La Crosse Fishery of the USFWS.

The world expert on the Higgins' Eye Pearly mussel is a largely self-taught La Crosse resident whose daughter's science fair project led to a consulting business. Marian E. Havlik, a registered nurse who attended St. Francis School of Nursing, became interested in freshwater mussels in 1969, when her daughter, Rosemarie, chose shells for a fifth grade science fair project. Intrigued by what she learned by helping her daughter do research on mollusks, Marian continued to read, observe, and accumulate knowledge. She met with commercial clam buyers in the early 1970s and became angry when she learned their concerns about the river habitat had been ignored by the Wisconsin and Iowa Departments of Natural Resources. Marian decided it was time to do something about these hidden river monitors. In 1976, she received a scholarship from the Bush Foundation in Minneapolis to do a summertime independent study with freshwater mollusk expert, Dr. David H. Stansbery. Her study looked at the identification of freshwater mussels and their relationship to the Mississippi River ecosystem.

Mussels are filter feeders that keep our rivers clean by removing suspended particles. The Higgins' Eye mussel was put on the federal endangered species list in 1976. Marian learned that the Corps of Engineers was going to dredge in an area where she suspected Higgins' Eye mussels lived; she wrote the Corps. While she was studying in Ohio, the Corps proceeded with the dredging project even though she had confirmed that the Higgins' Eye mussel indeed lived in that area, the east channel of the Mississippi River at Prairie du Chien. Rosemarie also found a fresh-dead Higgins' Eye shell on the dredged material. Marian wrote to the Corps again and accused them of violating the Endangered Species Act. She sent copies of her letter to area congressmen, the President, and various government and environmental agencies. "All heck broke loose," she recalled, "and my life has never been the same since."

In March 1977, the Corps of Engineers asked Marian to investigate the Minnesota River at Savage, Minnesota, where they were conducting a channel maintenance dredging project. "When you start being paid for your knowledge, you've started your own business," she said. Her firm, Malacological Consultants, does research on rivers, particularly surveys and mitigation for endangered freshwater mussels species. Since that time, Marian has used her expertise to protect the environment. She encountered frustrating times when her expertise was not respected because she lacked the usual academic credentials in her field. However, Marian continued to receive contracts for survey work from various governmental bodies, to publish articles in professional journals and popular magazines, and to testify as an expert witness. Although she is called "The Clam Lady," Marian pointed out that the more accurate nickname would be "The Mussel Lady" because the Higgins' Eye is a freshwater mussel, not a clam.[48]

Environmental Activists

Barbara Conway also challenged the Corps of Engineers. In response to the Corps' plan to dredge the main channel of the Mississippi River, she organized Save our Shores (SOS). The dredging, which was designed to increase barge traffic, would have washed away the riverbank on which she and several other families lived. Barbara applied her energy and wit to save the shoreline from the action of the Corps. In order to emphasize other environmental concerns, she joined committees of the La Crosse Chamber of Commerce and encouraged Barbara Frank and Rosalie Schnick to do the same. "They [the other members] didn't know what to do with us because we weren't your typical businessmen," said Barbara. "But, we educated the community about recycling, tested water samples of the La Crosse River for pollution, and kept abreast of energy and Mississippi River issues."[49]

Sandra Fletcher put her zoology education and land use planning experience to use as a community volunteer in the late 1960s and 1970s. Her desire to save the center of the city from being split by a highway led her to seek election to the La Crosse Common Council. When she was narrowly defeated in the spring of 1971, she went on to organize support for alternative forms of land use and transportation within the city and for conservancy zoning to protect the bluff lands from indiscriminant development. In 1974, Sandra combined her environmental concerns with her political activism and campaigned for the Democratic nomination for the 95th Assembly District. Her campaign platform also included improved housing, equitable property rights for housewives, and safe and inexpensive transportation alternatives. When Sandra finished second in the primary election, she turned her energies to developing the River and Bluffs Bicentennial Intracity Trail. What became known as the RABBIT hiking trail through Myrick Marsh was laid out to connect north with south La Crosse as well as the bluffs with the river. The plan, developed by a committee of eleven volunteers, also included a nature center.

Barbara Schieche Frank, who grew up in rural La Crosse County, referred to her mother as "my first environmental teacher." The efforts and accomplishments of the activist daughter echoed the success of the mother. When Barbara returned to La Crosse with her husband and their two children in 1968, she joined existing organizations with interests in preserving the environment and founded new groups. She gave her time to lobbying and education. As a Sierra Club volunteer lobbyist, she traveled to Washington, D.C., a number of times to speak with legislators about clean air and Mississippi River issues. From 1975 to 1982, she served on the Minnesota-Wisconsin Boundary Area Commission and in 1978 was selected chair of this advisory board dealing with Mississippi and St. Croix rivers corridor issues. The commission successfully lobbied for the establishment of the inter-governmental Great River Environmental Action Team (GREAT). In the 1970s, Leah Senff, who chaired the Viterbo College biology department, and Barbara founded Coalition for Regional Environmental Education Development (CREED). Leah, whose philosophy was "of course we can do this," advised, and Barbara implemented the citizen effort to develop environmental education curricula and programs for La Crosse area schools.[50]

In the early 1970s, Barbara Frank, Leah Senff, and Sandra Fletcher met with a filming team from the University of Wisconsin-Madison, which was producing a film about state-wide environmental activities and activists. The three women talked about local activities and toured some sites in La Crosse. Then the photographer rather petulantly asked why it was always women who were involved with these things. "When the film was completed, it contained only one woman, recognized briefly and somewhat unfavorably," Barbara recalled. "Although the contributions of women have not always been acknowledged, we'd like the record to show we were there."[51]

Cultural Pursuits

A variety of groups existed for personal edification as well as for community performance and cultural cultivation. Some were limited to either men or women; others opened their membership to both. There were study clubs in which women established libraries for their communities, read and discussed books to expand their own minds, and studied and performed music for their own pleasure and the pleasure of others. Local women also were involved in the visual and performing arts, some as the artist or performer, others behind the scenes as organizers and fundraisers.

Study Clubs

To extend their knowledge and stimulate their thinking, women came together for regular in-depth study meetings. Two such early groups in La Crosse were a reading club called the Coterie (1877) and the Ladies Art Class (1886) whose members "traveled in imagination through the cities and galleries of the Old World."[1] There also was a discussion group, the Fortnightly Club, which started the traveling libraries in La Crosse County.[2] When the nineteenth century ended, the Fortnightly Club disbanded and reorganized as the Twentieth Century Club. The last woman to preside over the Fortnightly Club was Mrs. Frank (Emily) Tiffany. Elsie Gile Scott became the first president of the newly formed Twentieth Century Club.

Campbell Library Association
Fauver Hill Study Club

The oldest, continuous study club in rural Wisconsin began as the Campbell Library Association.[3] Its original purpose was to select, purchase, and loan books to people in the community. The rural women who formed this group on March 15, 1901, were of English and Scottish descent. They lived on farms throughout the Town of Campbell. The first officers of the Campbell Library Association were Mrs. W. A. (Lizzie) Tripp, president; Lydia Dawson, vice-president; and Mrs. J. R. Hartley, secretary-treasurer. The group also appointed a Committee of Inspection and elected three librarians who kept portions of the collection in their homes. At their monthly meetings, members had lively discussions about which books to purchase. The hostess served a meal to the members and their families. After dinner, the men retired to another room for a game of cards, the children played, and the women gathered in the parlor for their study meeting.

After the county library was established in 1923, the Campbell Library Association changed its goal to acquire knowledge for self-improvement. Members studied classic literary works and discussed contemporary topics such as citizenship training, law enforcement, Wisconsin music and its composers. As times changed, so did the meetings. Automobiles, paved roads, radio, and television literally and figuratively expanded the realm of rural women's lives. As more college graduates became members, the quest for knowledge so evident in the early years of the club declined. Changes in the economy also sent many members into the workforce. Eventually, in-depth study was replaced by guest speakers, reports, and tours, and the large meal was replaced by dessert and coffee. In 1967, the group changed its name to the Fauver Hill Study Club. Minnie Kinney, who belonged to the club from 1915 until her death in 1984, described it as "one big family, talking over the many problems, sympathizing with all in joy and sorrow, thankful to our charter members for holding the candle high and filling an inner satisfaction at accomplishing our bit in life."

West Salem Study Club

The West Salem Study Club was organized in January 1914 by women interested in stimulating their minds through the review of history, literature, and art.[4] The club met every Monday afternoon, had thirty-six charter members and had an average attendance of twenty-five. The first officers were Mary Dudley, president; May Wakefield, vice-president; Pearl Wakefield, secretary; and Clara Kirmse, treasurer. Unlike similar groups which combined a social hour with their program, the West Salem Study Club never served refreshments.

Ibsen Club

The Ibsen Club began in 1899 when Helga Gundersen invited into her home a few women, lonely for their homeland and native language, to read the latest book of Henrik Ibsen, *When We Dead Awaken.*[5] For ten years, these women gathered informally for afternoon coffee and listened to Helga read Norwegian literature. Her daughter, Helga Gundersen Midelfort, recalled, "[my mother] was the only reader. She had a fantastic background to give ... her recollection of history ... tied in to make it meaningful to them."[6] As the core membership grew to twenty or thirty members, the organization became formalized, electing officers and taking minutes. The elder Helga was unanimously elected president each year for the next fifty years. Members of the group hosted the Friday afternoon meetings. Helga hosted an annual anniversary dinner party for members, husbands, and special guests who might be visiting from Norway. She could seat fifty guests in the reception hall of her home. During World War II, the Ibsen Club gave money to Finnish Relief, Norwegian Relief, Greek Relief, Red Cross, and Little Norway camp in Canada. Members also knitted "helmets" for Norwegian sailors. Because of the Nazi occupation of Norway, these sailors were cut off from assistance from their own countrymen and women. The younger Helga inherited the role of reader from her mother in the early 1950s until the group disbanded in the 1960s. By that time, many members were not fluent in Norwegian. "In fact, sometimes I wonder if I'm reading to myself," she reflected, " ... but they want to keep on; that's what's so funny! And it's great for me; I keep my Norwegian a little more alive than otherwise."[7]

La Crosse Music Study Club

When Mrs. Arthur Esperson moved to La Crosse in 1911, she promoted the idea of a music study club for married women. Mrs. George Heath hosted a meeting in November of that year to launch the La Crosse Music Study Club.[8] The first regular meeting was held on a bitterly cold day in January 1912. The hostess, Mrs. Robert C. Whelpley, served tea in front of a grate fire. Mary Austen played a group of piano numbers and Mrs. Whelpley sang. During its first year, the club devoted itself to in-depth studies of individual composers and music of all nations. During its second year, the group allowed unmarried women to join and decided to limit the number of members. Each prospective member submitted a letter which included a resumé of her activities and musical background plus sponsorship by three current members. At their meetings, which were held on Friday afternoons from fall through spring, members performed for one another. Viola Doerflinger Fellows became a member in 1915. Her sister, Leona Doerflinger Locke, joined in 1927. Together they performed for other club members. Viola, who had trained to become a concert pianist, accompanied as her sister sang.[9]

In addition to promoting the study and appreciation of music among its members, the club encouraged the cultivation of music in the community. From 1919 to 1926, the La Crosse Music Study Club sponsored performances of visiting artists of merit such as cellist Pablo Casals, coloratura soprano Luella Melius, and pianist Percy Grainger. Elise Lovold Cilley was an active member of the concert committee during the 1920s. One of her compositions was published: the musical setting for "In Flanders Field." When Elise died, the club paid tribute to her with organ, violin, and vocal perfomances in a service at the Congregational Church.[10] In 1930, the Music Study Club also began the Winter Concert Series which evolved into the Civic Choir and later the La Crosse Choral Union.

Wilma Scheffner recalled that when she and her husband, George, moved to La Crosse in 1959, most members of the Music Study Club came from prominent families, had husbands who were doctors or lawyers, and had an interest in music. Wilma had been performing as a singer since the age of seven and had sung for national radio commercials for Maytag appliances and Skelly gasoline during the 1950s. "Because we didn't have family connections and my husband sold farm machinery, I overheard other members say about me, 'She's just talented you know,'" Wilma said with a hearty laugh.[11] In 1976, the Music Study Club opened its membership to men and presented six high school students with awards for musical excellence. The group disbanded in 1986.

Campus Dames

Mrs. Ernest Smith, wife of the president of the La Crosse Normal School, organized Campus Dames in December 1925 to promote the social and literary interests of faculty wives and to offer helpful cooperation with the student life on campus. Twenty-three wives of faculty members responded to her invitation. They met twice a month to study literature, to discuss school spirit and the condition of the campus, and to enjoy a luncheon together. Because of wartime food shortages, the meeting format changed in 1940 from a morning meeting followed by a luncheon to an early afternoon meeting followed by tea. One meeting was described in minutes from 1942 as "Spring came to us at tea, and fancy sandwiches and flowerlike cakes grew on a pattern of lovely lace. A California centerpiece added the one touch which cleared our minds of war and horror. Then Mrs. (Grace) Rolfe gave us tea with a smile and lemon or cream." Members also sewed drapes for Camp McCoy, devoted one meeting a month to Red Cross work, and helped organize a club for veterans' wives. Campus Dames reorganized again in the 1960s when membership increased because the college faculty was increasing and when women's schedules changed because more were employed outside the home. The group made a point of welcoming newly-arriving faculty wives. Instead of large group daytime meetings which featured book reviews, smaller groups developed for arts and crafts, antiques, gourmet dinners, moms and tots, and couples bridge as well as books.[12]

American Association
of University Women

The La Crosse Branch of the American Association of University Women (AAUW) was organized in 1922. Until the 1930s, it was known as The College Club. The first officers were Mrs. T. H. Brindley, president; Helen B. Williams, first vice-president; Catherine Hayes, second vice-president; Mrs. George Bunge, secretary; Martha Skaar, treasurer; and Mrs. D. O. (Caroline) Coate, corresponding secretary. The group adopted as its first goals equal pay for equal work; assistance for needy students; women on local, state, and national boards; and education for intelligent voting.[13]

Within AAUW, some members established study groups. These groups grew in number in order to accommodate a variety of interests. Bookfellows was begun in 1935 under the guidance of Helen Dorset. A classical scholar herself, she was eager for other women to continue to read good literature. Each year, the group selected a theme and members presented papers for discussion. For many of the original members, participation in Bookfellows was a lifetime commitment and a source of intimate friendships as well as learning. The group continues to meet, still mindful of Miss Dorset's ardent words, "We must ever press onward in this our rewarding quest in human thought."[14]

Another AAUW study group begun in the early 1930s, International Relations, continues today as World Problems. Members studied the history, geography, and specific problems of nations throughout the world. The group was led, in the early days, by the vigorous history professor, Myrtle Trowbridge, and later by Mary B. Gundersen and Helen Leide. More recent AAUW study groups have included Contemporary Authors, Hearth and Home, Theater, Literature and Cinema, and Vital People.[15]

The Bookfellows coat of arms, painted by Owen Jackson, husband of one of the study club members, was a satire about women's noble pursuit of knowledge.

Bookfellows Study Club

Wisconsin Literature

Flora E. Wood Lowry championed Wisconsin authors.[16] She graduated from Stevens Point Normal School, attended the University of Wisconsin, and taught in the public schools of La Crosse where she met and married Robert B. Lowry on July 19, 1906. In their home at 1433 Wood Street, she wrote poetry and collected and catalogued the works of Wisconsin authors.

Her collection included Marion Manville Pope, whose verse, novel, and dramatic sketches were published at the end of the nineteenth century, and Norwegian native Palma Pederson, who came to America as a young adult and wrote poems, short stories, and novels in Norwegian because she felt she had not "sufficiently mastered the English language to use it as a medium for expression."[17]

Flora also enjoyed sharing her knowledge about Wisconsin authors as a lecturer at meetings of women's clubs and literary societies. She was prompted to do this while listening to a lecture on Wisconsin authors at a La Crosse women's club. "I was ashamed of myself," recalled Flora, "because I knew nothing about some of the authors mentioned and little enough about some of the others for one who was born in Wisconsin. I resolved then to know the authors of my state. I have been at work ever since."[18]

Visual Arts

From the time she was in second grade, Marion Cape Biehn knew she wanted to be an artist.[19] She studied at the University of Wisconsin in Madison, at the Chicago Academy of Fine Art, and she completed her bachelor's degree at the Chicago Art Institute. By the time she, her husband, and their two children moved to La Crosse in 1955, Marion had shown a stained glass window in the 1934 World's Fair, done free-lance work sketching fashion designs for advertising, and painted portraits, landscapes, and structures. Her medium was oil, but Art Hebberd, a colleague in the Sunday Painters, convinced her to try watercolor. In the 1960s, Marion began entering juried art fairs throughout the Midwest. Her work won awards for best watercolor, best painting, and best of show. For many years, she was a standard exhibitor at the Art Fair on the Green in La Crosse. In 1959, AAUW organized this juried art show which brought quality artists and their work to La Crosse. AAUW put the profits into its scholarship fund for local students attending the University of Wisconsin-La Crosse, Viterbo College, and Western Wisconsin Technical College. The group also provided scholarships and grants for non-traditional students and for teachers and students attending summer workshops.[20]

Betty and Dale Kendrick regularly featured Marion's paintings at their Behind-the-Brewery Gallery, especially in December and the month before

Mother's Day. "The ease with which [viewers] could put themselves into the paintings was a measure of the artistry and emotion which Biehn puts into every work," wrote Sandra (Fletcher) Gue in a review of one of Marion's shows.[21]

Betty Kendrick met Marion Biehn shortly after Betty married Dale and moved to La Crosse in 1962. "She was painting the little house we were living in in Greenwald Coulee," recalled Betty, "so I walked down the driveway and introduced myself." Shortly thereafter they became friends who shared a love and talent for art. About the time she moved to La Crosse, Betty began expressing herself in two and three dimensional stitchery.[22] In 1966, Betty and Dale started holding art shows at their home. In May of that year, they showcased work of four women artists: Marion Biehn's watercolors, Sherry Fiorini's pottery, Anne Swan's textiles, and Betty's stitchery. Since 1971, when they opened their Behind-the-Brewery Gallery, the Kendricks have exhibited their own artwork and that of others. Betty also taught many classes at the gallery and in the community. "That has always been a big part of my life, encouraging others in art," she said. In the mid-1970s, Betty quit stitchery and began exploring batik. Ten years later, she decided to concentrate on drawing. "I couldn't think of my life without art! It's always been a part of me and I would probably have a great sense of emotional loss without it," she said.

Reviving and preserving the heritage of needlecrafts has been the goal of two women's groups, Coulee County Chapter of the Embroiderers' Guild of America and La Crosse Area Quilters. When the local Embroiderers' Guild organized in 1978, a typical member was married with school-age or older children and could attend monthly morning meetings because she was not employed outside the home.[23] The first officers were Nancy Tompkins, president; Cheri Hood, vice-president; Linda Miles, secretary; and Betty Sundet, treasurer. The group promoted the art of embroidery through educational meetings for its members, sponsorship of an annual Oktoberfest Needlework Show, and workshops for children. In 1985, the Guild presented an appliqued and embroidered replica of the La Crosse City Seal which was hung in the city council chambers. In the 1990s, Guild members began smocking baby gowns for Lutheran Hospital and St. Francis Medical Center to give to parents of babies who died before or shortly after birth. Parents used them as burial garments or saved them as keepsakes.

American quilting has been a practical as well as a creative artform. Colonial and pioneer women pieced precious scraps of cloth into quilt tops to add warmth and color to their homes. Conversation around the quilting frame was not limited to gossip. "By the 1850s women were giving time and effort to causes such as anti-slavery and temperance. These issues were heatedly discussed around the quilting frames."[24] Susan B. Anthony's first talk on equal rights for women was delivered at a church quilting party in Cleveland, Ohio.[25]

The La Crosse Area Quilters organized in 1980 to bring quilters in touch with one another and to learn from and share their techniques and talents with each other.[26] May Parnow took the lead when she called a few quilters she knew and invited others with a notice in the newspaper. Fifteen women attended the first meeting. By the third year, the group had to find a community meeting place because the membership was too large to fit into a private home. Women of all ages who were nurses, teachers, secretaries, sales clerks, bank clerks, farm wives, homemakers, and retired have met monthly. Their interests ranged from traditional to contemporary designs for bed coverings, wall hangings, and clothing. A number of special interest groups developed within the club. Harriet Bott instituted the "quilt-in-a-day" project. In a modern day version of quilting bees, nine quilters toted their sewing machines to the home of one in the group. The hostess had planned the quilt, cut the pieces, and determined the method for assembling them. The stitchers sewed from nine in the morning to three in the afternoon, stopping for lunch provided by the hostess. Mary Herzog recalled one memorable session.

> *Stepping down just one step, I lost my balance and fell. Of course I was embarrassed to be so clumsy. I got up and hobbled to my sewing machine and sewed for a couple of hours. Sitting there I didn't feel too bad, until I tried to get up for lunch. Then I knew something was wrong. I called my long-suffering husband who came and hauled me off to the emergency ward. I had a broken hip, so the day ended in surgery. The first thing the next morning, my hostess appeared bearing the completed quilt top. It remained on my [hospital] bed, causing much comment, for the ten days of my stay there.*[27]

Performing Arts

Depending on their interests and how they wanted to spend their time, women belonged to one, a few, or several organizations. Because of Mrs. F. A. Douglas' interest in music, she was active in both the La Crosse Music Study Club and the La Crosse Community Concert Association. She belonged to the Music Study Club during the 1930s and 1940s and served as the first president of Community Concerts during its charter year, 1932-33.[28]

Community Concerts

La Crosse Community Concert Association was formed by men and women interested in bringing first class musical performances to the community. The group was part of a network associated with a New York City-based agency that sent soloists and groups into some eight hundred U. S. cities. During its approximately fifty years of existence, the Concert Association was led by just six presidents, the first and last of whom were women. Mrs. Douglas was succeeded by John Felton (1933-54), Albert P. Funk (1954-57), Emerson Wulling (1957-69), Hubert Schleiter (1969-76), and Betty Mielke (from 1976).[29]

"If you can sit still, you can go to the concerts," Olga and Hubert Schleiter would tell their elementary school age daughters, Linda and Jane. "It was a treat for us," recalled Linda Schleiter Sherwood. "My parents' dinner table conversation included contract negotiations, budgeting, and scheduling....My father and Emerson Wulling were presidents of Community Concerts, but my mother and Jean [Wulling] did most of the work. If the vocational school auditorium held 1200, then they would get on the phone during the one-week membership drive and sell 1200 season subscriptions; the more they sold, the more money there was for better musicians."[30]

"The vocational school was a very busy place," remembered Linda, "so pianists would come to our house [at Seventeenth and Pine streets where the University of Wisconsin-La Crosse Murphy Library was built in 1969] to practice before the concert and then return for a dinner party prepared by my mother following the concert. My father did the fun work — meeting the artists and negotiating contracts with them — while my mother and Jean did the grunt work." During the 1970s, events sponsored by Community Concerts moved to the new fine arts facility of Viterbo College. Eventually, the function of Community Concerts was taken over by the fine arts programs and buildings at Viterbo and the University of Wisconsin-La Crosse.[31]

Vocal Music

La Crosse citizens also organized to sponsor musical and theatrical productions in which they performed. La Crosse florist Till Lund's love of music led her to join Sweet Adelines, the female counterpart to barbershop singers. She loved the performing and the camaraderie even if her membership in the late 1940s and early 1950s did not give her the tenor voice for which she secretly wished.[32]

Women and men performed vocal music in groups ranging from church choirs and the former Civic Choir to current performing groups such as the La Crosse Chamber Chorale and Best of Broadway. Virginia Larkin, a charter member of the Chamber Chorale which formed in 1986, said, "choral singing is a most important part of my life so I'm thankful for a group such as this" which performs vocal chamber music from the sixteenth century to the present.[33]

In the early 1980s, Wilma Scheffner realized, "I was starting to hear, in my mind, my voice students doing all these wonderful show tunes. So I put together a recital but soon realized it really was a musical revue. We've expanded it a little more each year."[34] A loyal local audience and conventioneers from out of town have been enjoying the singing and acting "with plenty of schtick and humor" at the Pump House since 1984.

Community Theatre

In the 1930s and 1940s, the American Association of University Women (AAUW) brought children's theatre touring companies to La Crosse. In the 1950s and 1960s, AAUW members and their friends put their time and energy into producing theatre for children. They did everything from props and publicity to performing. Wilma Scheffner, who played the Beast in "Beauty and the Beast," recalled, "We performed in the old Coleman [vocational school] Auditorium. The place would be packed with kids, and we had to speak over them. There was no amplification. But Liz Staley dressed up as a jester and, before each performance, talked with the kids about theatre manners."[35] As membership and members' discretionary time began to decrease in the 1960s, AAUW started a joint venture with the university theatre department to continue performances for children.

Members of Christ Episcopal Church were looking for ways to raise money to furnish their new Christian education building when they decided upon a musical revue for the community. The group presented "Hey, Look Us Over!" on November 29, 1962, at the vocational school auditorium. Sally Cremer produced the review of one hundred years of La Crosse history portrayed in song and dance. Pleased with its success, a core group of planners and performers decided to form La Crosse Community Theatre (LCCT). When longtime members of LCCT gathered in 1994 to reminisce about the group's history and accomplishments, they singled out three people who were "most interested and influential in starting LCCT."[36] Those three, all women, were Sally Cremer, Allan Trane, and Betty Hood. Sally was "an organizer, a 'mover and doer,' a 'shaker upper.'" Allan and Betty were "extremely important" in the early stage of LCCT's development because "they had clout ... and were able to go to the moneyed people in town and to the business community for support of this fledgling group."[37]

La Crosse Community Theatre incorporated on February 27, 1963, in order to extend the good times experienced during the production of "Hey, Look Us Over!" The founding members planned to provide live entertainment in La Crosse (of which "there was a dearth" in the 1950s and 1960s), and to serve as an outlet for performers and others who wanted to exhibit their creative potential. Several members, often without theatre training or much experience, developed their talents as LCCT needed them. Roxanna Morgan and Sue Brailey, housewives, designed and created costumes. Karen Pederson became proficient at stage make-up.

LCCT also wanted a "home of its own." In its early years, the group rehearsed in various churches, constructed scenery in rooms of the Diocese of La Crosse, and mounted productions in auditoriums throughout the city and even under tents. The group recalled there was a lot of volunteer support in the beginning, "It was the 'in thing' to be involved with LCCT — probably because of the trend to support the arts in the 1960s." Some volunteer enthusiasm was lost when LCCT moved into its own building on Fifth Avenue and hired a technical director in 1968. JoAnn Jenkins made a lifetime career as the business manager.

LCCT also proved to be an acceptable place for women to socialize and a way for men and women to meet and date. Julia Steinke and Al Saterbak met during the production of "The Remarkable Mr. Penneypacker" and married in 1977.[38]

A Home for the Arts

In 1976, women and men, musicians and artists, representatives of cultural groups and individual patrons of the arts came together to form Western Wisconsin Regional Arts (WWRA). The arts council's first president was Audrey Kader. Its first investment was a good quality typewriter nicknamed "Old Blue." Its first home was a small office in the Grandview Building at 1707 Main Street. With those assets, WWRA tackled its first project, a monthly calendar of area arts events to help member groups coordinate their schedules and to inform the community. It did not take long to realize more space was needed for meetings as well as exhibits and performances. WWRA set its sights on the city water works pumping station built in the 1890s. A combination of funding helped WWRA get established and start renovating its new home, dubbed the Pump House. A "City Spirit" award from the National Endowment for the Arts provided the salary for the group's first paid administrator, Lenore Italiano. She applied for Comprehensive Employment and Training Act (CETA) money to hire multi-talented people. Lenore became known as "housemother to the CETA workers" who spent part of their time renovating the building and the other part on the road spreading news of the arts throughout the region as representatives of the Pump House. One of these was Lynn Zampino who doubled as the first janitor and as a traveling musician. Lynn was hired in 1978 and eventually served as program director at the Pump House. Most of these CETA artists did not fit the image of traditional arts groups. "But we were the envy of all the other arts councils in the state because of the creative energy here," Lenore recalled.[39]

The first period of stability for the Pump House came during Sonia Baker's seven years of administrative leadership, from 1980 to 1987. Board members credited her with overseeing basic building improvements, establishing a plan for private and public funding, developing volunteers to staff the Pump House, and inspiring young artists.[40]

Eastbank Artists

A chance meeting in a shopping center parking lot in 1976 was the spark for Eastbank Artists, a group with very close ties to the Pump House. When painter Pat Swartz, multi-media artist Janet Larson Kruk, and stain painter Sonja Adams met, they asked each other, "Are you still doing your art? Is your work selling?" Each one realized she was not alone in her frustration about market places for her artwork. "We didn't have a model for an art group around here. We visited galleries in Madison and the Twin Cities to get ideas. That's when we realized we needed to develop our own identity," Sonja said.[41] Pat, Janet, and Sonja met with other artists who were "serious about their work" to discuss forming a group that insisted on standards and juried admission for membership. Fiber artist Kathy Gresens, potter and sculptor Martha Schwem, weaver Gloria Jackson, painter Nancy Ellingson, stained-glass artist Barbara Starner, soft sculptor Constance Mahairas, and visual artist Margaret Anderson formed the core of the group that held its first two Christmas shows, in 1976 and 1977, in members' homes.

In its quest for gallery space, Eastbank Artists gave significant support to WWRA and the Pump House. Members lobbied the city council about leasing the building. They also gave their physical labor to create an exhibition area in the Pump House and were the first group to use it. "Our collective naivete was immense," Janet recalled. "I thought all we would have to do was to hang our work." Before the walls were ready for display, they were stripped of high-gloss green enamel paint, then plastered and painted. Since that show, Eastbank Artists has rented Pump House gallery space year-round.[42]

Public Service

Ours has been a movement of the soul;
let us hope it finds its way into
the soul of everywoman.
Carrie Chapman Catt

The First Step:
Getting the Right to Vote

The American woman's desire for equality and the right to vote dates back to the American Revolution. Abigail Adams wrote to her husband, John, as he was helping to form the new laws that would govern a new nation, "I desire you would remember the ladies ... we will not hold ourselves bound to obey any laws in which we have no voice or representation."[1]

The first formal demand in the United States for woman suffrage came from the women's rights meeting organized by Lucretia Mott and Elizabeth Cady Stanton and held in Seneca Falls, New York, on July 19, 1848. Various speakers called for women's moral persuasion to end slavery, to advance temperance, and to obtain more humane working conditions for women. In her speech that day, Elizabeth Cady Stanton claimed it was not right that "drunkards, idiots, horse-racing, rum-selling rowdies, ignorant foreigners, and silly boys" had the privilege of voting while the same was denied to women.

The first amendment granting women the right to vote was introduced into Congress in 1868. The following year, in November, Elizabeth Cady Stanton visited La Crosse.[2] Her autobiography, *Eighty Years and More*, included her thoughts during that visit which compared the struggle for equal rights to the Mississippi River:

> *... I found myself in a pleasant room in the International*
> *Hotel at La Crosse looking out on the Great Mother of Waters, on*
> *whose cold bosom the ice and the streamers [sic] were struggling*

for mastery. Beyond stretched the snowclad bluffs, sternly
looking down on the Mississippi as if to say, "Thus far shalt
thou come and no farther" — though sluggish, you are
aggressive, ever pushing where you should not; but all attempts
in this direction are alike vain; since creation's dawn we have
defied you and here we stand, today, calm, majestic,
immovable...

As I listened to these complacent hills and watched the poor
Mississippi weeping as she swept along to lose her sorrows in
ocean's depths, I thought how like the attitude of man to
woman...

From the 1840s, Elizabeth Cady Stanton devoted her life's work to the emancipation of women. Like the river which was confined by the bluffs, she felt that the struggle for women's rights was stymied by the attitude of man. Unfortunately, her death in 1902 prevented her from exercising one of the rights she struggled for, the right to vote.

In 1885, the Wisconsin legislature passed an act granting suffrage to women in any election pertaining to school matters. This action was approved by the state's voting citizens, i.e., men, in November 1886. Suffrage leader Olympia Brown tested that law the next year by trying to vote in a municipal election in Racine. Her vote was refused. Although Circuit Court Judge John B. Winslow rendered a decision that women were entitled to vote for all candidates at any election, the state supreme court reversed his decision. Wisconsin women continued to be prohibited from voting until 1901 when the legislature provided for separate ballot boxes for women.[3] In that way, women's votes could be distinguished from men's and not counted in any but school-related elections.

The second version of a woman's suffrage amendment, drafted by Susan B. Anthony, had been introduced into Congress in 1878: "The right of citizens of the United States to vote shall not be denied or abridged by the United States or by any state on account of sex." In November and December of 1886, national suffrage leaders visited each of Wisconsin's nine congressional districts. Olympia Brown and Susan B. Anthony addressed over two hundred people at Norden Hall in La Crosse on November 23rd. An article in *The Morning Chronicle* described the main speaker:

Miss Anthony speaks without particular oratorical advantage
and her speaking compels attention chiefly through the
earnestness of the speaker and the clear, well directed style of

her propositions to the one central idea, but she has a keen and somewhat savage style of sarcasm that frequently comes by way of direct thrust, or as an aside, to spice the dryness of her mere argumentative propositions. Her earnestness occasionally approaches closely to eloquence, especially when she touches upon subjects that recall her early history and interest in the abolition of the slaves.[4]

Like many women in the suffrage movement, Susan B. Anthony had honed her skills in earlier campaigns such as abolition, temperance, and improved labor conditions.

Olympia Brown, who had tested Wisconsin's suffrage law in 1887, opened the evening presentation with "the nature of the necessities for organization."[5] She closed by announcing that Leila W. Usher, Harriet Myers, and Jennie Stimble were organizing a local association. Other collaborators in forming the La Crosse Branch of the Woman Suffrage Association were "Mrs. Charles S. Benton, Mrs. Jacobs, the dressmaker, and Mrs. Myers, the photographer."[6] The group met at the homes of its members on the first and third Friday of each month at 7:30 in the evening. The last known records of the association include the minutes of the October 9, 1897, meeting and a listing in the 1900 city directory.[7]

The 1912 Suffrage Referendum

For the 1911-1912 suffrage campaign, national and other state suffrage organizations sent salaried organizers to Wisconsin. In an effort to win the November 4, 1912, referendum, they carefully and laboriously built up at least fifty "active, solvent dues-paying locals [suffrage associations]" in Wisconsin.[8] On January 15, 1912, Harriet Grim, representing the National Woman Suffrage Association, and the Reverend Olympia Brown, president of the Wisconsin Woman Suffrage Association, spoke to the Women's Christian Temperance Union (WCTU), the La Crosse Women's Club, and several members of the Twentieth Century Club in the parlors of La Crosse's Hotel Stoddard.[9] Later that afternoon, "thirty of the most prominent women of La Crosse went into secret session" to organize a local suffrage committee. They refused to divulge the names of the committee members but did announce that they would organize "the towns and wards of the county and city for the fight which will be waged at the fall election when the question of giving women the right to vote will be decided by referendum vote."[10] On January 25, 1912, between thirty and forty women met at the home of Mrs. R. J. Russell to sign the constitution of and elect officers for the newly organized La Crosse Equal Suffrage society.[11] The newspaper report of the meeting indicated that anyone desiring "membership may procure same by applying to Miss Mary Alice Smith, librarian, and paying the membership fee of twenty cents."

The La Crosse Equal Suffrage League sponsored a lecture by Rachel Foster Avery of the National Woman Suffrage Association on February 15, 1912. She addressed two hundred women at city hall with a history of the woman suffrage movement which "originated in the United States and gradually spread to the countries of Europe" but was not making much progress in this country. She went on to say that was because, in the United States, "we must first lobby for woman suffrage and if we are fortunate we may succeed in getting the

Women Vote in Six States

Why Not in Wisconsin?

Believing that the Men of Wisconsin
are as just and fair as the Men of

Wyoming
Utah
Colorado
Idaho
Washington
California

And believing that the women of Wisconsin are as trustworthy as the women of these states, we ask you to vote for Woman Suffrage in November, 1912.

"Wisconsin Next"

EQUAL SUFFRAGE LEAGUE,
LA CROSSE, WIS.

FORM OF BALLOT.

Shall Chapter 227 of the laws of 1911, entitled, "An act extending the right of suffrage to women" be adopted? | Yes |

Equal Suffrage League flyer in support of the 1912 referendum which would have given Wisconsin women the right to vote.

Special Collections, Murphy Library,
University of Wisconsin-La Crosse

legislature to enact a bill calling for a referendum vote. Then we have to get a majority of the men to vote for woman suffrage before we can gain enfranchisement."[12] The two-step process of convincing the legislature and then the electorate consumed tremendous amounts of time and energy.

Later that month Carrie P. Daniels, of the La Crosse Equal Suffrage League, made an appeal for funds in the newspaper.[13] She pointed out that "women of wealth may feel that they have all the rights they need; however, they should remember that there was a time when married women could not hold and enjoy their own property.... The wife was a mere chattel in her husband's household." She also called upon the women "holding good positions with adequate salaries made possible by the past generation of women who lectured, petitioned the legislature, worked up sympathy among men, until they actually worried, shamed and convinced the legislators" to make progressive changes.

When the La Crosse Equal Suffrage association met on April 15, 1912, it accepted an offer from "the Political Equality League of Milwaukee to send prominent speakers to tour La Crosse County in automobiles later in the season."[14] Also at that meeting, the group elected Carrie P. Daniels as first vice-president and Mrs. N. E. Cameron, corresponding secretary. It seems, however, that Carrie Daniels was doing the public corresponding. Another one of her letters to the editor appeared in mid-July.[15] It began, "While wandering about the Copeland Park on the birthday of American Independence in the company with a large crowd of humanity, all looking, listening and apparently desiring some form of entertainment to help pass away the time, it occurred to the writer what a fine opportunity was presented for some equal suffrage speaker." When Carrie approached the committee on arrangements, her request was denied. Therefore, she made her points about suffrage in a letter to the editor which she ended with a quotation from "Woman Voter." It described New York women who believed women should stay at home rather than vote and who came to Wisconsin to say so:

> *They have packed their trunks and satchels*
> *They are rushing for the train.*
> *They are going to Wisconsin,*
> *Bound to fight with might and main.*
> *They have left their home and children,*
> *From their husbands far they roam,*
> *Just to tell the other women*
> *That a woman's place is home.*[16]

Just six weeks before the November 4th referendum, the Reverend Anna Howard Shaw, a Unitarian minister who had inherited the leadership of the suffrage movement from Susan B. Anthony, spoke in La Crosse. During the weekend of September 21 and 22, 1912, she addressed an audience at the La Crosse theater on Saturday evening and occupied the pulpit of St. Paul's Universalist Church the following morning.[17]

Just ten days before the referendum, the Franklin Club sponsored a debate, "Resolved, that the voters of Wisconsin should ratify the amendment to the state constitution granting woman's suffrage." Clara F. Wolfe of

Toledo, Ohio, and Rose Keefe of La Crosse argued the affirmative while Harry Robinson, Professor H. G. Hayden, and W. E. Barber "sustained the negative." A news article declared it "one of the most interesting and most largely attended debates of the year."[18]

During the campaign of 1911-12, suffragists made speeches, lobbied legislators, and developed support for a bill that would put to referendum a constitutional amendment giving the women of Wisconsin the right to vote. When the bill passed that spring, the suffragists began their statewide campaign to convince the male citizens to vote YES. Throughout the year, supporters spoke at every meeting, convention, and county fair, distributed pamphlets, marched in parades, and made an automobile tour during which they stopped to make speeches from the back of the vehicle. Late in 1911, however, strong opposition developed from the German-American Alliance and from the network of brewers, distillers, and distributors. The organized opposition combined with the conservatism of male voters defeated the referendum. Although 135,000 voters supported giving women the right to vote, more than 200,000 voted against the referendum.

The Nineteenth Amendment

World War I temporarily interrupted the suffrage campaign. However, Wisconsin women, with several decades of experience behind them, were ready when the U.S. Constitutional amendment was sent to the states for ratification. It generally has been taught that, because of the state's great progressive tradition, Wisconsin was the first state to ratify the Nineteenth Amendment. This is disputed by Genevieve McBride, author of *On Wisconsin Women*: "The progressive movement was neither very progressive nor a movement for Wisconsin women."[19] In her book about woman suffrage in Wisconsin, she wrote that Wisconsin was the first state to ratify because Wisconsin women were better organized. They had been fighting for their rights almost continuously for eighty years. In other states, which had granted the vote to women years before, suffrage groups had relaxed or disbanded. On June 10, 1919, the Illinois legislature ratified the amendment, more than one hour before Wisconsin. Nonetheless, Wisconsin was the first to deliver certification of ratification to Washington, D.C. Ada James, of Richland Center, who had worked tirelessly throughout the state for women's right to vote, convinced her father, former Senator David G. James, to deliver the ratification papers to the nation's capital so that Wisconsin might be given credit as the first state to ratify the Nineteenth Amendment.

Voting for the First Time

Even before the Nineteenth Amendment was ratified on August 26, 1920, local women were preparing to vote. In the spring of 1920, the La Crosse County Community Council developed a plan, under the direction of Helen Dorset, to acquaint women with voting. In April, the council sponsored classes at the Chamber of Commerce on voting and election methods.[20] As soon as the amendment became law, a registration day for women was set. The Community Council arranged to have two women at each polling place to assist other women when they registered to vote one week before the September 7th election. The newspaper announcement encouraged "every woman in La Crosse who has reached the age of 21 years" and lived in the city for one year and in her ward for ten days to register. The article assured each woman "she will not be asked to give her age, and will only be asked in a general way if she is 21 years old."[21]

By noon of registration day, it appeared that local women were "taking a deep interest in their new voting power and that a number much larger than was anticipated will be registered as bona fide electors of the state of Wisconsin."[22] The newspaper report continued, "The fact that they this morning left their housework in a season when canning is at its height, was taken to indicate that by closing time — 8 o'clock — tonight the total number of women registered will be large."

The Trades and Labor Council took steps "to familiarize the wives, daughters and mothers of the organized workers with the ballot" and to organize committees of women in every ward to get out the vote on election day. The Ladies' Auxiliaries of the brotherhoods of Locomotive Firemen and Engineers, Railway Trainmen and Car Repairers held a mass meeting at Woodman Hall on La Crosse's north side to hear speeches about candidates.[23]

On September 7, 1920, local women voted in their first election. A sample ballot for the election printed in the *La Crosse Tribune and Leader-Press* listed seventy-two candidates, all of whom appeared to be male, for seventeen offices ranging from governor to county surveyor. Ella Heider was the first of 114 women to cast her first vote in West Salem. Mrs. Math Oines was the first of forty-five women in the Town of Hamilton.[24]

The Next Step:
Serving in Public Office

Election Officials

In September 1920, three Holmen women became members of the election board: Mrs. Adolph Johnson and Mrs. Storm Gilbertson, ballot clerks; and Miss Nina Gullickson, election clerk. According to the newspaper report, "there will be one or two mere men hanging around but the women will do the work. The men are only going to sort of supervise the new officials."[25]

Tillie Zein was the first city of La Crosse woman to serve as an election official when she was the ballot clerk in the twelfth ward for the March 22, 1921, city primary. According to Tillie, her appointment was not related to women winning the vote. "As a matter of fact when they called me ... I thought it was a joke. Then it was explained they wanted me to serve in the absence of my husband who was ill."[26] Tillie, an employee of Doerflinger's Department Store for thirty-nine years, served as twelfth ward ballot clerk until 1933.

In 1924, the West Salem Study Club attempted to have women named to the election board. Despite arguments that "'green women' would slow up the count and that they must sit up until long after midnight counting the ballots," women were named as inspectors on the village election board.[27]

Lilian B. Tracey became Onalaska's first female clerk of elections, in 1934. Sixteen years later, all three clerks in the city were women: Floyde Sias, Clementine Thill, and Zaida Berg.[28]

Jury Duty

On February 6, 1922, many spectators, most of them women, crowded the circuit court room to witness the swearing in of the first women to serve on a jury in La Crosse. The female jurors were Susan Swarthout, Louise Tenneson, Bertha T. Hickisch and Cora M. Bangsberg, La Crosse; Anna Cullman, West Salem; Julia Mayo and Mabel Boersma, Onalaska. In his formal remarks to the jury (which also included William Kathary, Gus

Voight, W. J. Wsetecka, Fred Cook, and Albert Johns), Judge E. C. Higbee
said,

> *This is the first occasion in this circuit court when ladies have
> been called for jury service.... The struggle by women for equal
> participation in the affairs of government has been a long and
> arduous one and sometimes discouraging, but now that it is an
> accomplished fact, we are all more concerned with the question
> as to whether it is going to result in benefits to society or
> whether it is a detriment.*[29]

The jury found the defendant not guilty of arson.

Once women began to serve on juries, they also were appointed by the circuit court judge to be bailiffs. Cora Olson, who served as a bailiff from 1925 to 1950, believed the presence of a woman bailiff made female jurors "feel more at ease during their first unfamiliar experience in court procedure."[30] She also commended the women who served:

> *... in the past two years we have had about 125 women who
> have served, and none have ever been late for jury service. Many
> times it is a great effort for these women to serve as some of
> them drive over country roads that are muddy and slippery
> with snow and ice. I recall one woman juror who lived on a
> farm in one of the townships who arose at four-thirty and
> milked twenty-one cows each morning before coming to serve on
> the jury. Another woman juror had five little children and
> dropped one or two off at each neighbor as she came to jury
> service each morning, and each evening on her way home she
> picked them up again.*

Women took their new responsibility seriously.

School Board

When Ida Tilson was elected to the West Salem School Board in the 1920s, she became the first woman to hold that office.[31] In a 1941 referendum, Onalaska citizens voted 121 to 96 in favor of an elected school board. In the next election, voters chose Edna Schaller and Ida P. Johnson to fill two of the five seats.[32]

In December 1904, the Twentieth Century Club petitioned the mayor and city council of La Crosse to appoint at least one woman to the school board, preferably one from the north side and one from the south side of the city. "We further ask that her duties and privileges be the same in every respect as other members of the board."[33] In 1920, the La Crosse County Community Council adopted a resolution to support putting a woman on the school board. Mrs. E. C. Thompson led the vigorous campaign in which Community Council ward captains lobbied their aldermen.[34] When Flora E. (Hawkes) Lueck was named to the La Crosse School Board, a page-one story of the December 11, 1920, *La Crosse Tribune and Leader-Press*, declared her the "first of her sex in La Crosse elected to hold a city office." This was not exactly true because La Crosse citizens did not directly elect the school board until 1968, after a persistent campaign by the Citizens Education Committee. The day after the council's decision, the newspaper reported "a large gathering of women attended the [La Crosse city] council meeting Friday night and announcement of the election of Mrs. Lueck was greeted with a hearty sound by the audience."[35]

Through the years, the city council appointed a few women to serve on the school board. In 1968, Elizabeth Staley became the first woman selected in a direct election. In a 1970 interview, she said, "Woman's traditional role has been to care for people. Politicians are making important decisions about people (education, housing, environment, and using their hard-earned money), and women as well as men have a responsibility to become active in making these decisions."[36] After Carol Gundersen became the second elected female member (in 1970) and Linda Neumann the third (in 1971), the *La Crosse Tribune* published an article entitled "Women's Lib on School Board." It began, "They aren't burning any bras yet over at the La Crosse Area Public School District Board of Education, but the Women's Lib movement is gradually challenging this hallowed area of male dominance." The reporter did acknowledge that these three members of the board were interested in innovative programs for education, programs for students who were not college bound, increased emphasis on the board's public image, and equality of opportunity for girls, particularly in athletics. However, the article included phrases like "three of the fairer sex." It also mentioned that if two more were elected it would be "five girls and four men" and having women on the board is "distracting for reporters covering the sessions — after all none of the aldermen or county supervisors would do very much for a bikini."[37]

City Government

In 1926, Carrie Saunders became the first woman in Onalaska city government when she was elected to the first of her two terms as city treasurer. She was succeeded by Jessie Hammond in 1934 and Mabel Dunlap during the 1940s.[38] Since 1951, when Alice Dixon became the first woman to serve as city clerk in La Crosse, that position has been held by women: Alice Dixon, 1951-67; Shirley Tomalka, 1967-73; O'Nieta Thorsen, 1973-75; Aubrey Kroner, 1975-93; and Teri Lehrke, 1993-present.

Women began serving on city councils much later. In 1980, Ruth E. Root became the first woman elected to the Onalaska City Council. Seven years earlier, Sharon Imes was the first elected to the La Crosse Common Council on which she served until 1979. In the middle of her term, Sharon received a Bush Foundation Fellowship to earn a master's degree in public administration at the University of Wisconsin-Madison. "I was thinking about running for mayor," she said, "and thought it would be beneficial to have a broader knowledge of government than just the local perspective." When she lost her bid for mayor in 1979, Sharon applied to a new program to train people to mediate and arbitrate disputes between labor and management. She was one of thirteen selected to handle the workload expected to result from Wisconsin's new binding arbitration law for public sector employees. Sharon combined that training with her experiences in teaching and as an elected official to launch a new career as a labor-management arbitrator.[39]

Town and Village Government

When Minnie Kinney succeeded her husband as treasurer upon his death, she became the first woman official in the town of Medary. She served as treasurer from 1955 to 1958.[40] Della Berg of Bangor also succeeded her husband, Oscar, as treasurer of the village of Bangor when he died in 1972. When that term expired, she ran for election and re-election, eventually serving for twenty years. "The busiest part of my job was figuring and making out the tax bills. That was in the days before computers," she said. When Bangor combined the responsibilities of village clerk and treasurer in 1984, Della was elected to the new position. In addition to scheduling meetings and preparing minutes and reports, she collected dog license fees and paid bounties. In order to receive their bounty, people brought body parts of the animals to the village hall. "They brought them in glass jars, and I had to count mole feet and gopher tails, pay the bounty, and report to the county clerk," she recalled.[41]

County Government

When Lars Instenes died while serving as clerk of the circuit court in 1941, Judge Robert S. Cowie appointed Instenes's deputy, Gertrude Hoedebeck, to fill the position for the rest of the term. She was the first woman to hold that post, and she appointed Instenes's widow, Pearl, to serve as her deputy. In his announcement, Judge Cowie stated, "There have been a number of very creditable applicants for this important position, but I am making this appointment purely in the interests of the best service possible in the office. Miss Hoedebeck has been schooled under the leadership of Mr. Instenes for more than eight years and has proved her fidelity, ability and complete competency."[42]

Esther Domke, county clerk from 1927 to 1972, had a reputation as "a real polite politician. She was political all the time and you didn't even know it," said some of the men who met for coffee every morning at the Elite in downtown La Crosse.[43] Esther had been deputy clerk for five years when her predecessor died in office and she was appointed to succeed him. Her election to the post in 1928 was the first in a long series of primary and general election victories. She was the La Crosse County Republican Party's first female candidate for any public office, and she never lost an election. Although she always was active in the Republican Party, "she was never accused of playing political favorites," said former state senator Raymond Bice. "She was trusted and loved by everybody." Esther, a La Crosse native who grew up in the multi-ethnic neighborhood called "Goosetown," had a reputation for extraordinary service. She was known to open up the office at night or on weekends to help someone in need of fishing, hunting, marriage, or car licenses. "She took duplicate hunting licenses home with her. If they [hunters] lost them, they could come right to the home and get them," recalled the current county clerk, Sharon Mahlum Lemke.[44]

Alice Moore was the first woman to serve on the La Crosse County Board. In 1960, she was appointed to complete the last year of Donald Merwin's term when he resigned. Mary Hinsberger was the first woman elected to the county board. She served from 1962 to 1963 and then became the civil defense director for the county and the city. Mary was instrumental in establishing the civil defense warning siren which is tested on the first Monday of each month.[45]

Elizabeth (Betty) Gundersen was the first woman elected to the county board to serve multiple terms.[46] In 1972, she defeated longtime incumbent, Warner "Shorty" Kish. According to the initial count, Betty lost by eighteen votes. "However, someone from the Shelby Town Board called me to say something wasn't right," Betty recalled. "So I asked for a recount. Shelby was still using paper ballots then, and there were more ballots than there were people who had voted." Betty was declared the winner when the recount showed she had forty-five votes more than the incumbent. Her first resolution called for county meetings to be posted (on a bulletin board at the entrance to the county building). Prior to that time, there was no public notice of the meetings. Because she was the only woman on the county board, other members asked her, "What are you doing here? You should be home taking care of your children."[47]

In 1974, Sally Oswalt increased the female membership on the thirty-four member county board to two when she defeated the incumbent in her district. When asked how she was treated by the men, Sally said, "I felt like a piranha because I had defeated the man who had chaired the county board for quite some time. During the campaign, he said 'I've got some woman running against me, but I'm not worried at all.'"[48]

Two years later, Joyce Arthur defeated Sally Oswalt. "That was the first woman to woman election and a lot of people, especially women, didn't know what to do, how to vote," recalled Joyce who wanted to serve in order to have an impact on social services and the growing environmental issues.[49]

Pat Wiffler and Shirley Holman joined the county board in 1977 and 1978, respectively. Shirley recalled Pat's attempt to become a member of the county highway committee:

> *Some men told her they would support her but, when the vote came, they voted against her. Later someone told her that when the highway committee took trips, 'sometimes they needed to make a stop and go [relieve themselves] behind a tree and they wouldn't know what to do about that if she was on the committee and traveling with them.' So, at the next county board meeting, we women brought in three-pound coffee cans with a note on top that said, 'For your highway stops.' Some of them became angry.*[50]

Joyce, who retired from the board in 1984, said that public office "gave me a perspective far beyond the walls of home. I liked the issues, there were lots of them." Pat, who retired in 1986, enjoyed "the human dynamics. There was a perspective you just can't get from the newspaper. You had lots of information, people calling, and talking to people at parties about the issues." As Betty looked back on her fourteen years of county board service, she said, "I loved every minute of it. I love to argue. I love to fight. I love the issues. And I liked having a say in government, in changing something I thought needed to be changed." Shirley, whose service on the board spans three decades, continues to make progress in the areas that first interested her. "While doing volunteer work at Oak Forest Nursing Home in the late 1960s and early 1970s, I saw that it needed some things the county could and should supply. So I started going to county board meetings and thought, 'I can do as good a job as these men.'"

Political Parties and Organizations

Jean Wulling could not imagine herself as a member of the non-partisan League of Women Voters. "You have to behave yourself if you sit on the fence," she said. Jean gave her time to the La Crosse County Republican Women, an organization founded by Floyde Sias of Onalaska to support the cause of Republican candidates. Floyde enjoyed displaying her party loyalty in a variety of ways. She collected elephants, wore elephant jewelry, and named her German Shepherd "GOP." She was active at all levels, from helping a local candidate, to serving as president of the state's Federation of Republican Women, to being a delegate to the national convention. While the La Crosse County Republican Party members who were men did the strong-arm fundraising, the La Crosse County Republican Women held fundraising teas, boosted political party membership, and did the grassroots campaign work. Beginning with the Barry Goldwater presidential campaign in 1964, Jean staffed the local Republican headquarters. "I would be in headquarters every day from July through the November election organizing other volunteers to do mailings, make phone calls, and distribute literature," she said.[51]

For several years, Jean Wulling, Mina Satory, and Olga Schleiter contacted people by phone to renew their Republican membership. When Olga died in 1990, some people joked they would not have to pay their

Republican dues anymore. Olga's daughter, Linda Sherwood, said, "a lot of people just couldn't say no to her. She was so nice and always persistent, in a nice way. Some people probably voted Democratic but paid Republican dues because of her. I don't know for sure, but I think my mother was always a Republican. I remember that when one of her brothers ran for office in the county as a Democrat, she and her sisters were mortified." When Olga met Steve Gunderson in his bid for the U.S. Congress in 1980, she liked him. "Mother was his first supporter in this area, and she was determined that he would be elected, so she convinced influential La Crosse Republicans to support Steve," Linda said and then added, "I think it was a rather astute choice on her part because Steve has represented the district well and lasted a long time. Whenever he came back to the district, he visited my mother."[52]

Mary Muehr grew up in a Democratic household during Franklin Roosevelt's administration. She officially joined the Democratic Party when her hero, Adlai Stevenson, ran for President in 1952. The next year, she became secretary of the local party and, for four years, kept the minutes and sent out meeting notices for what she called the "party of the people." From 1959 to 1973, Mary kept "very good track" of the organization's money as its treasurer. When asked why she gave so much time to the party, she jokingly said, "No one else wanted the job." She also remarked that her philosophy was "if you believe in something, then you have to help the cause in any way possible."[53]

History professor Jean Helliesen joined the local Democratic Party in 1960. A few years later, she was spurred into action by her opposition to the war in Vietnam. Jean joined others who were disillusioned with the U.S. government policy and looked for a peace candidate to run against the incumbent president, Lyndon Johnson. She spent the first three months of 1968 trying to persuade voters to support Eugene McCarthy in Wisconsin's April presidential primary. "I'm not sure how LBJ's announcement on March 31st that he wouldn't run for re-election affected the outcome [but] the primary went off wonderfully. McCarthy took eight of the ten districts in Wisconsin," she said. That summer Jean attended the Democratic National Convention held in Chicago. She described it as a "fantastically brutal time … Robert Kennedy had been assassinated but there was a Kennedy faction at the convention and a McCarthy faction and an LBJ-Hubert Humphrey faction … and Chicago was under the control of Mayor Daley." There were delegations against the war and some concerned with issues of race. "The Mississippi black delegation's challenge to the white delegation at the 1964 convention in Atlantic City still had not been ironed out," she recalled. "Those of us in the Wisconsin delegation moved over on our seats to make room for some of the black delegates from southern states." The following summer, Jean was elected to the State Administrative Committee of the Wisconsin Democratic Party.[54]

During the 1970s and 1980s, many local Democratic politicians relied on Muriel Blackdeer's organizational skills. Sometimes she volunteered her time; other times she was paid for her abilities to organize the campaign volunteers, publish the candidate's schedule, and keep the news media informed about events and issues. In 1980, she served as paid office manager for the Al Baldus campaign for Congress. When John Medinger ran for the state senate in 1984, Muriel and Ellen Rosborough managed the campaign office.

From 1975 to 1981, U.S. Congressman Al Baldus employed Muriel as receptionist, secretary, office manager, and case worker in his local district office. Muriel met with constituents, listened to their problems, and did what she could to solve them. Veteran and Social Security issues could often be handled locally. She referred others to Washington, D.C., for action. Her "most satisfying case was helping Jimmie Gillmeister get his Air Force discharge changed from dishonorable to honorable."[55] The Air Force veteran's efforts through the Veteran's Administration, the American Legion, the Veterans of Foreign Wars, and previous third district congressmen had been unsuccessful. In 1975, Al Baldus assigned the problem to Muriel. "I made many, many phone calls and set up appointments for Jimmie so he could tell his story to the people that could make the change," she said.[56]

Without Political Affiliation

Other community women have been effective in politics without declaring a party affiliation. Local politician John Medinger described Sister Rita Jeanne Abicht, a member of the Franciscan Sisters of Perpetual Adoration, as, figuratively speaking, "carrying 100 votes in her hip pocket." Well-advised candidates learned that an interview with Sister Rita Jeanne was an important part of any campaign. When she decided to support someone, that candidate received an invitation to St. Rose Convent to address the sisters in residence. On election day, Sister Rita Jeanne scoured every nook of the convent to make sure each sister voted.

In the early 1970s, women who wanted to see more women in elected and appointed office organized the La Crosse County Chapter of the National Women's Political Caucus.[57] Although many already were active in the

Republican and Democratic parties, the League of Women Voters, and UW-La Crosse's Organization for Campus Women, they were extremely interested in an organization that focused on women's issues and involved women in politics. The Caucus held "So you want to run for office" workshops and campaigned for women who did seek public office. The first candidate to receive Caucus help was O'Nieta Thorsen, who ran for and was elected city clerk in 1973. Sally Oswalt was the second. In Sally's bid to unseat a major county board figure, "We knocked on every door in her district," recalled Caucus member Patricia Muller. The Caucus also endorsed candidates and made financial campaign contributions, "most commonly the queenly sum of $25."

During the decade of its existence, from the early 1970s to the early 1980s, the La Crosse Women's Political Caucus (WPC) helped raise the consciousness of the larger community. In response to La Crosse Mayor Patrick Zielke's comment that there were few women on city boards and committees because he did not know any qualified women,[58] the Caucus developed a list of well-qualified and interested women for his consideration.

Caucus members also lobbied for changes in how women were identified. They joined a statewide effort initiated in 1975 by the Wisconsin National Organization for Women (NOW) to require telephone companies to include a married woman's first name in the same listing with her husband's as the standard form in telephone directories. As part of DIAL (Directory Identity Action League), La Crosse members of WPC and NOW talked with telephone company representatives, solicited petition signatures, and obtained news coverage of their cause. Joan Rausch, who was appointments chairperson for La Crosse WPC, spoke at the Public Service Commission hearing in Madison on June 22, 1976. Although the attorneys representing the telephone companies raised several objections with the speakers, they did not object even once when Joan recounted her experience:

> *At a chance meeting with the Mayor of La Crosse on a*
> *Tuesday, I learned that there was an appointive position open*
> *on the Western Wisconsin Technical Institute Liaison Board*
> *and he would like the suggestion of a woman from the north*
> *side of La Crosse. I learned of someone through another source*
> *knowing only her first and last name. By the time I found her*
> *after calling several people to find out to whom she was*
> *married, contacted her and received her answer, by the time I*
> *contacted the Mayor on Friday afternoon, he was gone. By the*
> *time I contacted him on Monday, he had already made the*
> *appointment and therefore this valuable opportunity for this*
> *woman was lost.*[59]

Caucus members encouraged the *La Crosse Tribune* to refer to a woman by her own first name instead of her husband's and to end its practice of classifying employment advertisements by gender. Members also tried to convince one of the local medical centers that married women could be financially responsible persons in their own right. Therefore, they said, upon a woman's request, the clinic should send the bill to her in her name rather than in her husband's name.[60]

Not everyone appreciated the efforts of this group. When Caucus members marched in the 1975 Oktoberfest Maple Leaf Parade costumed as early feminists, they were alternately cheered and booed.

Members of Women's Political Caucus, National Organization for Women, American Association of University Women, La Crosse County Republican Women, La Crosse County Democratic Party, Business and Professional Women and the Girl Scouts marched in the Oktoberfest Maple Leaf Parade in La Crosse, 1975.

La Crosse Chapter of the National Women's Political Caucus

Social Causes

*We have no platform unless it is the care of women
and children and the home, the latter meaning the
four walls of the city as well as the four walls of brick
and mortar.*

General Federation of
Women's Clubs President, 1910

Clubs gave women an organized way to express their concerns about
social ills and to translate their ideas into social action. Some groups operated
on the local level only while others were local chapters of larger
organizations. By implementing their leadership skills, women became
important molders of public opinion. "The women of the early years of the city
were the ones most responsible for the establishment of our welfare
institutions," wrote Gloria Jackson in an article for the La Crosse County
Historical Society.[1] The fact that all of the organizations described in this
chapter, except for the La Crosse Woman's Industrial Exchange and the
La Crosse Women's Trade Union League, still serve the community today is a
testament to the clarity and commitment with which these groups defined
their original missions and then evolved with the changing times.

Young Ladies Mission Band
La Crosse Home for Children

Prominent young women of La Crosse formed the Young Ladies Mission
Band in 1883. To raise money for charities, it sponsored the community's first
Charity Ball in 1884. For years, this fundraiser was the social event of the
season. In 1888, the group determined that elderly, deserted, or destitute
women and neglected children were in need of care and shelter. Therefore,
they founded the Society of the La Crosse Home for Friendless Women and

Children and established a residence for them.[2] At first the board of managers, which was composed of fifteen women, sold membership subscriptions to raise $2,000 to support the Home for the Friendless. They supported the home in other ways, too. For instance, each morning Mrs. Gideon C. (Ellen J. Pennell) Hixon sent milk to the home from the cows kept in the Hixon barn.[3]

In 1937, the board narrowed its focus to caring for dependent or neglected children and changed the name to the La Crosse Home for Children. When board member Mrs. Harry (Eleanora) Gund died in 1958, she left her Cass Street residence to the children's home. It would have been very costly to alter the Gund house to comply with safety codes and to update the existing home, located at Eleventh and Ferry streets, which had aged considerably since it was acquired in 1891. Therefore, the board decided to sell both properties and build a new facility. When it came time to acquire new property, Mary Gundersen negotiated with the landowner to get the best price possible for the parcel at Weston Street and Losey Boulevard. The new home was dedicated on November 24, 1963. A few years later, men joined the board for the first time in the organization's history. In 1983, the La Crosse Home for Children merged with the La Crosse Family Welfare Association to form the Family and Children's Center. The new agency continues to devise and revise programs and services to meet the changing needs of families and children.

La Crosse Woman's Industrial Exchange

Some of the same women who served on the board of directors of the Home for the Friendless founded another early philanthropic organization in 1893, the La Crosse Woman's Industrial Exchange. No matter how desperate the need for an income, at the turn of the century there was a social stigma for the married woman who worked in public.[4] Like other communities across the country during an era of social activism, La Crosse established the industrial exchange to provide a way for women to earn some money without working outside the home by selling homemade goods through its store and restaurant.[5] One hundred fifty-seven La Crosse women signed on as initial subscribers and paid two dollars each to support it. The board met monthly to deal with the responsibilities of finding a good location, hiring managers, and raising additional funds.

Women looking for a way to earn some money brought in baked and preserved goods, needlework, and other handicrafts and were called depositors. They paid a flat fee of one dollar in order to sell through the Exchange plus a ten percent commission on each item sold. In November 1893, all but two or three of the depositors were self-supporting women. Because the Exchange preserved the anonymity of the depositors in order to preserve their dignity and pride, it is not known how many more than the original seventeen depositors participated.

The La Crosse Woman's Industrial Exchange conducted business in at least two downtown locations and employed three successive managers to keep track of the enterprise. Monthly sales income averaged just over $200 for the store and almost $150 for the restaurant, while commissions added $25. This income barely or rarely met the regular expenses of weekly payments to depositors; the manager's salary of $25 a month; groceries, meats, and sundries for the restaurant; rent, utilities, and advertising. The Exchange subscribers, many of whom belonged to leading social clubs of the community, sponsored dinners, musicales, ice cream socials, and a cookbook to raise additional funds. They also solicited contributions from businesses and other organizations.

The last entry in the La Crosse Woman's Industrial Exchange record book is dated April 3, 1895, and lists the board of directors, the officers, and members of the advisory board and of the committees for 1895-96. Available records do not reveal how long the Exchange existed, but it is clear that one hundred years ago women helped women in need by providing an outlet for selling their homemade goods.

La Crosse Women's
Trade Union League

Prior to World War I, many young women worked in domestic service. When factory jobs opened up for them during the war, they found the higher pay and weekends off very attractive even if other aspects of factory work left something to be desired. Protective legislation enacted in 1911 regarding working hours for women was meant to preserve their health and efficiency.

The law limited them to ten hours of labor in one day and fifty-five hours in a week. Night shift workers were limited to eight hours a night and forty-eight hours a week.[6]

Studies of working conditions and wages for women by the Wisconsin Industrial Commission (1913-14) and the Wisconsin Consumers' League (1918) revealed, first, that "wage earning women were not working for 'pin money'" and, second, that, in jobs held predominantly by women such as "in 10-cent stores, candy factories, shoe factories, and tobacco warehouses," the wages were low. During this period, the La Crosse Women's Trade Union League joined with Madison, Milwaukee, and Racine trade union leagues and the Young Women's Christian Association to campaign for better working conditions, specifically minimum wage standards.[7]

Young Women's Christian Association

In March 1903, the La Crosse Young Women's Christian Association (YWCA) opened its first facility in one room above Coren's Dry Goods, Cloaks, and Ladies Furnishings Store at 420 Main Street. Reflecting its concern for "the temporal, moral and religious welfare of self-supporting women," the organization offered classes and clubs in English, German, French, mandolin, Bible study, and sewing. Sunday Vespers featured local musicians and speakers — all with a religious background.

Continually looking for more space, particularly for physical activity, the YWCA relocated, in 1905, to the Mons Anderson house at Fourth and Cass streets and, in 1918, to the second and third floors at 420 Main Street. The second floor served as reading and rest space, club rooms, and offices; the third floor was converted to a full-sized gymnasium with showers and dressing rooms. During its early years, the YWCA served thousands of meals to working women who took advantage of the Y's Noon Rest program. It also served as a clearinghouse for women seeking work as domestics in the community. However, young women with enough ambition to move from the country to the city often wanted employment other than domestic service, something they had been all too familiar with at home. To meet this desire, the YWCA began to offer training in office skills.

In 1920, the La Crosse Business Women's Club raised money to purchase "Houck's Rest" on French Island and turned it over to the YWCA for operation as a camp for self-supporting women. Members of the fundraising campaign committee were Emma Roundblad, Wisconsin Pearl Button works; Anna Mashek and Mary Devine, public schools; Ella Ingwersen, La Crosse Hospital; Mae Hindmary, F. W. Kruse Company; and Otillie Sjolander, Torrance Foundry. Several young women who could not afford the time or money for a long vacation enjoyed an outdoor holiday at Camp Rest-A-While for just twenty-five cents a night. Three years later, the YWCA sold the French Island property and purchased land on Pettibone Island for a new camp, "The Open Door." The location, which was more convenient to the city, offered swimming, tennis, and miniature golf. Mrs. Ray Brink and Mrs. Charles (Mary) Hickisch managed the camp "until the ever changing Mississippi flooded the banks, washed away the tennis court, and the swimming pool became a dangerous whirlpool."[8]

In 1931, the YWCA purchased the Elsie Gile Scott home at Main Street and West Avenue. The cash down payment of $5,000 came from the endowment fund which was started when Sarah Clinton made a $100 bequest in 1910. Volunteers worked tirelessly to spruce up the spacious home and to convert the large stone coach house to a gymnasium. The mortgage of fifteen promissory notes of $1,000 each plus interest was paid off in fourteen years.

For three decades, the YWCA used the Scott home to offer programs to women and girls, sponsor lawn parties, and provide a lovely setting for various social events such as weddings, receptions, and teas. The elegant home and grounds also offered a meeting place for other organizations, religious and cultural. By the late 1950s, it was apparent that the YWCA needed better facilities and its own swimming pool to serve its members. Although the YWCA and the YMCA voted unanimously against merging in 1963, the two groups decided to embark on a cooperative effort to raise money for a new facility which they would share. More than 5,000 people attended the November 24, 1969, open house for the new structure.

In 1978, on the eve of its seventy-fifth anniversary, the La Crosse YWCA had over five thousand members, a history of one thousand programs and eight hundred volunteers, a budget of a quarter of a million dollars, and one-half of a three million dollar building. Attorney Maureen Kinney, who joined the board of directors that year, recalled that, "board meetings could not start until one-thirty in the afternoon so women could be at home to make lunch for their husbands. Now [nearly twenty years later] the meetings have to be at seven in the morning so board members can get to their own jobs."[9]

The Loreto Club

The Catholic Women's League (CWL) provided a similar facility and services for the Catholic community. The CWL, organized in 1915, received a home of its own in 1924 when Bishop Alexander J. McGavick offered property at the corner of Cass and Eleventh streets in La Crosse as a Catholic Community Center. The Loreto Club, so named by the bishop, was inspected by six hundred visitors when it opened on January 4, 1925. In addition to serving as a meeting place for CWL and other organizations, the Loreto Club also operated as a residence for self-supporting Catholic women. A 1925 newspaper article described this function as:

> *one of the most successful features of the club. On account of the strong demand for rooms, the transient guest room has been discontinued during the school year. It was deemed unwise to refuse regular residence to a self-supporting girl in order to care for the less constant transients. The occasional transient girl in need of help is cared for under club supervision by a cooperative arrangement with the Franciscan sisters. All the rooms are now filled by eager students or busy young working women. A few of the girls make daily use of the kitchenette, others take advantage of facilities only at weekends. All appreciate the artistic individual rooms, the liberal guest privileges, and the home-like atmosphere of the house.*[10]

Mary Louise Crotty, the social service secretary, was the first person in charge of the Loreto Club. By 1927, the directors realized a housemother was needed and hired Margaret Hambacher. The Loreto Club also organized the Joan of Arc Club for business girls, the St. Therese Club for girls engaged in domestic service, and the Junior League for high school girls.

The CWL undertook various fundraising activities to pay for the upkeep of the Loreto Club: annual food sales at Barron's Department Store, Aquinas cookie sales and bazaars, rummage sales, movies at the Rivoli and Hollywood theaters, a dance at the Avalon Ballroom, traditional card parties, and the popular "vanishing card parties." According to Genevieve Koenig, such parties were initiated by a hostess whose three guests paid for the opportunity to play cards. At the end of the afternoon, the guests "vanished" to their own homes where, on another day, they hosted their own parties. As the number of card parties and guests grew, so did the amount of money raised.

The Loreto Club also received income by renting rooms to students, mainly from the La Crosse Normal School, and to various community groups. Rosalie Lyga's dancing school brought in funds in 1931. When money was tight in the early years, individual members made low interest loans to cover continuing expenses, and the phrase "to pay bills as far as the money will reach" was frequently used.

Although CWL members did much of the cleaning and restoration, by 1946 the expenses of the aging, deteriorating house had become difficult to meet. Bishop John P. Treacy agreed to accept the property on behalf of the Diocese of La Crosse and to reimburse the CWL for the value of the furnishings and equipment. The following year the Loreto Club house was converted into La Crosse's first seminary.[11]

Red Cross

Although the first officers of the La Crosse Chapter of the American Red Cross were men, the first planning session was held in the home of Mrs. B. C. Smith in December 1915, and the first Red Cross office was located in the home of Emma Seide at 611 Pine Street. Emma served as the chapter's executive secretary from 1929 to 1954. The American Red Cross was chartered in 1881 by the U. S. Congress to provide special services to members of the U. S. Armed Forces and to disaster victims. During World War I, local volunteers made surgical dressings, bandages, garments, and comfort kits to be sent overseas.[12] On the homefront, they dealt with the deadly influenza epidemic which killed twenty-seven million worldwide. When the epidemic reached its peak in the United States in late October 1918, twenty-one thousand perished from the virus in just one week. Cora Olson went into homes to take care of the sick, especially young mothers and little babies who were the most vulnerable to the flu. Cora's daughter, Florence Whiting, recalled, "not any of us in our family ever got that deadly flu.... Mother wore a white uniform ... and she would take her clothing off in a little porch outside ... and she used to wash all the door knobs with Lysol."[13]

The very first group of Red Cross volunteers in La Crosse worked at the headquarters at 522 Main Street during World War I.

American Red Cross, La Crosse County Chapter

Eva Wolff's tenure as chapter chair spanned the years of Depression and war, from 1929 to 1946. When Eva's investigation revealed the number of children in need in the community, the Red Cross established the Children's Dental Clinic. After the need had been successfully demonstrated and met, the city of La Crosse took over the Dental Clinic in the 1930s.

During World War II, the Red Cross was a very important link between soldiers and their families. Trained volunteers staffed an office to help families of servicemen. There was a high level of activity in the area because of the close proximity of Camp McCoy.

An article on the women's page of the January 26, 1942, *La Crosse Tribune and Leader-Press* chided women who were not spending their time to the best advantage, i.e., doing volunteer work for the war effort. The article specifically mentioned the importance of Red Cross work.[14] Individuals and organizations met the challenge. Several women donated worn-out sheets which were ripped into widths of two, three and four inches and rolled "very, very tightly" into bandages. Others worked in production centers making kit bags for servicemen. During six months in 1944, the La Crosse chapter was expected to produce 982 kit bags. Each one had several compartments filled with articles for personal use plus a "housewife." The latter contained needles, safety pins, buttons, and thread. In August of that year, when Mrs. Emery (Minne A.) Leamer, production chair, announced that the quota had been reached in half the time allotted, she credited the work of Anna Bell and Nettie Hall. Anna had made 401 of the kit bags; Nettie had assembled 630 "housewives."[15]

Muriel Mitchell, wife of La Crosse State Teachers College president Rexford Mitchell, did Red Cross volunteer work almost full-time. Her daughters, Mitzi Carroll and Jane Aarstad, remembered that she used her background as a teacher of speech to publicize the work of the Red Cross. She spoke on the radio and addressed Rotary Clubs and PTAs. She also wrote articles for newpapers to reach readers in southwestern Wisconsin, southeastern Minnesota, and northeastern Iowa.[16]

The value of donated blood was proven during World War II. Badly wounded soldiers who received blood and plasma recovered more quickly. Therefore, the American Red Cross became involved in a blood donor program in 1946. Eleanore Wollschlaeger, affectionately known as "Mrs. Bloodmobile," recalled that the La Crosse chapter's first blood drive was held in 1950. It was sponsored by the Trane Company and yielded over 1,000 pints of blood in one week. Eleanore, who had been tapped by the Red Cross in 1929 to circle her block collecting money because "it was a good way to meet her new neighbors," received her "65 Years of Service" pin in 1994.[17]

The local Red Cross chapter provided disaster relief in its own backyard when the rivers flooded in the spring of 1965. The Mississippi River crested at 17.9 feet on Tuesday afternoon, April 20th, and held for four days before starting to recede.[18] The Red Cross and the Salvation Army began preparing in March and were still assisting flood victims into the summer. At the peak of the flood, the Red Cross fed hundreds of volunteer flood fighters and helped 137 families move their furniture to the former Auto-Lite building. Two hundred forty-six flood victim families registered with the Red Cross so it was able to respond to numerous inquiries from family and friends around the country. It also established a shelter at the Naval Reserve Training Center. The Andrew and Evelyn Vetsch family moved to the shelter when the river broke through a dike and flooded their home at 501 Sumner Street. "I could hear the noise of the water coming; it sounded like thunder. Our house was surrounded in ten minutes," Andrew said. "I was washing clothes and Rosie was outside hanging them up," Evelyn said. While she and their daughters gathered some of their belongings, Andrew went to get gas in the car. When he returned, the yard was covered waist-deep with water.[19]

Auxiliaries

Auxiliaries, groups that function in a supporting capacity, began emerging in late-nineteenth-century America. Many women's auxiliaries formed as parallel associations to men's work-related, patriotic, or fraternal organizations. For example, in 1900, wives of Onalaska lumbermen formed an organization to provide social activities for their families. The men's group was the Modern Woodmen; the women belonged to the Royal Neighbors of America.[20]

Patriotic Auxiliaries

One of Wisconsin's first patriotic women's societies was founded at La Crosse on June 26, 1884. The Wisconsin Chapter of the Woman's Relief Corps, the counterpart to the Civil War Union Veterans Association, assisted Union veterans and helped Civil War widows and orphans.[21]

When the Sons of the American Revolution refused admission to women, the female descendants of revolutionary soldiers formed the Daughters of the American Revolution (DAR). The La Crosse Chapter of the DAR was established December 11, 1896. Mrs. Angus (Mary Baker) Cameron, a founder of the La Crosse Chapter, became the first DAR national vice-president general elected from Wisconsin.[22] During the Spanish-American and world wars, the La Crosse chapter gathered items needed by soldiers and gave relief to veterans and their families. In 1916, the DAR sponsored Jane Addams's visit to La Crosse and entertained William Howard Taft after he left the presidency but before he ascended to the U. S. Supreme Court. The next year, members held teas for soldiers and gave a grand ball which raised six hundred fifty-three dollars for the Red Cross. The DAR participated in naturalization ceremonies for new citizens and sponsored the annual DAR Good Citizenship contest in La Crosse area high schools.[23]

Health Care Auxiliaries

A number of auxiliaries have supported private and public health care institutions. The La Crosse Shrine Auxiliary for Crippled Children was organized May 9, 1924, by twenty-three women who paid annual dues of one dollar each. The typical member from the 1920s to the 1960s was married and a full-time homemaker. That began to change in the 1970s when many members became more active outside the home — in professions, in business, and in other community organizations, sometimes employed, often as volunteers.

The purpose of the organization, to contribute funds and supplies to the Shrine Hospital for Crippled Children in Minneapolis, has remained constant. Through the years, the fundraising events have changed. Teas, desserts or salad luncheons paired with style shows were typical social and fundraising events until the late 1970s. Sometimes the Obreicht sisters, Mae and Julie, provided the music. Local shops, such as Kruezer's, Aletta's, Lottie's, and Kauma's, provided the furs, hats, and stylish apparel. These events eventually gave way to Syrian dinners, chili luncheons, and spaghetti dinners. The group sold cook books, de-linters, fruit cakes, and chances on an afghan, and sponsored bakeless bake sales and rummage sales. A rummage sale held in 1976 netted $200 "on a day that had at least 100 rummage sales listed" in the paper. In the early days, Shrine Auxiliary members were more likely to knit mittens to send to the hospital. As their fundraising became more successful, especially from the Cotton Ball dinner-dance and the Holiday Fair craft booth in the 1960s and 1970s, they sent larger and larger cash donations.[24]

In 1903, trustees of La Crosse Lutheran Hospital invited the wives of the ministers who were corporate members to set up a "ladies visiting board." It was not until 1950, however, that a small group of women, encouraged by nursing superintendent Bennora C. Lee, organized the La Crosse Lutheran Hospital Auxiliary.[25] The first officers of the group, also known as the Senior or the Women's Auxiliary, were: Mrs. Lawrence (Esther F.) Thrune, president; Mrs. Herman (Irene) Tietz, first vice-president; Dorothy Kumlin, second vice-president; Mrs. Carsten O. (ZeDona E.) Christiansen, treasurer; and Mrs. Robert (Murilla A.) Molzahn, secretary.

These volunteers assisted in recruiting nursing personnel, worked with the local Diabetes Reception Center, and helped with the Red Cross Blood Bank Program and blood drives. They also rolled surgical dressings, assisted newly-admitted patients to their rooms, made phone calls for nurses, delivered mail to patients, and helped in one office or another where needed.

Auxiliary members were on hand, too, to help clean up after the fire of February 1961. One of those, Mary Patros, was at the Cerise restaurant, playing cards, when she heard that Lutheran Hospital was on fire and the fire was out of control. "In those days, we wore high heels and were dressed up. I had my fur coat on," Mary remembered. Water from the fire hoses had frozen, so, when Mary arrived after the fire,"the whole street was like glass. Policemen weren't letting anyone in but I ran right between them into Emergency and said, 'What can I do?' They gave me a hospital gown and some boots and sent me up to the third floor where Dr. Robert Aiken and I swabbed the floor with sheet blankets."[26]

The auxiliary began raising money from its inception. An annual Silver Tea, a shopping cart to deliver small items such as candy bars and magazines to patients' rooms, a gift shop, and items handmade by the sewing committee provided $10,000 in the first ten years to purchase isolettes, medical books, wheelchairs, a Hubbard tank for physical therapy, and a resuscitator. Fundraising efforts intensified as membership grew in the 1960s and 1970s. In addition to augmenting hospital equipment, the auxiliary established endowment funds of $40,000 each for health career studies at Western Wisconsin Technical College, Viterbo College, and the University of Wisconsin-La Crosse.

In 1953, the Senior Auxiliary sponsored the formation of a Junior Auxiliary for working and university women, ages eighteen to thirty-five. There were sixteen charter members. The first officers were: Frances Fregin, president; Dagne Sivertson, vice-president; Mrs. John Ness, secretary; and Bonnie Wrobel, treasurer. Their efforts benefited the children's ward in particular and the hospital as a whole. The most successful fundraisers have been newborn baby portraits, the hospital's Flower Mart, and the biennial follies originally called "Pills-A-Poppin." The Junior Auxiliary, which eventually opened its membership to men, merged with the senior group in 1981 to become the Lutheran Hospital Auxiliary.

✧ ✧ ✧

One of the 105 charter members of the St. Francis Auxiliary said of women in the 1950s, "We were so unaware of what we were all about. No charter members worked outside the home. We made a career of volunteering." In 1952, these women set out to serve St. Francis Hospital and its patients, and to conduct fundraising projects in harmony with the hospital's philosphy. One of its earliest projects was the St. Francis Gift Shoppe. Members not only gave, they also gained. Their involvement in service and fundraising developed and exercised their administrative skills. They also learned some new ones, e.g., computer skills.[27]

From the beginning, the typical St. Francis auxiliary member was married with children. The membership more than tripled in the 1960s to 375 but then dropped to approximately 200 as women returned to work, diversified their volunteer activities, and spent more time with their children's increasing extracurricular activities. When St. Francis Hospital hired a paid director of volunteer services in 1968, the auxiliary began focusing more of its energies on fundraising. Both the hospital and the larger community have benefited. Since 1952, this all-volunteer group has raised almost one million dollars for equipment and services, scholarships, and needy patient accounts. Some of the more innovative fundraising projects initiated in the 1980s have been copied by other Wisconsin auxiliaries. These include the Geranium Sale for nursing scholarships, the Season of Lights to fund needy patient accounts, and the Tiny Tim Christmas Fantasy dinner-auction to benefit healthcare and community projects such as the St. Clare Health Mission for those with low income and no health insurance, New Horizons shelter and services for victims of domestic abuse, and D.A.R.E. drug education for school children sponsored by the La Crosse Police Department. As government and insurance funding of healthcare has changed, members have become more aware of the importance of what they have done and continue to do.

At one time, La Crosse County owned and managed three public health care institutions: the Poor Farm located at the south end of La Crosse; the Insane Asylum near West Salem; and the Oak Forest Tuberculosis Sanatorium in Onalaska. In 1953, the county opened a new 170-bed facility, called the La Crosse County Home and Infirmary, on the Poor Farm property. Except for two years, when she was treated for TB at Oak Forest, Marian Schnell was the activity director of the La Crosse County Home from 1953 until 1985. Looking for volunteers to help with activities for the residents, Marian initiated the first nursing home auxiliary in Wisconsin.[28] The La Crosse County Home Auxiliary organized in 1967. When the institution changed its name to Hillview, the group became the Hillview

Health Care Auxiliary. Members of the Hillview Auxiliary assisted with social hours, pancake breakfasts, church services, parties, picnics, and trips to parks and restaurants. They also sponsored bake sales, auctions and flea markets, chicken-cues and ice cream socials to raise money. Each Christmas they have given gifts to the residents. They have beautified the grounds by planting flowers each spring. In addition to serving others, they also have enjoyed friendship and fun with one another by "going out to breakfast or lunch several times a year" to celebrate the birthdays of auxiliary members, most of whom, in 1994, were retired or of retirement age.

When Oak Forest Nursing Home, the former tuberculosis sanatorium, closed in 1981 and Hillview was converted to small retirement apartments, the residents moved into a new 204-bed health care center. The Oak Forest Auxiliary, which had organized in 1971, disbanded but some of its members continued to bring joy and community involvement to county nursing home residents through the Hillview Auxiliary. In 1951, Katherine Schaller of Onalaska began playing organ for the weekly church services conducted at Oak Forest. When Oak Forest consolidated with Hillview, she just drove farther down the road to continue her volunteer music.[29]

Muriel Blackdeer began her volunteer work with the county nursing homes in 1960. "I was a member of the American Legion Auxiliary and heard about another member, living at Hillview, who would enjoy company. So I took my ukelele and sat at her bedside and played and sang. The nurses asked me to come back, so I returned to play the uke and the piano for more of the residents," she said. Music also was an integral part of Muriel's time at Oak Forest. She either volunteered or worked at the nursing home from 1970 until it closed. While she was an activities director, she organized the nursing home residents into the "Acorns" rhythm band. "In those years, people were in nursing homes because they had no place else to go. They weren't there because they were deathly sick or in wheelchairs or anything like that. They still were mobile; they just didn't have family. They felt special being part of a band," she said about the group which performed in other nursing homes in the area.[30]

La Crosse Association for
Responsible Citizens

A group of parents, led by Jule Kish, Irvin Otto, and Wilbert Wick, attended a fall 1954 La Crosse School Board meeting to request help in transporting their children to "a special class for mentally-retarded students." Although blind and deaf students from all over the school district were given free transportation to attend school at Washburn, these parents had to drive their children to and from the daily two-hour class at Jefferson Elementary. Because it was not always possible for working parents to meet this schedule, some had to count on an unreliable cab service which charged seventy-five cents one way. Within one week of their request, the city of La Crosse began paying for taxi service until arrangements were made for a school bus.

This was the beginning of LARC. The group incorporated in May 1955 as the La Crosse Association for Retarded Children. It later changed the name to La Crosse Association for Responsible Citizens. LARC worked closely with the La Crosse school district and, in particular, with Evan Lowrey, supervisor of special student services. The members set ambitious fundraising goals for 1955-56. Their aims were to establish a sheltered workshop, education and recreation programs, teacher scholarships, parent education, and a nursery. "We did lots and lots of fundraising," said Helen Senn, one of the original members. "We sold fresh baked goods at the Holiday Fair every year, held card parties, dances, and rummage sales, and went door-to-door asking for support." With the money, LARC provided scholarships to encourage teachers to become certified in special education. The early certified teachers, like Margaret Stark, Helen Nichols, and Dena Aldrich, were dedicated and often joined the organization.

The first members of LARC developed programs to benefit their own children. In 1956, Esther Wigdal's idea of a recreation program was put into action by Dorothy Wick, Eileen Otto, Clarabelle Brickson, Doris Williams, and Adeline Baumgartner. The children met one day a week during the summer at the Myrick Park shelter. "We started the day with crafts," said Dorothy, "and then the children visited the zoo animals while we set up lunch. High school girls volunteered to supervise. And supervision was essential because there always were 'runaways' who disappeared into the adjoining cemetery and other hiding places." Eventually the La Crosse Park and Recreation Department took over this program.

In 1958, LARC established a daycare center for all ages of developmentally-disabled citizens. It was one of five in the state licensed to operate with a staff of volunteers. Our Redeemer Lutheran Church donated the space. When more room was needed in 1967, it moved to the old Medary School on Highway 16. Eileen Otto, Bette Ware, Annette Felton, Eunice Frisbee, and Doris Williams were the volunteer staff. Lee Gaumer Cantwell Belles was the director.

The hard work of LARC volunteers and the one paid employee, administrative coordinator Margaret Sanford, has gone beyond benefiting their own children. Their commitment improved the lives of special needs citizens of all ages. The Coulee Region Developmental Center was organized to serve pre-schoolers. Cooperation with the schools has improved education for school-age children. Sheltered workshops such as Riverfront and ORC (Occupational Rehabilitation Center) made it possible for developmentally-disabled adults to earn an income and be semi-independent. In 1974, LARC purchased a house and remodeled it into a group home so mentally-handicapped adults in La Crosse and those returning from state institutions would have a supervised home in which to live.[31]

Daycare

Although there may have been private nursery schools and kindergartens as well as in-the-home babysitters, public nursery and daycare centers for young children did not exist until World War II. With money from the Lanham Act, the La Crosse School Board funded centers to take care of the children of women who had gone to work for the defense effort. Rose Bellerue was hired as program director of the centers which were housed at Roosevelt, Hamilton, and the La Crosse Adult and Vocational schools. They offered nursery daycare for two, three, and four year olds and extended daycare before and after school for children ages five through thirteen.[32]

When the war ended, so did the federal funding, and these centers shut down. Rose Bellerue, with board members and interested citizens, decided to continue a similar program "to serve the needs of working mothers and their children while helping the community benefit from the skills of women in such fields as nursing and teaching."[33] Until her retirement in 1971, she accommodated forty children on weekdays between the hours of 6:30 a.m. and 5:30 p.m. at the La Crosse Day Nursery at 1234 Ferry Street.

In the mid-1960s, Sharon Hughes began to wonder whether or not there was a need for more daycare services in the community. Sharon, whose background was nursing, was staying at home with her two pre-school age children. She also was a member of the League of Women Voters which, since 1955, had raised money for its treasury by conducting the biennial census required by state law of children under nineteen. The school district paid the League about eight cents per child identified in the census. Sharon agreed to chair the 1967 school census if she could also include a survey about daycare.[34]

Sharon Hughes was accompanied by her children as she conducted the school census and daycare survey by the League of Women Voters in La Crosse in 1967.

La Crosse Tribune

It took two months that spring for volunteers to visit every household in the La Crosse School District. The 1967 survey revealed that 1,583 of the households had children younger than thirteen, and that the mother worked outside the home in 841, or more than half, of those families. The women held jobs in offices, professions, factories, sales, service, and domestic work. Fourteen of them were students. The survey also found that more women wanted to be employed if only there were child care facilities available.[35]

Charlotte "Chardy" Shealy decided to join the League of Women Voters a year or two after moving to La Crosse in 1966. At the only League meeting she attended, she learned that a current project of the group was to finish the daycare survey and do something about the results. "That sounded interesting ... and I never had time to go to another League meeting because the daycare project seemed to take all my waking hours," she said. She gathered people she knew would be working members of a board, and they established the La Crosse Area Child Development Association, Inc. The board's first task was to convince the community of the need and to raise the money for a daycare center. At one Rotary Club meeting, Chardy was challenged by "a vocal group of irate men who believed women ought to stay at home." She countered with the survey results which showed the number of women with young children who already were in the workforce and in need of decent child care. "They still were not convinced," she recalled. "So I asked these men what would happen if they became injured or disabled and weren't able to work anymore and the only way for the family to survive was for their wife to go to work.... You could hear the dust fall."[36]

From left, The Rev. Ronald McMenamin, Mrs. Edward (Gerry) Perry and Robert Carroll were the founders of the Mobile Meals program, 1975.

La Crosse Tribune

Mobile Meals

When she was traveling in England, Gerry Perry learned about programs which delivered nutritious meals to elderly, ill and disabled people. In 1970, that idea came back to her while visiting an elderly member of her church. "She always looked so gray, and all she seemed to ever have for lunch or dinner was coffee," Gerry said about the housebound woman. "And, I thought, why can't we do that [prepare and deliver meals] in La Crosse?"[37]

Gerry contacted county supervisor Robert G. "Kootch" Carroll because "he was always helping others and was especially concerned about nutrition for the elderly. I also knew that he knew who else to tap." They enlisted the Reverend Ronald McMenamin, pastor of the North Presbyterian Church of La Crosse, and together these three organized Mobile Meals. The program established a board of directors and arranged with St. Francis Hospital to prepare the meals. Lutheran Hospital quickly offered to participate as well. Volunteers, recruited through a network of churches and service groups, delivered the daily noon-time meals. Mobile Meals served the first ten clients in November 1971. As the program approaches its twenty-fifth anniversary, hundreds of people receive not only nutritious food but also a friendly visit from the volunteer delivering the meal.

Reproductive Health Care

Birth of a Family Planning Clinic

"When my last pregnancy resulted in twins, I started thinking about women dealing with unexpected pregnancies," recalled Sally Steele Schaldach Salisbury. "I had been prepared for a fourth child, not fourth and fifth children. When I moved back to La Crosse with my husband and children in 1969, birth control devices were called 'indecent articles.' So I wondered what did women who didn't want to be pregnant do?"

What Sally did was join forces with her obstetrician, Dr. Jerome Gundersen, who had been conducting a family planning clinic one morning a week. She also attended a meeting of the Wisconsin Family Planning

Coordinating Council which fired her enthusiasm. Next she contacted several people who believed family planning should be available to all women, regardless of income. The group of supporters selected Edie Williams as chair and decided the center should act both as a referral service for those needing to see a social service agency or a doctor and as an educational outlet for providing information on the different types of birth control methods and their effectiveness. Dr. Clarence Van de Steeg, a local optometrist, donated two upstairs rooms in his office building at 125 North Fourth Street, for the center's use. Volunteers spent long, backbreaking hours painting walls and ceilings, refinishing donated furniture, and scrubbing floors in preparation for the February 1972 opening.[38]

The La Crosse Family Planning Center was financed by federal programs through the Wisconsin Health and Family Service Department. Beth Kilen, a nurse practitioner with the Community Action Program (CAP), gave family planning counseling training to volunteers who provided premarital counseling in relation to family planning and information on voluntary sterilization for both men and women, infertility, and adoption. Many of the first clients were married Catholic women with large families. Because of the Catholic Church's opposition to birth control, these women were reluctant to discuss family planning with their doctors who were associated with St. Francis Hospital. Unbeknownst to these women, Jerome Gundersen had enlisted support of other obstetricians/gynecologists in town. Therefore, "Sometimes the only service we provided these women was telling them their own doctor would help them in this regard," Jerome said. There also were sexually-active teenage girls in the community who, in seeking services from the clinic, were experiencing their first medical encounter beyond pediatrics and their first discussion about sexuality with an adult. Some critics thought the center was promoting out-of-wedlock sex, when, in reality, counselors presented a strong case for abstinence as well as methods of birth control.

Although sexuality issues were controversial, much of the community stood behind the clinic. Individuals from the university, St. Francis and Lutheran hospitals, clergy, county social services, and community leaders offered support. The only threat to the success of the fledgling La Crosse Family Planning Center came from the now defunct Western Wisconsin Health Systems (WWHS). The purpose of WWHS was to review health organizations in the area to prevent duplication of services and to cut health care costs. There was a period of nearly one year when the La Crosse Family Planning Center was constantly called before WWHS to defend its operations. "It amounted to harassment," said Marian Ramlow, who was not alone in believing local Right To Life activists, who strongly objected to the mission of the center, were prompting the review. The center prevailed.

For the first decade, most of the center's work was done by volunteers. The medical aspects of the clinic were supervised by Beth Kilen. In addition to Beth, Pat Mattie, a family planning outreach counselor for CAP, worked twenty hours a week at minimal pay. She held educational meetings in people's homes. "They were similar to Tupperware parties," said Pat, "except dessert and coffee were followed by movies and talk about birth control." She visited individual women in their homes, counseled clients at Riverfront, and provided schools with booklets entitled *Know Your Body*. "Blessed Sacrament Catholic School was the first school to request copies," Pat said.

In 1975, the family planning portion of CAP merged with the La Crosse program to form Coulee Region Family Planning Center, Inc., (CRFPC). In addition to La Crosse, the center served the counties of Crawford, Monroe, Richland, and Vernon. The center hired its first nurse practitioner in early 1979. Public policy and funding changed during the 1980s, and the clinic changed from being a referral service to one which provided comprehensive services. After several moves, the clinic found a permanent home in 1991 when it remodeled and subsequently purchased the Ben Franklin store on Caledonia Street on La Crosse's north side. At the same time the clinic, which had grown to six nurse practitioners and six family planning assistants, adopted a new name, "Options in Reproductive Care, Inc."

Birthright

In 1976, a group of women met in the La Crosse home of Mariel Carlisle to talk about initiating a crisis pregnancy service. What they wanted to do was give unconditional support to young women who were distressed by unwanted pregnancies. Although each of these women described herself as "pro-life," they did not want the group to have that image.[39] "We were not interested in political activity, and we did not want to be linked with any group that took a strong position on the controversial topic of unwanted pregnancy," said one of the original members, Judy Schmidt, who added, "we started out on a thread and a prayer." Their first step was to be listed in the phone book. Calls then were routed to the homes of volunteers on duty. The group, which thought it would take time for the word to spread, received twenty-six calls during the first month. The demand has continued with an average of four hundred calls each year.

Birthright never had to worry about money. At first the clinics provided free pregnancy testing. Then doctors took turns privately paying for pregnancy testing kits from their clinics. Clergy and psychiatrists donated counseling time. When a call came in, the first objective was to determine if the young woman was pregnant. Judy recalled one college student who, thinking she might have become pregnant during Oktoberfest, brought her urine specimen in a beer cup: "We thought that was ironic."

Test results were always given in person, never over the phone. If the results were positive, a member of Birthright was willing to be a support and a conduit to medical, professional, and/or psychological services the client might need. "We would go along when she told her parents, if she needed support in doing that. We were willing to help her through the pregnancy or to counsel her after an abortion — we knew that a certain percentage would choose abortion. What we wanted to do was help her understand all the possibilities before she made her own choice, and then stand by her if she needed us," Judy said.

New Horizons

In the late 1970s, as they became more aware of and alarmed about domestic violence, a few women started meeting to determine what they could do for battered women.[40] Sue Mercier, the adult and children creative activities director for the local YWCA, attended a day-long conference at UW-La Crosse on spousal abuse. "It was the first time I'd really thought about that issue," she recalled. Mary Anderson, head nurse at Lutheran Hospital's emergency room, had seen the physical evidence of abuse when women came in for treatment. Rita Jenks and Margaret Treu, who were teaching nursing at Viterbo, had learned about the problem from women they had counseled during a clinical part of their graduate work. "It was a real eye opener as I listened to my clients," Rita said.

The group's initial discussion spawned nearly as many ideas as there were people in attendance. One idea was a birthing house, another was an art gallery. The idea of a gallery as an outlet for women's creative works and a source of income for women in need was reminiscent of the La Crosse Woman's Industrial Exchange of the 1890s. However, there was a core that believed whatever was done for victims of domestic violence needed to be something that would be easy to articulate to the community. The group decided to focus on a shelter for the victims of domestic abuse who had nowhere else to go. New Horizons was established in 1978 as a program of the YWCA, and Sue became the liaison between the two.

La Crosse was the third community in Wisconsin to have a shelter in addition to a program of services. Other communities had programs but no shelters. The first of New Horizons' shelters was in the Lutheran Hospital Nurses Home. Although the location was confidential, one time a man came to the hospital looking for his wife and children. "He asked enough questions around the hospital until he found his family," recalled Maureen Kinney, who was on the YWCA board of directors and the advisory committee for New Horizons. Maureen took the woman and children into her own home for a week. "On the drive from the hospital to my house, the woman dove to the floor when she thought she saw her husband's car," Maureen recalled.

From the beginning, the YWCA and New Horizons worked to educate and gain the support of the community. The responses and reactions were mixed. In the political arena, State Assembly Representative John Medinger and State Senator Paul Offner were strong advocates. In the legal community, Roger LeGrand, who was district attorney at the time (1983-84), instituted mandatory arrest whenever violence was reported. Some of the "old guard" members of the police force were reluctant to get involved because they thought others should not interfere in what they considered family problems. However, Rita Jenks recalled that Jerry Patchell, of the La Crosse Police Department, was a strong supporter from the beginning. In the corporate medical community, St. Francis Hospital regarded New Horizons as an entity in its own right and responded favorably whenever asked for help, whereas Lutheran Hospital was interested in running the program itself. After a few months, the shelter shifted to a new location, an old house on Jackson Street offered by St. Francis Hospital.

In 1979, New Horizons worked with county extension agent Steve Taff to obtain funding for the county to buy a home for New Horizons to use. Because a zoning variance was needed to use the property as a shelter, the YWCA and New Horizons notified neighbors and invited them to an informational meeting. Some of the neighbors attended the public hearing and complained. "They didn't know what to expect," Sue said. "They imagined men with guns roaming their neighborhood looking for the women in the shelter. We hadn't been around long enough to have a track record. Mostly they were afraid of the unknown." When interviewed by a reporter after the meeting, Sue said, "I'm sure if the good Lord moved next door, neighbors would complain because too many people would come to visit."

Members of the county board spanned the spectrum from opponent to supporter. Ferdinand Sontag told Maureen, "I can't believe you would be involved in something like this — breaking up families and promoting divorce." Robert "Kootch" Carroll, however, asked key questions so representatives of New Horizons could make their points at county board meetings. New Horizons still uses the home the county purchased plus another large home which the group bought in 1989 after a successful fund drive.

As the group reflected on the reality of New Horizons, Sue said, "It's probably the greatest thing I've done — except for my four kids." That sentiment truly reflects the lives of many mothers. They have worked outside the four walls of their homes to improve the world around them, yet rank the raising of their children as their most important accomplishment — a sentiment that takes this book back to where it began: taking care of others.

✧ ✧ ✧

As early as the mid-nineteenth century, women's volunteer activities benefited La Crosse County and the world beyond. Their domestic skills of child rearing, sewing, and cooking served to develop youth into responsible citizens and to raise money for various causes. Their organizational, fundraising, and leadership skills improved life for the inhabitants of the community.

La Crosse echoed the social activism evident throughout the nation in the late nineteenth and early twentieth centuries. Local women identified problems and formed organizations to resolve them.

When the Nineteenth Amendment was finally ratified in 1920, it not only gave women the right to vote but also opened up opportunities for them to serve in official public capacities. There were a few pioneer jurors, school board members, and city officers.

During the Great Depression of the 1930s, a time when charitable efforts were needed more than ever, women met the challenge. They also tended to the cultural needs of the community by forming new literary and music societies to augment those already in existence.

Although, during World War II, the nation's needs required women to go into paid employment in support of the war effort, women still balanced volunteer work with their housework and employment.

After the war, women were encouraged to return to the home. They joined auxiliaries for local hospitals, served as school volunteers, and established new groups to serve the needs of their children.

Major changes in society began to occur in the 1960s. The environmental movement took on a new sense of urgency. Prior to that time, local women had protected Grandad Bluff, preserved natural habitats, and studied the condition of the water supply. However, Rachel Carson spawned a new era of environmental concern when she published *The Silent Spring* in 1962. Her book called public attention to the wasteful and destructive use of pesticides. Local teachers, scientists, and activists took up the call and worked to convince others to improve and protect the quality of our environment.

In 1963, Betty Friedan, in her book, *The Feminine Mystique*, protested the society that put pressure on women to be housewives only and not to seek a career. Her book was a turning point. Women, who had been active in the civil rights movement of the 1950s and 1960s, began campaigning for their own rights in the 1960s and 1970s. Women began to serve in leadership positions throughout the community previously held by men.

As a larger percentage of women joined the workforce, organizations adjusted to the reduced amount of time women had for volunteer activities. For example, church groups scheduled meetings less frequently and emphasized education of their members instead of time-consuming, labor-intensive projects.

In the 1970s, women concentrated on electing women to public office and judging candidates by their stands on issues of importance to women, such as the environment, welfare of women and children, reproductive choice, nutrition, education, the arts, and equal rights. Women also took action. They established daycare centers, a family planning clinic, home delivery of meals, and a shelter and program for victims of domestic violence.

The national trend to support the arts was reflected locally in the establishment of theatre and arts organizations as well as groups to promote the revival of traditional handwork such as embroidery and quilting that would encourage women in their creative endeavors.

The struggle for an amendment to guarantee equal rights absorbed women's energies in Wisconsin and throughout the nation during the 1970s. The federal version, "Equality of rights under the law shall not be denied or abridged by the United States or any state on account of sex," was first introduced in 1923, passed Congress in 1972, and died in 1982 when it fell three states short of the thirty-eight needed for ratification. The struggle for equal rights was much like that for the right to vote — time consuming and frustrating. Yet, to date, an equal rights amendment has not succeeded.

The community reaped tremendous benefits from women's volunteer work. In serving others, the women also gained. They broadened their own skills in fundraising, planning, and leadership. They acquired a more sophisticated understanding of the world around them. They formed lasting bonds of respect and affection for those with whom they worked toward a common cause.

Post–1980: A Snapshot

For decades and generations, women generally worked behind the scenes to improve their communities. Their efforts made it possible for women's roles to expand. While many women continue to work quietly, others have assumed more visible roles. These are some of the ways women have had an influence in the life of La Crosse County since 1980.

1981

La Crosse Lutheran Hospital formalized RTS Bereavement Services, which gives support to families whose babies die during pregnancy or at birth. The program was based on the practice of nurses Carolyn Smiley and Kathryn Goettl and directed by Rana Limbo and Sara Rich Wheeler.

Joan Pickett founded the La Crosse affiliate of the education and advocacy group, Alliance for the Mentally Ill (AMI).

Thomas and Jacqueline Rand, John and Barbara Burgess and Father James Mason organized the first La Crosse Community Thanksgiving Dinner.

1982

The Franciscan Sisters of Perpetual Adoration established the Franciscan Spirituality Center. Kathleen Kenkel, FSPA, was named the first director of the center for adult spiritual formation.

✧

Sylvia Boma was elected La Crosse County Sheriff.

1983

AVANT - Women in La Crosse Business Leadership was organized to give women a way to develop a business network similar to the ones men had enjoyed for decades.

Hixon Forest Nature Center was established by a citizen group as part of the network of nature trails through Hixon Forest and Myrick Marsh. Among the many hard-working environmentalists was Bobbie Wilson who volunteered as the center's director from 1983 to the fall of 1987.

1984

Skemp Clinic established the Center for Women's Health. The center's holistic approach included massage therapy and counseling services.

1986

The food pantry, West Avenue Food Emergency Resource (WAFER), directed by Phyllis Borleske, began to provide non-perishable food to the hungry.

1987

Beverly Simone was named district director of the Western Wisconsin Vocational, Technical and Adult Education District and chief executive officer of Western Wisconsin Technical Institute.

Anita Froegel, Patricia Heim, and Beverly Simone joined Rotary of La Crosse, the first women to become members of the previously all-male service club.

Women of Christ Episcopal Church established the Friendship Program to help the growing number of Southeast Asian refugees settling in the La Crosse area to learn the language and culture of their new home.

267

1988

Maureen Kinney became a co-leader and spokesperson for the Marsh Coalition, a collection of citizen groups working to preserve Myrick Marsh.

1991

Judith Kuipers was selected as chancellor of the University of Wisconsin-La Crosse.

Bridget Belgiovine became Athletic Director at the University of Wisconsin-La Crosse.

1992

Citizens concerned about the need for affordable housing established a Habitat for Humanity affiliate and began to build, restore and help finance homes. Sharon Kannenberg served as the group's first president.

April Ulring Larson was elected bishop of the La Crosse Synod of the Evangelical Lutheran Church of America. Her election made her the first woman in the nation and the second worldwide to serve in that post of the Lutheran Church.

Sharon Imes became president of Rotary of La Crosse.

1993

St. Clare Health Mission opened its doors to provide health care to those who otherwise would receive none. Sister Leclare Beres, R. N., a member of the Franciscan Sisters of Perpetual Adoration, was named director of the Mission.

Pauline Jackson, a psychiatrist at Gundersen Clinic and Lutheran Hospital, was elected president of the State Medical Society of Wisconsin.

1994

La Crosse Central High School girls' basketball team placed second in the Wisconsin Interscholastic Athletic Association Divison I championship series in 1994 and 1995.

1995

Amy Mills was named conductor and music director of the La Crosse Symphony Orchestra.

Sylvia Finch was elected president of the Village of Holmen.

✧

Holmen High School girls' basketball team won the Wisconsin Interscholastic Athletic Association Division 2 championship.

✧

Ramona Gonzalez was elected La Crosse County Circuit Court Judge.

✧

Brigit E. Brown became the first woman and the first UW-La Crosse student to serve as the student member of the University of Wisconsin System Board of Regents.

✧

Barbara Frank served as chair of the Lutheran Hospital Corporation Trustees and was one of the key members of the committee that planned and directed the merger of Gundersen Clinic with Lutheran Hospital.

✧

Shirley Holman was elected president of the Wisconsin Counties Association.

1996

Aquinas High School girls' basketball team won the Wisconsin Independent Schools Athletic Association state championship.

Just under twenty percent of the physicians at Franciscan Skemp Healthcare and at Gundersen Lutheran Medical Center were women.

Notes

INTRODUCTION

1. Nancy M. Neuman, *The League of Women Voters in Perspective 1920-1995* (Washington, D.C.: League of Women Voters of the United States, 1994), p. 4.
2. "City Woman Recalls Early Days of U.N.," *La Crosse Tribune*, Oct. 22, 1967, p. 15.

IN THE HOME

1. "The Homemaker and Her Working Conditions," Co-operative Extension Work in Agriculture and Home Economics, State of Wisconsin, n.d. [late 1930s/early 1940s?].
2. Linda K. Kerber, *Women of the Republic*.
3. Jeanne Boydston, "The Pastoralization of Housework," in L. Kerber and J. DeHart, *Women's America*, pp. 148-161. Other books which provided a helpful description of the evolution of the American woman's role in the home and beyond include: Ruth Schwartz Cowan, *More Work for Mother*; Sheila M. Rothman, *Woman's Proper Place*; and Susan Strasser, *Never Done*.

CAREGIVING

1. "Priscilla Anderson Dvorak Interview," Jan. 25, 1995.
2. "Della Feak Berg Interview," Feb. 1, 1995.
3. "Campus Dames Book Group Interview," Jan. 24, 1995. Members present were Jane Aarstad, Joyce Arthur, Terry Coulombe, Diane Gagne, Beth Roskos, Mary Lou Ryan, Karen Taylor, Mary Fran Winrich and Kathy Witzke.
4. Ibid.
5. Ibid.
6. "Mildred Nelson Interview" by La Crosse Central High School student Anna Collins, Nov. 30, 1994.
7. "Campus Dames Book Group Interview."
8. "Della Feak Berg Interview."
9. "Marian Schlabach Ramlow Interview," Jan. 23, 1995.
10. "Donald 'Chick' Meinert Interview," Aug. 22, 1995.
11. "Flora Brooks Interview," June 14, 1994.
12. "Campus Dames Book Group Interview."
13. "Della Feak Berg Interview."
14. "Thelma Orr Zumach Stokes and Marion Zumach Hopkins Interview," Nov. 16, 1994.
15. The Social Security Act of 1935 established the La Crosse County Department of Social Services. "Social Services Have Been Expanded," *La Crosse Tribune*, Sept. 20, 1979, p. 45.
16. "Beverly Broadhead Ranis Interview," Dec. 28, 1994, and Jan. 16, 1995.
17. "Sue Strehl Interview," Jan. 18, 1995.
18. "Martin and Martina Twite: A History of the Twite Family," compiled by Josie Broadhead and Tina Tangen, 1990; "Broadhead Ancestral Treasures," compiled by Josie Broadhead, 1981.
19. "Josie," a collection of Josie Broadhead's writing, 1994.

LABOR INTENSIVE HOUSEKEEPING

1. "Ruth Snodgrass Interview," Feb. 25, 1995.
2. Ibid.
3. "Betty Lamb Dell Hyde Interview," Dec. 29, 1994, and Jan. 12, 1995.
4. "Mary Lou Brown Rudolph Interview," Apr. 28, 1995.
5. Recollection of Marian Ramlow and Margaret Fish, Mar. 13, 1995.
6. "Florence Munson Interview," Oct. 7 and 8, 1980.
7. Estella Krohn Bryhn, *Around the Coulees*, pp. 133-4.
8. Susan Strasser, *Never Done*, p. 78.
9. "Mary Lou Brown Rudolph Interview."
10. "Della Feak Berg Interview," Feb. 1, 1995.
11. "Ruth Snodgrass Interview."
12. Strasser, *Never Done*, p. 131.
13. "Helen Hanson Interview," Aug. 16, 1994, and Apr. 3, 1995.
14. "Della Feak Berg Interview."
15. Strasser, *Never Done*, p. 272.
16. "Irene Radcliffe Interview," Nov. 7, 1994.
17. Doug Connell, ed., *La Crosse Time Trip, 1944* (La Crosse, Wisconsin: La Crosse History Works, 1994), p. 8.
18. "Ruth Snodgrass Interview."
19. "Mary Lou Brown Rudolph Interview."
20. "Jean Wulling Interview," Dec. 7, 1994.
21. Interview with Suellen Hoy on National Public Radio's "Weekend Edition," Aug. 6, 1995. Hoy is the author of *Chasing Dirt: The American Pursuit of Cleanliness*.
22. Ibid.

DOMESTIC SCIENCE

1. Susan Strasser, *Never Done*, p. 212.
2. "Betty Lamb Dell Hyde Interview," Dec. 29, 1994, and Jan. 12, 1995.
3. "Doris Flick Interview," Jan. 16, 1995.
4. This section based on: "Silver Anniversary of La Crosse County Homemakers Association, 1920-1945" printed program; Evelyn Burand Young, *Historical Review of La Crosse County Homemakers* [1980?]; various project circulars prepared by Home Economics Extension Service, College of Agriculture, University of Wisconsin, Madison, and by Cooperative Extension Programs, University of Wisconsin-Extension; various newsletters from La Crosse County extension home economists; La Crosse County Extension Homemakers, *Club Histories*; and Cora Olson speech to Webster Homemakers Club, n.d. [1930s?].
5. "Marge Hughes Gollnik Interview," Nov. 2, 1994.
6. La Crosse County Extension Homemakers, *Club Histories* (La Crosse County: 1981), p. 56.
7. Shelley Goldbloom, "Emerson Club Members Thrive on Enthusiasm," *La Crosse Tribune*, n.d. [1978/1979?].
8. Various undated announcements and articles promoting the "Save a Woman" campaign from local March 1972 newspapers collected in a September 1970 - September 1972 scrapbook about La Crosse County Extension Homemakers provided by Marge Gollnik.
9. "Marge Hughes Gollnik Interview."
10. Interview with Alice Nuttleman by Mary Meehan-Strub and Marge Gollnik for *The Impact of Her Spirit*, A 50th Anniversary Project of Wisconsin Extension Homemakers' Council, Inc., June 1986.
11. Interview with Effie Knudson and Helen Hulberg by Judy Rommel and Marge Gollnik for *The Impact of Her Spirit*, June 1985.

RURAL LIVING

1. Hazel Heider correspondence with West Salem High School student Jennifer Keller; Hazel Rahn Heider, *Along the Waterloo Road*, p. 73.
2. "Irene Kreisel Schaller Interview," Nov. 18, 1994.
3. Forrest McDonald, *Let There Be Light,* pp. 10, 81-3, 281-2; Trempealeau Electric Cooperative, "Official Notice of 25th Annual Meeting and Operating Report for Year 1961," Oct. 6, 1962; Yung-Sze Tso, "Rural Electric Co-ops in Wisconsin" (Master's thesis, University of Wisconsin [Madison], 1949).
4. Yung-Sze Tso, "Rural Electric Co-ops in Wisconsin," p. 22.
5. "Marge Hughes Gollnik Interview," Nov. 2, 1994.
6. Dolbier and Dolbier, *From Sawmills to Sunfish*, pp. 87-88; "Eleanor Kinney Robinson Interview" by Onalaska High School student Kasey Heth, Dec. 12, 1994.
7. Dolbier and Dolbier, pp. 79-80.
8. "Vernetta Witte Romskog Interview," Nov. 21, 1994, and Aug. 14, 1995.
9. "Shirley Dummer Interview," Dec. 30, 1994, and Jan. 18, 1995.
10. Shirley Dummer, *NFO in Wisconsin — A Dream, A Challenge, A Reality* (National Farmers Organization of Wisconsin, 1984).
11. Priscilla Salant, William Saupe & John Belknap, "Highlights of the 1983 Wisconsin Family Farm Survey," The Research Division of the College of Agricultural & Life Science, University of Wisconsin, Madison, Publication R3294.

MAKING DO

1. Errol Kindschy, *Leonard's Dream*, p. 85.
2. Cora Olson speech to Webster School Homemakers Club, n.d. [1930s?].
3. "Carroll Gundersen Interview," 1972 and 1973.
4. "Priscilla Anderson Dvorak Interview," Jan. 25, 1995.
5. "Florence Munson Interview," Oct. 7 and 8, 1980.
6. "Campus Dames Book Group Interview," Jan. 24, 1995.
7. "City Food Stores Close at 6 P.M.," *La Crosse Tribune and Leader-Press*, Jan. 26, 1942, p. 2.
8. "Community Joins Country to Register for Rationing Books," *La Crosse Tribune and Leader-Press*, May 5, 1942, p. 1.
9. "Housewife's Headaches Commence as Point Rationing Sales Start," *La Crosse Tribune and Leader-Press*, Mar. 1, 1943, p. 1.
10. "Ruth Snodgrass Interview," Feb. 25, 1995.
11. "How to Live for Less," *La Crosse Tribune and Leader-Press*, Jan. 25, 1942, p. 2.
12. "Mitzi Mitchell Carroll and Jane Mitchell Aarstad Interview," Feb. 1, 1995.
13. "Send Shipment of Nylon, Silk Hose from City," *La Crosse Tribune and Leader-Press*, Feb. 23, 1943, p. 3; Advertisement, *La Crosse Tribune and Leader-Press*, Apr. 1, 1943, p. 5.
14. "Ruth Snodgrass Interview."
15. "Remaking Garments, Food Preparation, Repair of Equipment, Popular School Women's Classes," *La Crosse Tribune and Leader-Press*, Dec. 5, 1943, p. 7.
16. "Lilly Hendrickson Interview," Jan. 9, 1995.
17. "La Crosse Girls All Out at McCoy Service Club Dances," *La Crosse Tribune and Leader-Press*, Nov. 23, 1943, p. 12; "Priscilla Anderson Dvorak Interview."
18. "New Residents Shivering from Cold, Wonder about Heat for Their Rooms," *La Crosse Tribune and Leader-Press*, Nov. 14, 1943, p. 9.
19. "Della Feak Berg Interview," Feb. 1, 1995.
20. "Eleanore Wollschlaeger Interview," Dec. 11, 1994.
21. "Florence Olson Whiting Interview," June 14, 1994.

BEYOND THE HOME

1. "Florence Olson Whiting Interview," June 14, 1994.
2. Brett Harvey, *The Fifties*, p. 129.
3. Ibid., p. 71.
4. Ruth Schwartz Cowan, *More Work for Mother*, pp. 178-9.
5. This section based on Joann Vanek, "Time Spent in Housework," *Scientific American* 231 (November 1974), pp. 116-120; and Cowan, *More Work for Mother*.
6. "Campus Dames Book Group Interview," Jan. 24, 1995.
7. Alice Kessler-Harris, *Women Have Always Worked*, p. 130.

IN THE WORKPLACE

1. Alice Kessler-Harris, *Women Have Always Worked*, pp. 77 & 80.
2. Ibid., p. 80

HEALERS AND HELPERS

1. The general historical framework for this section on nursing was condensed from background information prepared for this book by Mary Van Atta. Her sources included: Celia Davies, ed., *Rewriting Nursing History*; Barbara Melosh, *The Physician's Hand*; Martha Vicinus, *Independent Women*.
2. Virginia Marcotte Larkin, "A Tradition of Caring," *Past, Present & Future*, La Crosse County Historical Society, Vol. 11, No. 4, July 1989, pp. 12-16.
3. Ibid., p. 12.
4. Lutheran Hospital - La Crosse Nursing Alumnae reminiscing session, Oct. 26, 1994, attended by Irene Barsness Albrechtson (1931), Agnes Burt Garthus Amble (1931), Inga Sorenson Larsson Benrud (1930), Clarissa Larson Espeland (1930), Marguerite Schroeder Figge Goodermote (1932), Margaret Steuernagel Griffel (1930), Evelyn Harder (c. 1930), Dorothy Ahlstrom Harman (1926), Myrtle S. Onsrud (1932), Helen Thompson Revor (1931), Frances T. Spande (1924), Vivian Paulson Veum (1932), and Effie Nelson Vigness (1931).
5. Melosh, *The Physician's Hand*, pp. 77-111.
6. "Evelyn Hoover Interview," Dec. 11, 1994.
7. Lutheran Hospital - La Crosse Nursing Alumnae reminiscing session.
8. "Lilly Hendrickson Interview," Sept. 11, 1995.
9. Melosh, *The Physician's Hand*, p. 70.
10. Ibid., pp. 182-3.
11. "Sister Grace Clare Beznouz Interview," Dec. 1, 1994.
12. Notes compiled by La Crosse Central High School student Kristin Duresky based on "A Day of Study in the Busy Life of a Student Nurse," *La Crosse Tribune*, Nov. 17, 1966, p. 9.
13. Sister Theodine Sebold, FSPA, *Continuity and Change*, p. 116.
14. "Sister Grace Clare Beznouz Interview."
15. "Maddeline Schuldes and Florence Campbell Interview," Nov. 30, 1994.
16. Ibid.
17. "LPN Dorothy Mercier is Scrub-Nurse for Neurosurgeon, Dr. C. N. Shealy," *The Accolade*, Coleman Technical Institute, La Crosse, Wisconsin, February 1968, p. 5.
18. "Schuldes and Campbell Interview."
19. "Opening Day is Auspicious," *La Crosse Daily Republican and Leader*, May 14, 1901, p. 2.
20. "Head of Hospital in City Succumbs," *La Crosse Tribune and Leader-Press*, Mar. 16, 1942, pp. 1-2.
21. "Miss Horn Retiring as Hospital Administrator; Phelps Named," *La Crosse Tribune*, May 27, 1956, p. 5.
22. "Evelyn Hoover Interview."

23. "Nancy Fitzpatrick Interview," Dec. 13, 1994.
24. "June Kjome Interview," Dec. 1, 9, 21, 1994.
25. Melosh, pp. 134-5, 153-7.
26. "Priscilla Anderson Dvorak Interview," Jan. 25, 1995.
27. This section based on "Helen Hanson Interview," Aug. 16, 1994, and Apr. 3, 1995; notes compiled by Myrna Peacock in her review of Annual Reports to the La Crosse County Board by the County Nurse, 1919-1971.
28. "Health Board Acts To Curb Polio Here," *La Crosse Tribune and Leader-Press*, Sept. 19, 1945, p. 1.
29. "1954 Field Trials Launched Polio Vaccine Success Here," *La Crosse Sunday Tribune*, Apr. 8, 1962, p. 4.
30. This section based on John and Joan Dolbier, *From Sawmills to Sunfish*, pp. 243-4; Ken Brekke, "TB: Dreaded Killer of Years Past," *La Crosse Tribune*, Apr. 10, 1988, pp. 1 & 10; and "Myrtle Carlson Interview," Feb. 24, 1995.
31. Karen E. Glasser, Cynthia Delano, and Paul D. Silva, "The History and Current Status of Nurse Midwifery in Wisconsin," *Wisconsin Medical Journal*, February 1992, pp. 67-70. Marilyn Van Wyk synthesized the articles, interviews and notes collected for this section on midwifery.
32. Information on the life and work of Mary Gerrard based on Carol Westerlund Gundersen's research on midwifery in La Crosse.
33. Carolyn Nelson, "La Crosse Healers: A Checklist of Physicians, Midwives, Dentists, Chiropractors and Miscellaneous Practitioners in the City of La Crosse from the 1840s to the 1940s" (La Crosse, Wisconsin: Murphy Library, University of Wisconsin-La Crosse, 1977).
34. Judith Walzer Leavitt, "Public Health: Then and Now," *American Journal of Public Health*, October 1988, pp. 1353-60; Judith P. Rooks, "Nurse-Midwifery: The Window Is Wide Open," *American Journal of Nursing*, December 1990, pp. 31-36.
35. Rooks, *"Nurse-Midwifery,"* p. 31.
36. Lutheran Hospital - La Crosse Nursing Alumnae reminiscing session.
37. "Campus Dames Book Group Interview."
38. Letter from J. R. Richter, M.D., to Joyce Arthur, July 23, 1969.
39. Letter from Maureen Guillan to Joyce Arthur, July 17, 1969.
40. "Campus Dames Book Group Interview."
41. "Cynthia Thompson Delano and Linda Hirsh Interview," Feb. 28, 1995.
42. Virginia Sapiro, *Women in American Society*, pp. 148-9.
43. Joan Janis synthesized the articles, interviews and notes collected for this section on physicians.
44. Ida Tilson, "Dr. Mary Elizabeth Lottridge," La Crosse County Historical Sketches; "2nd Woman Doctor in U.S. Practiced Here for 40 Years," *West Salem (Wis.) Journal*, Feb. 6, 1969; Richard Boudreau, "Books Ignore Medical, Feminist Pacesetter," *St. Paul Sunday Pioneer Press*, Wisconsin Edition, Sept. 21, 1975, p. 8.
45. Nelson, "La Crosse Healers."
46. "The Swarthout Family," *Past, Present & Future*, La Crosse County Historical Society, Vol. 11, No. 2, March 1989, pp. 1, 3-6.
47. "New Main Floor Offices for Physician Latest Improvement Made at State Teachers College," *La Crosse Tribune and Leader-Press*, Nov. 2, 1941; Marjorie Von Arx, R.N., "History of the Health Service, Wisconsin State University, La Crosse, Wisconsin," June 1967, for *New Perspectives in College Health Nursing*; George R. Gilkey, *The First Seventy Years*, pp. 149, 151, 155; "La Crosse State Teachers College Student Health Service, Second Semester 1942-43," In Student Health Service file, Special Collections Department, Murphy Library, University of Wisconsin-La Crosse; "Dr. Sarah Bangsberg Resigns Position at Teachers College," *La Crosse Tribune*, July 16, 1944, p. 12.
48. Dolbier and Dolbier, *From Sawmills to Sunfish*, pp. 262-3.
49. "Gretchen Guernsey Interview," Feb. 1, 1995.
50. Ibid.
51. "Mary Scheurich Maney Interview," Feb. 2, 1995.
52. "Ruth Dalton Interview," Jan. 30, 1995.

53. Richard Boudreau, "She Ran Clinic's 'One-Man Pharmacy,'" *La Crosse Tribune*, Sept. 20, 1979, p. 34; Stanley L. Sims, *La Crosse Lutheran Hospital*, p. 136.
54. "Women Win St. Francis Award," *La Crosse Tribune*, Dec. 16, 1994, p. B-5.
55. Mary Lou Ryan synthesized the articles, interviews and notes she collected on hospice: 1995 conversations with Terri Pedace, director of Unity Home Health Care, and Marilyn McElligott, director of volunteers at Lutheran Hospital; St. Francis Hospice brochure; Unity Hospice Volunteer Program training materials; and her personal journal entries from 1982 when she volunteered with St. Francis Hospice.

EDUCATORS

1. Catharine E. Beecher, *An Essay on the Education of Female Teachers* (New York, 1835), cited in Sheila M. Rothman, *Woman's Proper Place*, p. 57.
2. The general historical framework for this chapter based on Alice Kessler-Harris, *Out To Work*; Ruth De Young Kohler, *The Story of Wisconsin Women*; Sheila M. Rothman, *Woman's Proper Place*; Kathryn Kish Sklar, "Catharine Beecher: Transforming the Teaching Profession," in L. Kerber and J. DeHart, eds., *Women's America*, pp. 171-8.
3. Virginia Sapiro, *Women in American Society*, pp. 363-6.
4. Information on the brief teaching career of Mary Eveline Bagley Smith compiled by Gloria Bailey Jackson from *History of La Crosse County, Wisconsin*, p. 515; Albert H. Sanford and H. J. Hirshheimer, *A History of La Crosse, Wisconsin*, 1841-1900, p. 61; H. Shepardson, "Early School Days in the Old Third Ward School Recalled by First Pupils," *La Crosse Tribune and Leader-Press*, Jan. 27, 1924, p. 9; and La Crosse County Register of Deeds, *Marriage Records*, Vol. 1, p. 13.
5. Errol Kindschy, *Leonard's Dream*, p. 22.
6. Estella Bryhn, *Early Schools of La Crosse County*, pp. 128-9; "Mrs. Ida Tilson, County Pioneer, Dies at Hospital," *La Crosse Tribune*, Feb. 7, 1936, p. 1.
7. Kay Boyd synthesized and condensed the articles, interviews and notes collected for this section on rural education in La Crosse County.
8. Recollection of Eleanor Kinney Robinson, May 1, 1995; Randy Erickson, "School Days," *Holmen Courier / Onalaska Community Life*, July 28, 1994, p. 11B.
9. "Mildred Lee Streeton Interview" by Bangor High School student Rhonda Rueckheim, January 1995.
10. "Jane Leicht Kaiser Interview," June 15 and Aug. 6, 1994.
11. "Bob Leicht Interview," Apr. 2, 1996.
12. Hazel Leicht, "My Years as La Crosse County Superintendent of Schools," in Bryhn, *Early Schools*, pp. 180-2.
13. Bryhn, *Early Schools*, p. 178.
14. Ibid., p. 182.
15. "Jane Leicht Kaiser Interview."
16. "Florence Olson Whiting Interview," June 14, 1994.
17. Recollection of Charles Gelatt, Sept. 28, 1995.
18. "Name New High School for Anna Mashek," Letter to Editor, *La Crosse Tribune*, Apr. 2, 1965, signed by Alvida Ahlstrom, Helen Dorset, Clara Siepert, Hazel Stillman, Gertrude Thurow, Mauree Applegate Clack, Mrs. Forrest (Ruth) Edwards, Mrs. Hubert (Kay) Fuller, Mrs. Alf (Carroll) Gundersen, Mrs. Gunnar (Mary) Gundersen, Mrs. Arthur (Mary) Hebberd, Mrs. Owen (Stella) Jackson, Mrs. Adam (Betty) Heuslein, Mrs. Joseph (Margaret) Keller, Mrs. William (Clara) Laux, Mrs. Rexford (Muriel) Mitchell, Mrs. Arthur (Rebecca) Moody, Mrs. Robert (Marian) Ramlow, Mrs. Leo (Gertrude) Schnur, Mrs. Fred (Jane) Steele, Mrs. Robert (Marion) Whiteway and Mrs. Emerson (Jean) Wulling.
19. "Instructor's Death Shock to Many Here," unidentified newspaper, n.d. [July 1936].
20. Kay Spence, "Josephine Hintgen: Guidance Pioneer" (La Crosse, Wisconsin: Committee on Pioneer Women and Research of Theta Chapter of Delta Kappa Gamma, 1960), p. 19.
21. Ibid., p. 2.

22. Margaret K. Kosbab, "A History of the Guidance Program of the La Crosse Public Schools, Under the Leadership of Miss Josephine Hintgen, 1920-1957" (Seminar paper, Wisconsin State University-La Crosse, 1969), p. 19.
23. Spence, p. 5.
24. Terry Burt, "'Like a Big Family,' Old Grad Recalls," *La Crosse Tribune*, June 19, 1976, p. 1.
25. "Joan Pitzner Interview," January 1996.
26. Wisconsin Blue Book (1958), p. 172.
27. Leeward C. Lee, "Teacher Told Tales of Kickapoo Valley," *La Crosse Tribune*, Feb. 19, 1974, p. 3.
28. Information on the brief teaching career of Mary Eveline Bagley Smith compiled by Gloria Bailey Jackson.
29. "Elvern Ericksen Nyseth Interview," Aug. 8, 1994, and Apr. 8, 1996.
30. Notes compiled by West Salem High School student Jennifer Keller, December 1994.
31. Minutes of the June 2, 1942, meeting of the Board of Education, La Crosse, Wisconsin.
32. "Marge Schaller Interview" by La Crosse Central High School student Pam Hanson, 1994.
33. Recollection of Margaret Fish who taught in the Onalaska School District in the 1940s.
34. La Crosse Education Association response to "Hunting Our History Questionnaire," compiled by Barbara Schultz.
35. Interview with Geneva Ragland by Gloria Bailey Jackson and David Marcou for the La Crosse County Historical Society, Oct. 10, 1985.
36. A brief history compiled by Rose Erickson and Randi Brye included with the La Crosse Area Retired Educators Association response to "Hunting Our History Questionnaire."
37. "Florence Olson Whiting Interview."
38. Theta Chapter Delta Kappa Gamma Society response to "Hunting Our History Questionnaire."
39. La Crosse Education Association response to questionnaire.
40. "Marge Schaller Interview."
41. Anne Nicol Gaylor, "Meet Feisty, Independent Phyllis Grams," *Free Thought Today*, Freedom From Religion Foundation, May 1984, p. 5.
42. Ibid.
43. "Miss Keefe's School of Shorthand," *The Sunday Press*, La Crosse, Wisconsin, May 13, 1894.
44. Arla Clemons synthesized the articles, interviews and notes collected for this section on La Crosse Vocational School/Western Wisconsin Technical College: "Dedication Program: Vocational and Adult Schools Addition," Apr. 19, 1940; "The Old Team," *La Tech* Yearbook of Western Wisconsin Technical Institute, 1978, pp. 4-9; *The Rag-Tag and Bobtail: Personal Reminiscences of John B. Coleman* (La Crosse, Wisconsin: Western Wisconsin Technical Institute, 1971); notes compiled by Annette Niederkorn, librarian, Western Wisconsin Technical College, 1994.
45. George Kent, "A City that Goes to School," *The Reader's Digest*, February, 1942, reprinted by La Crosse Vocational and Adult School Press, La Crosse, Wisconsin, March, 1942.
46. "La Crosse School Boasts First U.S. Public Switchboard Operating Class," *La Crosse Tribune and Leader-Press*, Mar. 29, 1942, p. 3.
47. "Grim Looking Welders Here ... Are Really Pretty Young Girls," *La Crosse Tribune and Leader-Press*, Aug. 2, 1942, p. 14.
48. Recollection of Kathleen Lotze Rone, 1996.
49. "The Cookbook: Food for Thought," *La Crosse Tribune*, Mar. 12, 1978, p. 2.
50. Anonymous, "A Person that Changed My Life," April 1995.
51. This section on St. Rose Convent/Viterbo College based on Sister M. Mileta Ludwig, FSPA, *A Chapter of Franciscan History*, 1849-1949; Sister Theodine Sebold, FSPA, *Continuity and Change*; and "Sister Grace McDonald Interview," Sept. 20, 1995.
52. Ludwig, pp. 298-9.
53. "Sister Grace McDonald Interview."
54. "Virginia Marcotte Larkin Interview," Oct. 18 and 21, 1994.
55. Sebold, p. 40.

56. Ibid., p. 79.
57. Ibid., pp. 65-66.
58. "Sister Grace McDonald Interview."
59. This section on La Crosse Normal School/University of Wisconsin-La Crosse based on *The Catalyst*, A University of Wisconsin-La Crosse General Honors Program Publication, UW-L 75th Commemorative Edition, Volume VI, Number 1, October 1984; George R. Gilkey, *The First Seventy Years*; Susan T. Hessel, *Recollections 1909-1973; Women Who Forged the Way*, produced by Organization for Campus Women of the University of Wisconsin-La Crosse, 1994, videocassette.
60. Ida S. Rusedahl Hunter, "Let's Visit Valley View School," in Bryhn, *Early Schools*, p. 65.
61. Hessel, p. 105.
62. Jean L. Foss, "Emma Lou Wilder: She Came To Teach," in Marian J. Swoboda and Audrey J. Roberts, eds., *University Women, a Series of Essays, Volume I*, (Madison, Wisconsin: University of Wisconsin Board of Regents, 1980), pp. 53-55.
63. "Dr. Beatrice Baird Retires," UW-La Crosse *Racquet*, Dec. 5, 1974, p. 8; "Jean Foss Interview," Mar. 2, 1995.
64. Charles Haas, "Marie Park Toland, A Champion of the Arts," *The Catalyst*, October 1984, pp. 26-9.
65. Gilkey, *The First Seventy Years*, p. 180.
66. Kenneth G. Brown, "'Teach Writing as You Teach Art,'" *The La Crosse Sunday Tribune Family Magazine*, May 5, 1963; Susan McCabe, "Writing, Speaking and China Collecting Combine as Hobbies," *La Crosse Tribune*, Mar. 22, 1959, p. 9; Gilkey, p. 220.
67. "Margaret Chew Interview," Apr. 26, 1995.
68. "Olive Gershon Interview," May 24, 1995.
69. "AWS: A Handbook for and about the Women Students of Wisconsin State University, La Crosse," prepared by the Associated Women Students, 1967-68; "Carol Hettinga Bassuener Interview," Mar. 10, 1995.
70. "Norene A. Smith Interview," Mar. 2, 1995.
71. "Jean Foss Interview."
72. "Carol Hettinga Bassuener Interview."
73. "Jean Kessler Interview," Feb. 8, 1996.
74. This section on Women's Education Resources (WER) based on notes compiled by Shirley Haas who was coordinator of WER for its entire existence, 1974-86.
75. "Mary O'Sullivan Interview," Mar. 10, 1995.
76. The original committee members were Jean Foss, convenor; Judith Green, English; Shirley Haas, Women's Education Resources; Jean Helliesen, history; Susannah Lloyd, anthropology; Vivian Munson, history; Eileen Muth, physical education; Mary Gayle Pifer, foreign language; Joan Yeatman, English; and students Kay Heins, Kathryn Severance and Mary Weigers.
77. Sandra Krajewski and Judith McCaslin with Jean Foss and Judith Green, "Women and Education at UW-La Crosse: Recollections, Reflections and Re-Vision" (Women's Studies, University of Wisconsin-La Crosse, 1991), p. 5.
78. Ibid., p. 6.
79. Ibid., pp. 6-9.
80. Patricia Muller, "Highlights of OCW History," Organization for Campus Women (OCW) file, Special Collections Department, Murphy Library, University of Wisconsin-La Crosse.
81. Organization for Campus Women reminiscing session, June 13, 1995, attended by Judy Pace, Marilyn Wigdahl, Cris Prucha, Judith Green and Patricia Muller.
82. This section based on Shirley Haas's file on the April 1975 IWY (International Women's Year) Conference at the University of Wisconsin-La Crosse; and *Women Who Forged the Way*, videocassette.
83. Ann Beckman, "Women's Squabble Rises Amid Convention Glitter," *(Madison, Wisconsin) Capitol Times*, n.d., in Shirley Haas's file on IWY Conference.
84. Pat Moore, "Women's Confab: Big Deal or Ripoff?" *La Crosse Tribune*, Mar. 27, 1975, pp. 1 & 4.
85. "Proceedings of Adjourned Semi-Annual Meeting," Board of Regents of (Wisconsin) Normal Schools, Feb. 7-9 & 17, 1912, pp. 82-3.

86. Organization for Campus Women reminiscing session.
87. "Eileen Ryan Polizzotto Interview," June 29, 1995.
88. "Nancy Ellingson Interview" by La Crosse Central High School student Julie Sella, December 1994.

AT WORK IN INDUSTRY, OFFICE AND RETAIL

1. Alice Kessler-Harris, *Women Have Always Worked*, p. 82.
2. John and Joan Dolbier, *From Sawmills to Sunfish*, p. 120.
3. Research notes of Gloria Bailey Jackson, La Crosse County Historical Society.
4. Loretta Tennesen, "A Local History of Pearl Button Manufacturing," *Past, Present & Future*, La Crosse County Historical Society, Vol. 12, No. 10, July/August 1991, p. 1 ff.
5. Doug Connell, "Old Buttons Unearthed," *La Crosse Tribune*, June 22, 1987, p. 6.
6. Ibid.
7. Tennesen.
8. "Mary Longway Interview," Aug. 28, 1994.
9. Joseph A. Kidder, "Marinello Forerunner of Beauty Aid Business," *La Crosse Sunday Tribune*, Feb. 16, 1964, p. 8.
10. "Florence Munson Interview," Oct. 7 and 8, 1980.
11. Gloria Bailey Jackson, "The Leona," *Past, Present & Future*, La Crosse County Historical Society, Vol. 12, No. 2, March 1990, pp. 1, 3-5.
12. "Emma Raymond Fellows Interview," Apr. 5, 1977.
13. "Mary Lou Brown Rudolph Interview," Apr. 28, 1995.
14. "Jenny Ames Interview," Aug. 28, 1994.
15. "Florence Munson Interview."
16. Dolbier and Dolbier, p. 148.
17. "Rubber Mills Closes Today Until June 3," *La Crosse Tribune and Leader-Press*, May 21, 1942, p. 1.
18. "Betty Lamb Dell Hyde Interview," Dec. 29, 1994.
19. "Workers Like These Brought 'E' Award to Northern," *La Crosse Tribune and Leader-Press*, Dec. 3, 1942, p. 12.
20. "Florence Munson Interview."
21. "Lucille Wilkins Interview," Aug. 28, 1994.
22. "Donna Steele Lemke Interview," Nov. 17, 1994.
23. "Marilyn Stluka Interview," Aug. 28, 1994.
24. "Donna Steele Lemke Interview."
25. "Marion Zumach Hopkins Interview," Nov. 16, 1994.
26. This section based on notes compiled by Holmen High School student Keri Schermerhorn and her correspondence with Mrs. Kilmer (Lillian) Holter.
27. Estella Bryhn, *Around the Coulees*, pp. 63-4; "Ethel Holley Interview," Mar. 1, 1995.
28. "Donald 'Chick' Meinert Interview," Dec. 28, 1994.
29. Kessler-Harris, *Women Have Always Worked*, pp. 96-98.
30. "Violet Niedercorn Evans Berg Interview," Mar. 15, 1995.
31. "Mildred Anderson Nelson Interview," July 19, 1994.
32. "Lorraine Jandt Feit Interview," Mar. 22, 1995.
33. "Marilyn Koblitz Wigdahl Interview," Mar. 1, 1995.
34. "Anita Froegel Interview," Mar. 3, 1995.
35. Kessler-Harris, *Women Have Always Worked*, p. 99.
36. "Mitzi Mitchell Carroll Interview," Feb. 1, 1995.
37. Doug Connell, ed., *La Crosse Time Trip 1945* (La Crosse, Wisconsin: La Crosse History Works, 1995), p. 3.
38. "Sells Retail Store in City: Quillin Takes Over Rennebohm Grocery," *La Crosse Tribune and Leader-Press*, Sept. 12, 1945, p. 3.
39. "Estella Krohn Bryhn Interview," Dec. 6, 1994.
40. "Judie Weber Strauss Interview," Apr. 10, 1995.

41. "Aletta's Boasts All Hats in Shop Exclusive Models," *La Crosse Sunday Tribune*, Aug. 22, 1954, p. 9.
42. Dolbier and Dolbier, p. 44; Recollection of Mary Aiken, Mar. 8, 1995; "Dress Shop Owner Sees Style Changes Over Years," *La Crosse Tribune*, Mar. 28, 1954, p. 10.
43. "Betty Mielke Interview," Mar. 22, 1995.
44. "Sam Fellows Jr. Interview," Dec. 15, 1994.
45. "Mrs. Viola Fellows Is President of Company," *La Crosse Tribune and Leader-Press*, Oct. 4, 1939, p. 1.
46. "Mrs. Fellows, Doerflinger President, Dies," *La Crosse Tribune*, Aug. 26, 1954, pp. 1-2.
47. Nancy Oestreich Lurie, *Mountain Wolf Woman*, pp. 101-102.
48. Recollection of Ruth Lund Dadonna; "Anita Froegel Interview."
49. "Marion Whiteway Interview," Oct. 28, 1994.

SERVICES AND PROFESSIONS

1. John and Joan Dolbier, *From Sawmills to Sunfish*, pp. 52, 121-122.
2. "Art Soell Interview," Mar. 7, 1995.
3. "Wilma Peters Interview," Feb. 25 and 27, 1995.
4. "Sally Oswalt Interview," Mar. 9, 1995.
5. "Grace Van Steenwyk Interview," Oct. 29 and Nov. 5, 1970, p. 32.
6. "Della Feak Berg Interview," Feb. 1, 1995.
7. "Mildred Halderson Miller Interview," Mar. 15, 1995.
8. Recollection of Marilyn Wood, December 1994.
9. Pat Moore, "Ma's House Was Not A Home," *La Crosse Tribune*, Sept. 12, 1976, p. 13; Emily Hutson, *YWCA, La Crosse, Wisconsin*, 1903-1978 (La Crosse, Wisconsin: Young Women's Christian Association, 1978), p. 11.
10. "Betty Lamb Dell Hyde Interview," Dec. 29, 1994.
11. Kay Boyd synthesized the articles, interviews and notes collected for this section on libraries.
12. Unless cited otherwise, this section on the La Crosse Public Library based on an unpublished history of the library prepared by the La Crosse Public Library Archives staff.
13. "La Crosse Woman Heads Group Seeking New Library Program," *La Crosse Tribune*, Apr. 17, 1949, p. 28.
14. "She Brought Books, People Together," *La Crosse Tribune*, June 22, 1978, p. 11; "Muriel Fuller Killed in Showboat Upset," *La Crosse County Countryman*, June 22, 1978.
15. "It's Checkout Time for Local Librarians," *La Crosse Tribune*, Dec. 7, 1975, p. 15.
16. "More Than Just Books," *Milwaukee Journal*, Nov. 30, 1975.
17. Unless cited otherwise, this section based on an unpublished history of the La Crosse County Library.
18. Report of Supervising Librarian of County Traveling Library System for Year Ending Nov. 1, 1921.
19. Ibid.
20. Kindschy, *Leonard's Dream*, p. 107.
21. "West Salem Librarian Honored," *La Crosse Tribune*, Oct. 16, 1975, p. 25.
22. "Carol Lee and Madeline Anderson Interviews," May 3, 1995; Gayda Hollnagel, "Friends Remember Her as Modern Philospher," *La Crosse Tribune*, Oct. 8, 1982, p. 12.
23. "Emma Krause Interview," mid-1960s.
24. "Lucy Lonkoski Interview," Mar. 11, 1995.
25. "Nancy Westerhouse Tolvstad Interview," Mar. 4, 1995.
26. Floyde J. Sias obituary, *La Crosse Tribune*, Apr. 16, 1985; Gary Achterberg, "Her Help Just Phone Call Away," *La Crosse Tribune*, Apr. 19, 1985; Notes compiled by Onalaska High School student Kasey Heth, December 1994.
27. "Marce Mehren Interview," Mar. 14, 1995.
28. Dolbier and Dolbier, pp. 266-7.

29. Ibid., pp. 143-144.
30. "Hazel Dickinson Interview," May 3, 1995.
31. Unless cited otherwise, information on local women in photography based on Edwin L. Hill, "A History of Photography in La Crosse, Wisconsin, 1853-1930" (Master's thesis, University of Wisconsin-La Crosse, 1978).
32. "Helen M. Hoeft Dies at 75, Photo Pioneer," *La Crosse Tribune*, July 7, 1969.
33. "Barbara Showers Davidson Interview," Nov. 5, 1992.
34. Dolbier and Dolbier, p. 283.
35. Recollection of Marian Schlabach Ramlow, Mar. 13, 1995.
36. Gloria Jackson, "The Little Redhead: Eloda (Sitzer) Beach, Stage Actress of the 'Roaring '20s,'" *Past, Present & Future*, La Crosse County Historical Society, Vol. 10, No. 5 (September 1988), pp. 1, 3-4.
37. "State Industrial Commission Officer Calls Detention Home Tinder Box, Stirs Supervisors to Take Corrective Action," *La Crosse Tribune and Leader-Press*, July 26, 1942, p. 12.
38. "Joan Van Rossem Interview," Nov. 18, 1994.
39. "State Industrial Commission Officer Calls Detention Home Tinder Box, Stirs Supervisors to Take Corrective Action," *La Crosse Tribune and Leader-Press*, July 26, 1942, p. 12.
40. "County Detention Home 'Tinderbox' Eliminated by Supervisors' Action," *La Crosse Tribune and Leader-Press*, Sept. 18, 1942, p. 2.
41. Family and Children's Center response to "Hunting Our History Questionnaire."
42. Ibid.
43. Estella Krohn Bryhn, *Around the Coulees*, p. 20.
44. Notes compiled by Holmen High School student Sarah Wasley, December 1994.
45. "Thelma Orr Zumach Stokes Interview," Nov. 16, 1994.
46. Gayda Hollnagel, "Woman Pastor's Past Uncovered," *La Crosse Tribune*, Dec. 7, 1985; Notes compiled by Logan High School student Aleasha Amann.
47. Charles E. Haas, *Bless the Work of Our Hands*, pp. 217, 282.
48. Mary Schluter, "Women in Protestant Clergy Not New," *Coulee Gazette*, Sept. 27, 1978, p. 4.
49. Ibid.
50. Daniel Flaherty correspondence with the author, Feb. 24, 1995.
51. "Robert Joanis Interview," Mar. 19, 1995.
52. "City Lawyer Dies Thursday," *La Crosse Tribune*, Feb. 9, 1951, p. 1.
53. Susan T. Hessel, "Local Women Lawyers Skirt Feminist Causes," *La Crosse Tribune*, Aug. 9, 1975, p. 6.
54. "Women Safer Car Drivers Than Men, Opinion of Feminine Taxi Drivers," *La Crosse Tribune and Leader-Press*, Aug. 23, 1942, p. 13.
55. "Four La Crosse Girls Enlist in New Women's Auxiliary Corps," *La Crosse Tribune and Leader-Press*, Aug. 23, 1942, pp. 1-2.
56. "Mary Belle Ahlstrom Smith Interview," May 4, 1996; "Mary Belle Ahlstrom Gets Pilot's Wings in Auxiliary Ferry Service," *La Crosse Tribune and Leader-Press*, July 8, 1943, p. 10.
57. Kenneth G. Brown, "Frances E. Burgess Retires From Tribune," *La Crosse Tribune*, Sept. 20, 1970, p. 2; "Dave Burgess Interview," Feb. 16 and Mar. 6, 1995.
58. Notes compiled by La Crosse Central High School student Michelle Wilmot in her review of the *La Crosse Tribune* women's pages of the 1950s.
59. Susan M. McCabe, "Views Women's Page Changes Through 40 Years," *La Crosse Tribune*, Jan. 2, 1966, p. 9.
60. Bryhn, *Around the Coulees*, p. IV.
61. "Estella Krohn Bryhn Interview," Dec. 6 and 15, 1994.
62. "Della Feak Berg Interview," Feb. 1, 1995.
63. Jan McLain, "Gazette to Expand on May 2," *Coulee Gazette*, Mar. 28, 1979, p. 4.
64. Jan McLain, "Gazette Readership Survey '78," *Coulee Gazette*, June 14, 1978, p. 9.
65. "Jean Gitz Bassett Interview," Mar. 14, 1995.
66. "Bill Hoel Interview," Apr. 10, 1995.
67. "Judy Bouffleur Interview" by La Crosse Central High School student Annie Eide, December 1994; "Judy Burbach Bouffleur Interview," March 1995.

68. "Alice Osterhout Interview," Mar. 9, 1995.
69. "Lill Twining Interview," Mar. 10, 1995.
70. "Natalie Hartigan Interview," Mar. 11, 1995.
71. Julie McCabe, "The Swarthout Family," *Past, Present & Future*, La Crosse County Historical Society, Vol. 11, No. 2 (March 1989), pp. 1, 3-6; "Local Woman Acting Manager of Electric Light Company," *La Crosse Tribune and Leader-Press*, Mar. 14, 1937, p. 11.
72. Rita Schuettpelz synthesized the articles, interviews and notes collected for this section on Ethel Tausche. Carole F. Edland, "Ethel Olberg Tausche: A Woman General Contractor," Paper to accompany photographic documentary of the twenty-one houses she had built in La Crosse, Wisconsin, during 1925 to 1941, May 12, 1983; "Photo Display to Depict Female Builder's Life," *La Crosse Tribune*, May 29, 1983, p. 12.
73. Kathryn Tausche Smith, "A Special Person from My Past," a presentation to her PEO group in Muncie, Indiana, 1995.
74. Homes built by Ethel Tausche are located at: 343 and 357 South 23rd Street; 339, 357, 415 and 421 South 22nd Street; 201 and 207 South 21st Street; 322 and 333 South 20th Street; 2148, 2218, 2321, 2323, 2325 and 2327 Ferry Street; 1812 Cameron Avenue; 227 North 22nd Street; 427 North 23rd Street; 1008 South 7th Street; and 400 South 15th Street in La Crosse.

IN THE COMMUNITY

1. Albert H. Sanford and H. J. Hirshheimer, *A History of La Crosse, Wisconsin, 1841-1900*, p. 243.
2. Ibid., p. 244.

WOMEN AND THEIR FAITH

1. Clara M. Eid, La Crosse Circuit WMF historian, "History of La Crosse Circuit Women's Missionary Federation (Eastern District) From Its Organization in 1925 to the Year 1959," cited in Estella Krohn Bryhn, *Around the Coulees*, p. 76.
2. Bethel Lutheran Church Women of the Evangelical Lutheran Church of America response to "Hunting Our History Questionnaire," compiled by Lilly D. Hendrickson.
3. First Congregational Church of La Crosse response to "Hunting Our History Questionnaire," compiled by Charles Haas.
4. Ibid.
5. Our Savior's Lutheran Church of West Salem response to "Hunting Our History Questionnaire," compiled by Vernetta Romskog.
6. Ibid.
7. Bethel Lutheran Church response.
8. "Helen Hanson Interview," Aug. 16, 1994, and Apr. 3, 1995.
9. Bryhn, *Around the Coulees*, p. 76.
10. North Presbyterian Church of La Crosse response to "Hunting Our History Questionnaire," compiled by Arlene Boyle.
11. Recollection of Rachel Gutzke Gundersen.
12. Our Savior's Lutheran Church response.
13. "Helen Hanson Interview."
14. First Congregational Church response.
15. North Presbyterian Church response.
16. Our Redeemer Lutheran Church of La Crosse response to "Hunting Our History Questionnaire," compiled by Cindy Berg.
17. First Congregational Church response.
18. John and Joan Dolbier, *From Sawmills to Sunfish*, p. 43.
19. Holmen Lutheran Church response to "Hunting Our History Questionnaire," compiled by Pearl Johnson.

20. Bryhn, *Around the Coulees*, p. 76.
21. Our Savior's Lutheran Church response.
22. Asbury United Methodist Church of La Crosse response to "Hunting Our History Questionnaire," compiled by Mildred Olson.
23. "Irene Kreisel Schaller Interview," Nov. 18, 1994.
24. (St. Joseph the Workman) Cathedral Women's Organization response to "Hunting Our History Questionnaire," compiled by Lilly Lecheler.
25. Faith Lutheran Church of La Crosse response to "Hunting Our History Questionnaire," compiled by Arlene Bartig.
26. Our Redeemer Lutheran Church response.
27. Holmen Lutheran Church response.
28. Bethel Lutheran Church response.
29. Bryhn, *Around the Coulees*, p. 75.
30. Dolbier and Dolbier, p. 284.
31. Notes compiled by Holmen High School student Sarah Wasley.
32. Donald "Chick" Meinert, "Welcome to Goosetown," (1992), p. 3.
33. St. John's Lutheran Church, La Crosse, response to "Hunting Our History Questionnaire," compiled by Helen Berg.
34. Women of Olivet Lutheran Church response to "Hunting Our History Questionnaire," compiled by Neva Ritter.
35. First Congregational Church response.
36. Ibid.
37. Genevieve Koenig, "St. Elias Eastern Orthodox Church," *Past, Present & Future*, La Crosse County Historical Society, Vol. 12, No. 5, September 1990, pp. 16-18.
38. Armand Tuteur, "The History of the Jews of La Crosse," *The Reform Advocate*, Oct. 11, 1913, p. 5.
39. Jewish Women's League response to "Hunting Our History Questionnaire," compiled by Carol Ziff and Pam Strauss.
40. "Sally Levenstein Interview," Oct. 10, 1994.
41. Jewish Women's League response; "Sally Levenstein Interview."
42. Recollection of Marian Ramlow, October 1994.
43. L. DeAne Lagerquist, *From Our Mothers' Arms: A History of Women in the American Lutheran Church*, p. 93.
44. Catholic Women's League response to "Hunting Our History Questionnaire," compiled by Genevieve Koenig.
45. Mrs. George (Mercedes) Bracken and Blanche Haas, "Memoirs: 75th Anniversary of La Crosse Catholic Women's League, 1915-1990" (La Crosse, Wisconsin: Catholic Women's League, 1990).
46. Bryhn, *Around the Coulees*, p. 76.
47. Lagerquist, *From Our Mothers' Arms*, p. 192.
48. Court La Crosse #1183 of the Catholic Daughters of the Americas response to "Hunting Our History Questionnaire," compiled by Mary Blaschke and Marie Kabat.
49. "Catholic Daughters Operate Thrift Center 15 Years," *La Crosse Tribune*, Nov. 7. 1971, "Focus" p. 9.
50. Catholic Daughters of the Americas response.
51. Church Women United response to "Hunting Our History Questionnaire," compiled by Mary Kisken; Carrie Ann Seib, "Church Women United Praying for Peace," *Past, Present & Future*, La Crosse County Historical Society, Vol. 14, No. 5, September/October 1992, pp. 8-10.
52. "Patricia Sheehan Interview," May 13, 1996.
53. Shelley Goldbloom, "Womens Group Spawned in War, Wars on Hunger," *La Crosse Tribune*, Sept. 20, 1979, p. 40.

COMMUNITY INVESTMENT

1. Genevieve Koenig, "Looking Forward and Back," *Past, Present & Future*, La Crosse County Historical Society, Vol. 14, No. 3, May/June 1992, pp. 1,3,4.
2. "Della Feak Berg Interview," Feb. 1, 1995.
3. "Irene Radcliffe Interview," Jan. 12, 1996; Virginia Werner, "Smith Valley School Nearly 100 Years Old Preserved for Posterity," in Bryhn, *Early Schools of La Crosse County*, pp. 93-94.
4. La Crosse Chapter of the National Society, Daughters of the American Revolution response to "Hunting Our History Questionnaire," compiled by Laura L. Lane.
5. Carroll M. Gundersen file of minutes and correspondence of the La Crosse Historic Sites Commission, 1973-76.
6. "Joan M. Rausch Interview," Apr. 28, 1996; Joan M. Rausch with Dr. Richard Zeitlin, *Historic La Crosse Architectural and Historic Record: A Summary of an Intensive Survey Report* (La Crosse, Wisconsin: 1984). The complete 400-page report prepared for the La Crosse, Wisconsin, Planning Department by Architectural Researches, Inc., is on file in Special Collections, Murphy Library, University of Wisconsin-La Crosse.
7. Notes compiled by La Crosse Central High School student Angie Olson based on "Marion Cape Biehn Interview," 1984; Kathryn Fuller letter to editor, "Her Artwork is Treasured," *La Crosse Tribune*, Mar. 7, 1993, p. C-9; Pat Moore, "Tribute to an Artist," *La Crosse Tribune*, Feb. 21, 1993, p. C-1; James O. Holmlund, "Artists Preserve City's History," *La Crosse Sunday Tribune Family Magazine*, Feb. 25, 1968.
8. Chris Nudd, "La Crosse Scenes," *La Crosse Tribune*, Dec. 1, 1968, to Aug. 16, 1969.
9. Gloria Jackson, "Never Done: The Role of Women in the Making of La Crosse County," *Past, Present & Future*, La Crosse County Historical Society, Vol. VII, No. II, Summer 1985, p. 1.
10. Hazel Heider correspondence with West Salem High School student Jennifer Keller; Hazel Rahn Heider, *Along the Waterloo Road*, p. 73.
11. Joan Lybarger, "Pride in Heritage Spans the Ocean for Area Norse," *La Crosse Tribune*, July 18, 1976, p. 12.
12. This section on Borghild Olson compiled by Cris Berg Prucha based on "Interview with Borghild Olson," La Crosse County Historical Society; Interview with Tammy Potaracke, co-manager of Norskedalen, Dec. 15, 1995; Joan Lybarger, "Pride in Heritage Spans the Ocean for Area Norse," *La Crosse Tribune*, July 18, 1976, p. 12; Pat Moore, "One of Norway's Favorites: La Crosse Woman Getting St. Olaf Medal on Saturday," *La Crosse Tribune*, Apr. 5, 1991, p. B-2.
13. Bryhn, *Around the Coulees*, pp. 45-6.
14. Twentieth Century Club response to "Hunting Our History Questionnaire," compiled by Florence Whiting.
15. Notes compiled by La Crosse Logan High School student Barb Lysaker based on "City Women Organize for Defense Work," *La Crosse Tribune and Leader-Press*, May 25, 1917, p. 1.
16. Cora Olson speech to Webster School Homemakers Club, n.d. [1930s?]. During World War I, all people of German heritage were considered suspect. "German culture, so vital at La Crosse, became associated with anti-Americanism during the war. Berlin Street in North La Crosse, for example, became Liberty Street, just as sauerkraut became 'liberty cabbage.' The German Society changed its name to the Pioneer Club, and membership dropped. German congregations held their services in English rather than their native language." (Joan M. Rausch, *Historic La Crosse Architectural and Historic Record*, 1984, p. 9.)
17. Organizations and individuals affiliated with La Crosse County Community Council in 1929 were: Catholic Women's League, Central High School Mothers' League, Central High School P.T.A., City Public Health Nurse, County Nurse, County Superintendent of Schools, Daughters of Norway, Daughters of the American Revolution, Delphian Society, Ibsen Club, La Crosse Music Study Club, La Crosse Teachers' Club, La Crosse Woman's Club, Public Library, 7th District Nurses' Association, Service Star Legion, Social Service Society, YWCA, Washburn P.T.A., WCTU, American Legion Auxiliary, and the Homemakers Clubs of Bangor, Barre Mills, Brookside, Burn's Corner, East

Side, Franklin, Hamilton, Hogan, Holmen, Jefferson, Lincoln, Mindoro, Neshonec, Onalaska, Prairie, Roosevelt, Sand Lake, Tenth Ward, Union Mills, Washburn, Webster School, West Salem, and White School. "A Review of the Activities of the La Crosse County Community Council, 1919-1929" (La Crosse, Wisconsin: La Crosse County Community Council, 1929).

18. Ibid., p. 3.
19. Ibid., p. 5.
20. Ibid., p. 6.
21. "Silver Anniversary of La Crosse County Community Council, 1919-1944" (La Crosse, Wisconsin: La Crosse County Community Council, 1944).
22. "'Man of Year' is Still 'Woman of Day,'" *St. Paul Sunday Pioneer Press*, Feb. 19, 1950, p. 1.
23. "Fourteenth Annual Report of La Crosse Community Chest," for 1962, p. 3.
24. Margaret Fish file on Citizens Education Committee.
25. "Changing Scenes in Life of YWCA Fill Association's History with Colorful Events," *La Crosse Tribune*, May 19, 1935, p. 8.
26. Lutheran Hospital Auxiliary response to "Hunting Our History Questionnaire," compiled by Marilyn McElligott; "Gretchen Burns Interview," July 14, 1996.
27. Scrapbook of newspaper articles (1926 to 1929), office of La Crosse County 4-H and Youth Agent.
28. Molly Sacia correspondence with the author, January 1996.
29. Riverland Girl Scout Council, "History of Girl Scouting in La Crosse," no date; Mary Rohrer, executive director, Riverland Council, correspondence with the author, Jan. 12, 1995; "Marguerite Anderson, Nancy Hyde Gerrard and Fran Skemp Interview," 1994, videocassette.
30. Gayda Hollnagel, "Girl Pioneers: Roots Run Deep in La Crosse," *La Crosse Tribune*, Apr. 24, 1994, p. B-4.
31. Bethel #27 International Order of Job's Daughters response to "Hunting Our History Questionnaire," compiled by Mary Callaway.
32. "Irna Rideout Interview," Dec. 28, 1994.
33. "Mary Krum Munson Interview," Dec. 29, 1994.
34. "Pauline Weigel Connell Interview," Jan. 10, 1995.
35. "Don Iverson Interview," Jan. 29, 1996.
36. Jackson, "Never Done," pp. 6-7.
37. "Bicentennial Trail Dedication" printed program, Oct. 10, 1976; Lou Smith, "Hixon Trail Is Dedicated," *Coulee Gazette*, Oct. 18, 1976, pp. 1, 3.
38. "Katharine Martindale Wins Conservation Award," *La Crosse Tribune*, May 28, 1961, p. 7.
39. John and Joan Dolbier, *From Sawmills to Sunfish*, pp. 241-2.
40. "Pat Meir Shedesky Interview," Feb. 8, 1996; "Tribune Plans Locally Written Garden Column," *La Crosse Tribune*, Mar. 19, 1972, pp. 1-2.
41. Dolbier and Dolbier, pp. 260-2; Mae Peterson biographical file, Special Collections Department, Murphy Library, University of Wisconsin-La Crosse.
42. "Water Study" file, in the La Crosse County League of Women Voters collection, Special Collections Department, Murphy Library, University of Wisconsin-La Crosse.
43. "Laura Schuh Interview," May 1995.
44. Ibid.
45. Recollection of Nancy Goode who took the classes several times.
46. "Linda Malick Interview," May 1995.
47. "Rosalie Schnick Interview," May 1995.
48. "Marian Havlik Interview," June 1995; Marian E. Havlik biographical file, La Crosse Public Library Archives; curriculum vitae of Marian E. Havlik.
49. "Barbara Frank Interview," Mar. 6, 1996.
50. Ibid.
51. Ibid.

CULTURAL PURSUITS

1. Notes compiled by La Crosse Central High School student Alyssa Ablan based on Albert H. Sanford and H. J. Hirshheimer, *A History of La Crosse, Wisconsin, 1841-1900*, p. 243.
2. "Reports of Supervising Librarian of La Crosse County Traveling Library and La Crosse County Traveling Library Board to Board of Supervisors of La Crosse County," 1904-1924.
3. Fauver Hill Study Club response to "Hunting Our History Questionnaire," compiled by Irene Radcliffe and Eleanor Robinson.
4. Errol Kindschy, *Leonard's Dream*, pp. 83-4.
5. "Ibsen Club Celebrates Anniversary," *La Crosse Tribune and Leader-Press*, Jan. 7, 1942, p. 4; "Ibsen Club Adds Funds to War Relief," *La Crosse Tribune and Leader-Press*, Apr. 27, 1942, p. 4; "Ibsen Club Celebrates Golden Anniversary of Founding with 'Trettendagen,'" *La Crosse Tribune*, Jan. 11, 1950; obituary of Helga Isaksaetre Gundersen Midelfort, *La Crosse Tribune*, Apr. 23, 1995, p. B-7.
6. "Helga Gundersen Midelfort Interview," p. 36.
7. Ibid.
8. Notes compiled by La Crosse Central High School student Melissa Nash based on her review of La Crosse Music Study Club files, Special Collections, Murphy Library, University of Wisconsin-La Crosse.
9. "Sam Fellows Jr. Interview," Dec. 15, 1994.
10. "Music Study Club Pays Tribute to Memory of Elise L. Cilley, Composer and Concert Sponsor," unidentified newspaper, n.d., p. 4.
11. "Wilma Scheffner Interview," Feb. 13, 1996.
12. Campus Dames response to "Hunting Our History Questionnaire," compiled by Olive Gershon and Helen Brault; review of Campus Dames history prepared by Shirley Haas and presented at the May 1970 meeting of that organization.
13. American Association of University Women-La Crosse Branch response to "Hunting Our History Questionnaire," compiled by Marilyn Hempstead.
14. Letter from Helen Dorset to Bookfellows, Nov. 5, 1955. The founding members of Bookfellows were Helen Dorset, Lilly Borreson, Eleanor Bertelson, Mary (Ryerson) Hebberd, Gabriella Brendemuehl, Caroline Coate, Cora Desmond, Leona Farnam, Carroll Gundersen, Mary Gundersen, Margaret Keller, Sarah Lamb, Clara Laux, Eleanor Schlabach, Hazel Stillman and Katherine Wesson.
15. Virginia Rolnick, "Bookfellows 1935-1985" (La Crosse, Wisconsin: 1988).
16. "Mrs. Flora E. Lowry," *Reminiscences of Early La Crosse* (Liesenfeld Press, 1928), pp. 84-5.
17. "Marion Manville (Mrs. Charles A. Pope)," *La Crosse County Historical Sketches*, Series Six (La Crosse, Wisconsin: La Crosse County Historical Society, 1942) pp. 65-67; "La Crosse Woman is Making Mark as Poet and Author in Norske," *La Crosse Tribune and Leader-Press*, Aug. 20, 1922, p. 10.
18. "Mrs. Flora E. Lowry," *Reminiscences of Early La Crosse*.
19. Notes compiled by La Crosse Central High School student Angie Olson based on "Marion Cape Biehn Interview," 1984; Kathryn Fuller letter to editor, "Her Artwork is Treasured," *La Crosse Tribune*, Mar. 7, 1993, p. C-9; Pat Moore, "Tribute to an Artist," *La Crosse Tribune*, Feb. 21, 1993, p. C-1; James O. Holmlund, "Artists Preserve City's History," *La Crosse Sunday Tribune Family Magazine*, Feb. 25, 1968.
20. American Association of University Women-La Crosse Branch response.
21. Sandra Gue, "Marion Biehn Opens a Show!" *Revue*, Apr. 15, 1981, p. 5.
22. Notes compiled by La Crosse Central High School student Angie Olson based on her December 1994 interview with Betty Kendrick; Vita of Betty L. Perna Kendrick; "AAUW Members Demonstrate Special Skills," *La Crosse Tribune,* Dec. 7, 1965, p. 8; Sandra Gue, "Colorful Birds Roost on City Artist's Batiks," *La Crosse Tribune*, Oct. 17, 1981, p. 16; "She Creates Reality at the Drawing Board," *La Crosse Tribune*, July 25, 1987, p. 9.

23. Coulee County Chapter of The Embroiderers' Guild of America, Inc., response to "Hunting Our History Questionnaire," compiled by Maddeline Schuldes and Cindy Dietrich.
24. Lenice Ingram Bacon, *American Patchwork Quilts* (New York: Bonanza Books, 1980), p. 88.
25. Ibid.
26. La Crosse Area Quilters response to "Hunting Our History Questionnaire," compiled by Mary Herzog.
27. Mary Herzog, "Happiness is a Successful Quilting Group," *Quilt World*, August/September 1990, pp. 32-33.
28. La Crosse Music Study Club membership record book; Roland Nelson, "Concert Association Sings Praises to its Members," *La Crosse Tribune*, Mar. 8, 1977, p. 6.
29. Nelson, "Concert Association Sings Praises to its Members."
30. "Linda Schleiter Sherwood Interview," Oct. 5, 1995.
31. Nelson, "Concert Association Sings Praises to its Members."
32. Recollection of Ruth Lund Dadonna.
33. 1994-95 La Crosse Chamber Chorale brochure; Virginia Larkin correspondence with the author, Oct. 24, 1994.
34. "Wilma Scheffner Interview."
35. Ibid.
36. La Crosse Community Theatre response to "Hunting Our History Questionnaire," compiled by Sally Cremer, Jo Ann Jenkins, Libby Shirmacher, Julia Steinke Saterbak and Marilyn Wood; Julia Steinke, "Theater Curtain Rose in 1962," *La Crosse Tribune*, Oct. 1, 1976, p. 3.
37. Ibid.
38. Ibid.
39. Sandra Gue, "The Pump House, A Regional Center for the Arts: An Account of its Founding," *Artributes* (La Crosse, Wisconsin: Western Wisconsin Regional Arts, 1989) pp. 28-9.
40. "Sonia Baker Lives for the Arts," *La Crosse Tribune*, June 24, 1987, p. 4.
41. "Sonja Adams Interview," June 6, 1996.
42. Gue, pp. 28-9.

PUBLIC SERVICE

1. Letter from Abigail Smith Adams to John Adams, March 31, 1776.
2. "Recollections of 1869 La Crosse Visit," *La Crosse Tribune*, May 26, 1974, p. 11.
3. Ruth DeYoung Kohler, *The Story of Wisconsin Women*, p. 29.
4. "Susan B. Anthony's Lecture," *The Morning Chronicle*, Nov. 24, 1886, p. 1.
5. Ibid.
6. "Ellis Usher and Sister Present Handsome Gifts to the Normal Library," *La Crosse Tribune and Leader-Press*, Dec. 5, 1920, p. 9.
7. Minutes of October 9, 1897, meeting of La Crosse Branch of the Wisconsin Woman Suffrage Association, "La Crosse, Wis. Women's Suffrage" file, Special Collections, Murphy Library, University of Wisconsin-La Crosse. The members were: Mrs. L. O. Barlow, Mrs. Richardson, Elizabeth Looney, Ella Looney, Miss [sic] Dr. (Abby M.) Adams [physician and surgeon], Mrs. (Laura) Demmon, Mrs. Q. A. Daniels, Mrs. Ourat, Mrs. Blanchard, Miss (Lillie) Korsandra [teacher], Jennie Looney, Mrs. R. T. Wilson [boarding house proprietor], Mrs. Thurlow, Mrs. Scott.
8. Genevieve G. McBride, *On Wisconsin Women*, p. 208.
9. "Suffrage Boom Hits La Crosse," *La Crosse Tribune*, Jan. 15, 1912, p. 1.
10. "Suffragettes to Organize Party," *La Crosse Tribune*, Jan. 16, 1912, p. 1.
11. "Women Organize Suffrage Club," *La Crosse Tribune*, Jan. 25, 1912. The following officers were elected: president, Miss Rose Keefe; vice-president, Mrs. R. J. Russell; secretary, Mrs. Bullock; treasurer, Mrs. C. W. Levis. The committees appointed were: Ways and Means: Mrs. F. E. Davis, Mrs. Frank Winter, Mrs. C. W. Noble, Mrs. Leonard Kleeber, Mrs. Alex Hyslop; Publicity: Mrs. John Kroner Jr., Mrs. C. L. Jenks,

Mrs. L. Lueck, Mrs. Stratton, Mrs. Russell; Membership: Miss Mary Alice Smith, Mrs. F. E. Davis, Mrs. Gatterdam, Mrs. Bleekman.
12. "Suffrage Talk in City Hall," *La Crosse Tribune*, Feb. 16, 1912, p. 1.
13. "Need Funds for Suffrage Work," *La Crosse Tribune*, Feb. 29, 1912, p. 1.
14. "Suffrage Club Elects Officers," *La Crosse Tribune*, Apr. 20, 1912, p. 6.
15. "Wouldn't Allow Suffrage Speech," *La Crosse Tribune*, July 16, 1912, p. 6.
16. Ibid.
17. "Rev. Anna Shaw Here To Speak," *La Crosse Tribune*, Sept. 21, 1912, p. 1.
18. "Franklins Debate Equal Suffrage," *La Crosse Tribune*, Oct. 25, 1912, p. 12.
19. Ernst-Ulrich Franzen, "McBride Chronicles Wisconsin's Feminist Heritage," *Milwaukee Sentinel*, Apr. 16, 1994, pp. 1C-2C.
20. "Organize Second Class in Voting Tuesday Afternoon," *La Crosse Tribune and Leader-Press*, Apr. 19, 1920, p. 1.
21. "Registration Day for All Women is Set for Tuesday," *La Crosse Tribune and Leader-Press*, Aug. 29, 1920, p. 1.
22. "Women Register for Election in Numbers in City," *La Crosse Tribune and Leader-Press*, Aug. 31, 1920, p. 1.
23. "Women Active and Indications are Many Will Ballot," *La Crosse Tribune and Leader-Press*, Aug. 30, 1920, p. 1.
24. Errol Kindschy, *Leonard's Dream*, p. 97.
25. "Holmen Village Puts Women on Election Boards," *La Crosse Tribune and Leader-Press*, Sept. 6, 1920, p. 1.
26. Joseph K. Kidder, "Mrs. Zein First Woman Election Official Here," *La Crosse Tribune*, n.d. (1920).
27. Kindschy, p. 101.
28. John and Joan Dolbier, *From Sawmills to Sunfish*, p. 157.
29. Notes compiled by Onalaska High School student Lori Kish based on "Women First Began Serving on Circuit Court Jury Cases in La Crosse County 25 Years Ago," *La Crosse Tribune*, n.d. [1947?], in "La Crosse-History 1900-1950" file, La Crosse Public Library Archives.
30. Cora Olson speech to Webster School Homemakers Club, n.d. [1930s?]. Cora Olson also was the representative of the twenty-first ward to the La Crosse Community Council and was the volunteer who helped women of the twenty-first ward register to vote for the very first time in 1920.
31. Kindschy, p. 101.
32. Dolbier and Dolbier, p. 315.
33. Minutes of the Dec. 13 and 16, 1904, meetings, Twentieth Century Club.
34. "Woman Chosen as Member of School Board," *La Crosse Tribune and Leader-Press*, Dec. 11, 1920, p. 1.
35. Ibid.
36. "Local Women in Public Office," *La Crosse Tribune*, n.d. (early 1970s), in "La Crosse Women" file, La Crosse Public Library Archives.
37. Grant W. Blum, "Women's Lib on School Board," *La Crosse Tribune*, n.d. (1971).
38. Dolbier and Dolbier, p. 157.
39. "Imes to Oppose Zielke for Mayor's Seat," *Coulee Gazette*, Jan. 10, 1979, p. 8; Doug Svetnicka, "Political Women Still Exception, Not Norm," *Coulee Gazette*, July 11, 1979, p. A-2; "Sharon Imes," *La Crosse Tribune*, Apr. 28, 1985, p. 42; "Sharon Imes Interview," Mar. 11, 1995.
40. Dolbier and Dolbier, p. 265.
41. "Della Feak Berg Interview," Feb. 1, 1995.
42. "Cowie Appoints Deputy Clerk of Circuit Court," *La Crosse Tribune and Leader-Press*, July 16, 1941, p. 1.
43. "Robert Funke, Don Padesky, Ed Ryan and Bill Welch Interview," Dec. 13, 1994.
44. "Esther Domke, ex-County Clerk, Dies," *La Crosse Tribune*, Feb. 25, 1988, p. 9; Grant W. Blum, "County Clerk Served with Friendly Style," *La Crosse Tribune*, Feb. 27, 1988, p. 5.
45. Donald W. Affolter, "Mary Hinsberger Pleads, Yells, Pushes Civil Defense," *La Crosse Tribune*, Jan. 19, 1964, p. 10.

46. La Crosse Central High School student Jessica Bulk interviews with Elizabeth (Betty) Gundersen, Dec. 31, 1994; Joyce Arthur, Dec. 31, 1994; and Sally Oswalt, Jan. 1, 1995. "Elizabeth Gundersen, Joyce Arthur, Pat Wiffler Frechette and Shirley Holman Group Interview," June 14, 1995.
47. "Gundersen, Arthur, Wiffler and Holman Group Interview."
48. "Sally Oswalt Interview."
49. "Gundersen, Arthur, Wiffler and Holman Group Interview."
50. Ibid.
51. "Jean Wulling Interview," Dec. 7, 1994.
52. "Linda Schleiter Sherwood Interview," Oct. 5, 1995.
53. "Mary Muehr Interview," Feb. 21, 1995.
54. "Jean Helliesen Interview," Feb. 24, 1995.
55. "Muriel Onsrud Blackdeer Interview," Feb. 21, 1995.
56. "Honor Restored, City Man Lifts Head Again," *La Crosse Tribune*, May 3, 1976, p. 1; "Muriel Onsrud Blackdeer Interview."
57. La Crosse County Chapter of the National Women's Political Caucus response to "Hunting Our History Questionnaire," compiled by Sharon Ryan.
58. Ibid.
59. Testimony of Joan Rausch, "Before the Public Service Commission of Wisconsin: Petition of Harout O. Sanasarian, Florence K. Dickenson, and 28 Others regarding Telephone Directory Listing Practices," Volume I, June 22, 1976, pp. 69-70.
60. La Crosse County Women's Political Caucus newsletter, September 1975, p. 1.

SOCIAL CAUSES

1. Gloria Jackson, "Never Done: The Role of Women in the Making of La Crosse County," *Past, Present & Future*, La Crosse County Historical Society, Vol. VII, No. II, Summer 1985, pp. 1, 6.
2. "Family and Children's Center Records: Historical Background," Box 8, Folder 1, La Crosse Public Library Archives.
3. "Hixon," *La Crosse Tribune*, Oct. 21, 1976, in "La Crosse Hospital" file, La Crosse Public Library Archives.
4. Sheila M. Rothman, *Woman's Proper Place*, pp. 85-87.
5. "The Woman's Industrial Exchange of La Crosse" record book, La Crosse Public Library Archives.
6. Ruth De Young Kohler, *The Story of Wisconsin Women*, p. 120.
7. Ibid., pp. 120-21. (La Crosse Central High School student Loni Lundsten learned a frustrating lesson about research: sometimes one runs into a dead end. Although she checked the local library archives and the State Historical Society, she found no further information about the La Crosse Women's Trade Union League.)
8. Notes compiled by La Crosse Central High School student Erin Buros; Emily Hutson, *YWCA La Crosse, Wisconsin*, 1903-1978 (La Crosse, Wisconsin: Young Women's Christian Association, 1978).
9. Recollection of Maureen Kinney, Nov. 2, 1994.
10. "Activities of First Year at Loreto Club Summed Up in Annual Reports of Catholic Organizations Making Headquarters There," *La Crosse Tribune*, Feb. 28, 1926, p. 4.
11. Mrs. George (Mercedes) Bracken and Blanche Haas, "Memoirs: 75th Anniversary of La Crosse Catholic Women's League, 1915-1990" (La Crosse, Wisconsin: Catholic Women's League, 1990); Catholic Women's League response to "Hunting Our History Questionnaire," compiled by Genevieve Koenig.
12. "La Crosse County Chapter American Red Cross History" (La Crosse Red Cross, n.d.) and "A History of Helping Others" (American Red Cross, 1989, revised Feb. 1990) collected by La Crosse Central High School student Cerina Vollmer.
13. "Florence Olson Whiting Interview," June 14, 1994.
14. Ruth Millett, "You're Not Too Busy for Some War Work," *La Crosse Tribune and Leader-Press*, Jan. 26, 1942, p. 4.
15. "Two Red Cross Workers are Responsible for Kit Bags," *La Crosse Tribune and Leader-Press*, Aug. 15, 1944, p. 4.

16. "Mitzi Mitchell Carroll and Jane Mitchell Aarstad Interview," Feb. 1, 1995.

17. "Eleanore Wollschlaeger Interview," Dec. 11, 1994.

18. "A Report on The Record Flood at La Crosse in 1965," Special Flood Section, *La Crosse Tribune*, May 7, 1965, p. 2.

19. Ibid., p. 8.

20. John and Joan Dolbier, *From Sawmills to Sunfish*, p. 231.

21. Kohler, p. 94.

22. Ibid., p. 95.

23. La Crosse Chapter, Daughters of American Revolution response to "Hunting Our History Questionnaire," compiled by Laura L. Lane.

24. La Crosse Shrine Auxiliary for Crippled Children response to "Hunting Our History Questionnaire," compiled by Pauline Abel.

25. Lutheran Hospital Auxiliary response to "Hunting Our History Questionnaire," compiled by Marilyn McElligott.

26. "Mary Patros Interview," Dec. 12, 1994.

27. St. Francis Auxiliary response to "Hunting Our History Questionnaire," compiled by Marian Johnson.

28. Hillview Health Care Auxiliary response to "Hunting Our History Questionnaire," compiled by Vivian Strong.

29. Gayda Hollnagel, "Time Marches On and She Marches In," *La Crosse Tribune*, Apr. 16, 1995, p. A-1 ff.

30. "Muriel Onsrud Blackdeer Interview," Feb. 21, 1995.

31. La Crosse Association for Responsible Citizens reminiscing session, Oct. 27, 1994, attended by Helen Senn, Dorothy Wick and Margaret Sanford.

32. "Nursery Centers In Two Schools Given Approval," *La Crosse Tribune and Leader-Press*, Dec. 8, 1942, p. 9; "One Nursery Center Here Opens Today," *La Crosse Tribune and Leader-Press*, Jan. 18, 1943, p. 8; "Establish Child Care Centers In Six Public Schools of City," *La Crosse Tribune and Leader-Press*, Oct. 3, 1943, p. 7; "Five Centers in La Crosse Caring for Children of Working Mothers," *La Crosse Tribune and Leader-Press*, Jan. 9, 1944, p. 2; "Child Centers Aiding Parents," *La Crosse Tribune and Leader-Press*, June 11, 1944, p. 3.

33. "Rose Bellerue Honored as Woman of the Month," *La Crosse Tribune*, May 2, 1971, p. 17.

34. "Sharon Hughes Interview," Dec. 29, 1994.

35. "The League Speaks," *La Crosse Tribune*, May 19, 21, 22 & 23, 1968.

36. "Charlotte Shealy Interview," Mar. 5, 1995.

37. "Gerry Perry Interview," Nov. 10, 1994, and June 25, 1996.

38. Marilyn Van Wyk synthesized the articles, interviews and notes collected for this section: La Crosse Family Planning Center/Options in Reproductive Care reminiscing session, Jan. 4, 1995, attended by Margaret Fish, Jerome Gundersen, Pat Mattie, Marian Ramlow, Sally Schaldach Salisbury, and Edie Williams Woods; "Agency History" (Options in Reproductive Care, Inc., n.d.); Jan McLain, "Family Planning Center to Open," La Crosse Tribune, Jan. 30, 1972, p. 9; Pat Moore, "Family Planning Center Rouses Strong Feelings," *La Crosse Tribune*, n.d. [1976].

39. "Judy Schmidt Interview," Mar. 5, 1995; "Happy Birthday, Birthright!" *Birthright Newsletter*, November 1991.

40. New Horizons reminiscing session, Oct. 31, 1995, attended by Margaret Dosch, Maureen Kinney, Linda Madigan and Sue Mercier; "Rita Jenks Interview," Apr. 2, 1996.

Bibliography

Primary Sources

Interviews

Aarstad, Jane Mitchell and Carroll, Mitzi Mitchell. By author. Feb. 1, 1995.

Adams, Sonja. By author. June 6, 1996.

Ames, Jenny. By author. Aug. 28, 1994.

Anderson, Madeline and Lee, Carol. By author. May 3, 1995.

Anderson, Marguerite; Gerrard, Nancy Hyde; and Skemp, Fran. By Martha Koloski, TV-19. Videocassette. 1994.

Arthur, Joyce. By Jessica Bulk. Dec. 31, 1994.

Arthur, Joyce; Frechette, Pat Wiffler; Gundersen, Elizabeth; and Holman, Shirley. By author. June 14, 1995.

Bassett, Jean Gitz. By author. Mar. 14, 1995.

Bassuener, Carol Hettinga. By author. Mar. 10, 1995.

Berg, Della Feak. By Margaret Larson. Oral History Program, Special Collections Department, Murphy Library, University of Wisconsin-La Crosse. Feb. 1, 1995.

Berg, Violet Niedercorn Evans. By author. Mar. 15, 1995.

Beznouz, Sister Grace Clare. By Rita Jenks. Oral History Program, Special Collections Department, Murphy Library, University of Wisconsin-La Crosse. Dec. 1, 1994.

Biehn, Marion Cape. Oral History Program, Special Collections Department, Murphy Library, University of Wisconsin-La Crosse. 1984.

Blackdeer, Muriel Onsrud. By Erin Richardson. Feb. 21, 1995.

Bouffleur, Judy. By Annie Eide. December 1994.

Bouffleur, Judy Burbach. By author. March 1995.

Brooks, Flora. By Margaret Fish and Margaret Larson. Oral History Program, Special Collections Department, Murphy Library, University of Wisconsin-La Crosse. June 14, 1994.

Bryhn, Estella Krohn. By author. Dec. 6, 1994.

Burgess, Dave. By author. Feb. 16 and Mar. 6, 1995.

Burns, Gretchen. By author. July 14, 1996.

Campbell, Florence and Schuldes, Maddeline. By Rita Jenks. Nov. 30, 1994.

Campus Dames Book Group. By author. Jan. 24, 1995.

Carlson, Myrtle. By author. Feb. 24, 1995.

Carroll, Mitzi Mitchell and Aarstad, Jane Mitchell. By author. Feb. 1, 1995.

Chew, Margaret. By author. Apr. 26, 1995.

Connell, Pauline Weigel. By author. Jan. 10, 1995.

Dalton, Ruth. By Rita Jenks. Oral History Program, Special Collections Department, Murphy Library, University of Wisconsin-La Crosse. Jan. 30, 1995.

Davidson, Barbara Showers. By Mary Aiken. Onalaska Area Historical Society. Nov. 5, 1992.

Delano, Cynthia Thompson and Hirsh, Linda. By author. Feb. 28, 1995.

Dickinson, Hazel. By author. May 3, 1995.

Dummer, Shirley. By author. Dec. 30, 1994, and Jan. 18, 1995.

Dvorak, Priscilla Anderson. By author. Jan. 25, 1995.

Ellingson, Nancy. By Julie Sella. December 1994.

Fellows, Emma Raymond. Oral History Program, Special Collections Department, Murphy Library, University of Wisconsin-La Crosse. Apr. 5, 1977.

Fellows, Sam Jr. By author. Dec. 15, 1994.

Fiet, Lorraine Jandt. By author. Mar. 22, 1995.

Fitzpatrick, Nancy. By Rita Jenks. Oral History Program, Special Collections Department, Murphy Library, University of Wisconsin-La Crosse. Dec. 13, 1994.

Flick, Doris. By author. Jan. 16, 1995.

Foss, Jean. By author. Mar. 2, 1995.

Frank, Barbara. By author. Mar. 6, 1996.

Frechette, Pat Wiffler; Arthur, Joyce; Gundersen, Elizabeth; and Holman, Shirley. By author. June 14, 1995.

Froegel, Anita. By author. Mar. 3, 1995.

Gerrard, Nancy Hyde; Anderson, Marguerite; and Skemp, Fran. By Martha Koloski, TV-19. Videocassette. 1994.

Gershon, Olive. By author. May 24, 1995.

Gollnik, Marge Hughes. By Jean Marck and Margaret Larson. Oral History Program, Special Collections Department, Murphy Library, University of Wisconsin-La Crosse, Nov. 2, 1994.

Guernsey, Gretchen. By Rita Jenks. Oral History Program, Special Collections Department, Murphy Library, University of Wisconsin-La Crosse. Feb. 1, 1995.

Gundersen, Carroll. Oral History Program, Special Collections Department, Murphy Library, University of Wisconsin-La Crosse. 1972 and 1973.

Gundersen, Elizabeth. By Jessica Bulk. Dec. 31, 1994.

Gundersen, Elizabeth; Arthur, Joyce; Frechette, Pat Wiffler; and Holman, Shirley. By author. June 14, 1995.

Hanson, Helen. By author. Apr. 3, 1995.

Hartigan, Natalie. By author. Mar. 11, 1995.

Havlik, Marian. By Barbara Frank. June 1995.

Helliesen, Jean. By Erin Richardson. Feb. 24, 1995.

Hendrickson, Lilly. By author. Jan. 9, 1995, and Sept. 11, 1995.

Hirsh, Linda and Delano, Cynthia Thompson. By author. Feb. 28, 1995.

Hoel, Bill. By author. Apr. 10, 1995.

Holley, Ethel. By author. Mar. 1, 1995.

Holman, Shirley; Arthur, Joyce; Frechette, Pat Wiffler; and Gundersen, Elizabeth. By author. June 14, 1995.

Hoover, Evelyn. By Rita Jenks. Oral History Program, Special Collections Department, Murphy Library, University of Wisconsin-La Crosse. Dec. 11, 1994.

Hopkins, Marion Zumach and Stokes, Thelma Orr Zumach. By author. Nov. 16, 1994.

Hughes, Sharon. By author. Dec. 29, 1994.

Hulberg, Helen and Knudson, Effie. By Judy Rommel and Marge Gollnik for *The Impact of Her Spirit*. 1985.

Hyde, Betty Lamb Dell. By author. Dec. 29, 1994, and Jan. 12, 1995.

Imes, Sharon. By author. Mar. 11, 1995.

Iverson, Don. By Lisa Reinhardt. Jan. 29, 1996.

Jenks, Rita. by author. Apr. 2, 1996.

Joanis, Robert. by author. Mar. 19, 1995.

Kaiser, Jane Leicht. By author. June 15 and Aug. 6, 1994.

Kendrick, Betty. By Angie Olson. December 1994.

Kessler, Jean. By author. Feb. 8, 1996.

Kjome, June. By Margaret Larson. Oral History Program, Special Collections Department, Murphy Library, University of Wisconsin-La Crosse. Dec. 1, 9, 21, 1994.

Knudson, Effie and Hulberg, Helen. By Judy Rommel and Marge Gollnik for *The Impact of Her Spirit*. 1985.

Krause, Emma. Oral History Program, Special Collections Department, Murphy Library, University of Wisconsin-La Crosse. mid-1960s.

Larkin, Virginia Marcotte. By author. Oct. 18 and 21, 1994.

Lee, Carol and Anderson, Madeline. By author. May 3, 1995.

Leicht, Bob. By author. Apr. 2, 1996.

Lemke, Donna Steele. By Margaret Larson. Oral History Program, Special Collections Department, Murphy Library, University of Wisconsin-La Crosse. Nov. 17, 1994.

Levenstein, Sally. By author. Oct. 10, 1994.

Longway, Mary. By author. Aug. 28, 1994.

Lonkoski, Lucy. By author. Mar. 11, 1995.

Malick, Linda. By Barbara Frank. May 1995.

Maney, Mary Scheurich. By Rita Jenks. Oral History Program, Special Collections Department, Murphy Library, University of Wisconsin-La Crosse. Feb. 2, 1995.

McDonald, Sister Grace. By Pat Roslansky and Margaret Larson. Sept. 20, 1995.

Mehren, Marce. By author. Mar. 14, 1995.

Meinert, Donald "Chick." By author. Aug. 22, 1995.

Midelfort, Helga Gundersen. Oral History Program, Special Collections Department, Murphy Library, University of Wisconsin-LaCrosse. 1971.

Mielke, Betty. By author. Mar. 22, 1995.

Miller, Mildred Halderson. By author. Mar. 15, 1995.

Muehr, Mary. By Erin Richardson. Feb. 21, 1995.

Munson, Florence. Oral History Program, Special Collections Department, Murphy Library, University of Wisconsin-La Crosse. Oct. 7 and 8, 1980.

Munson, Mary Krum. By author. Dec. 29, 1994.

Nelson, Mildred. By Anna Collins. Nov. 30, 1994.

Nelson, Mildred Anderson. By Margaret Larson. Oral History Program, Special Collections Department, Murphy Library, University of Wisconsin-La Crosse. July 19, 1994.

Nuttleman, Alice. By Mary Meehan-Strub and Marge Gollnik for *The Impact of Her Spirit*. 1986.

Nyseth, Elvern Ericksen. By author. Aug. 8, 1994, and Apr. 8, 1996.

Osterhout, Alice. By author. Mar. 9, 1995.

O'Sullivan, Mary. By author. Mar. 10, 1995.

Oswalt, Sally. By Jessica Bulk. Jan. 1, 1995.

Oswalt, Sally. By author. Mar. 9, 1995.

Patros, Mary. By Margaret Larson. Oral History Program, Special Collections Department, Murphy Library, University of Wisconsin-La Crosse. Dec. 12, 1994.

Perry, Gerry. By author. Nov. 10, 1994, and June 25, 1996.

Peters, Wilma. By author. Feb. 25 and 27, 1995.

Pitzner, Joan. By Margaret Fish. January 1996.

Polizzotto, Eileen Ryan. By author. June 29, 1995.

Radcliffe, Irene. By author. Nov. 7, 1994.

Ragland, Geneva. By Gloria Bailey Jackson and David Marcou. La Crosse County Historical Society. Oct. 10, 1985.

Ramlow, Marian Schlabach. by author. Jan. 23, 1995.

Ranis, Beverly Broadhead. By author. Dec. 28, 1994, and Jan. 16, 1995.

Rausch, Joan M. By author. Apr. 28, 1996.

Rideout, Irna. By author. Dec. 28, 1994.

Robinson, Eleanor Kinney. By Kasey Heth. Dec. 12, 1994.

Romskog, Vernetta Witte. By author. Nov. 21, 1994, and Aug. 14, 1995.

Rudolph, Mary Lou Brown. By author. Apr. 28, 1995.

Schaller, Irene Kreisel. By Myrna Peacock and Margaret Larson. Oral History Program, Special Collections Department, Murphy Library, University of Wisconsin-La Crosse. Nov. 18, 1994.

Schaller, Marge. By Pam Hanson. 1994.

Scheffner, Wilma. By author. Feb. 13, 1996.

Schmidt, Judy. By author. Mar. 5, 1995.

Schnick, Rosalie. By Barbara Frank. May 1995.

Schuh, Laura. By Barbara Frank. May 1995.

Schuldes, Maddeline and Campbell, Florence. By Rita Jenks. Nov. 30, 1994.

Shealy, Charlotte. By author. Mar. 5, 1995.

Shedesky, Pat Meir. By author. Feb. 8, 1996.

Sheehan, Patricia. By author. May 13, 1996.

Sherwood, Linda Schleiter. By author. Oct. 5, 1995.

Skemp, Fran; Anderson, Marguerite; and Gerrard, Nancy Hyde. By Martha Koloski, TV-19. Videocassette. 1994.

Smith, Mary Belle Ahlstrom. By Lisa Reinhardt and Margaret Larson. May 4, 1996.

Smith, Norene A. By author. Mar. 2, 1995.

Snodgrass, Ruth. By Mandy Oertel and Aleecia Mueller. Oral History Program, Special Collections Department, Murphy Library, University of Wisconsin-La Crosse. Feb. 25, 1995.

Soell, Art. By author. Mar. 7, 1995.

Stluka, Marilyn. By author. Aug. 28, 1994.

Stokes, Thelma Orr Zumach and Hopkins, Marion Zumach. By author. Nov. 16, 1994.

Strauss, Judie Weber. By author. Apr. 10, 1995.

Streeton, Mildred Lee. By Rhonda Rueckheim. January 1995.

Strehl, Sue. By author. Jan. 18, 1995.

Tolvstad, Nancy Westerhouse. By author. Mar. 4, 1995.

Twining, Lill. By author. Mar. 10, 1995.

Van Rossem, Joan. By author. Nov. 18, 1994.

Van Steenwyk, Grace. Oral History Program, Special Collections Department, Murphy Library, University of Wisconsin-La Crosse. Oct. 29 and Nov. 5, 1970.

Whiteway, Marion. By author. Oct. 28, 1994.

Whiting, Florence Olson. By Jean Marck and Margaret Larson. Oral History Program, Special Collections Department, Murphy Library, University of Wisconsin-La Crosse. June 14, 1994.

Wigdahl, Marilyn Koblitz. By author. Mar. 1, 1995.

Wilkins, Lucille. By author. Aug. 28, 1994.

Wollschlaeger, Eleanore. By author. Dec. 11, 1994.

Wulling, Jean. By author. Dec. 7, 1994.

Responses to
Hunting Our History Questionnaires

American Association of University Women, La Crosse Branch. Compiled by Marilyn Hempstead.

Asbury United Methodist Church of La Crosse. Compiled by Mildred Olson.

Bethel Lutheran Church Women of the Evangelical Lutheran Church of America. Compiled by Lilly D. Hendrickson.

Campus Dames. Compiled by Olive Gershon and Helen Brault.

Catholic Daughters of the Americas, Court La Crosse #1183. Compiled by Mary Blaschke and Marie Kabat.

Catholic Women's League. Compiled by Genevieve Koenig.

Church Women United. Compiled by Mary Kisken.

Daughters of the American Revolution, La Crosse Chapter of the National Society. Compiled by Laura L. Lane.

Delta Kappa Gamma Society, Theta Chapter. Compiled by Pauline Abel.

The Embroiderers' Guild of America, Inc., Coulee County Chapter. Compiled by Maddeline Schuldes and Cindy Dietrich.

Faith Lutheran Church of La Crosse. Compiled by Arlene Bartig.

Family and Children's Center. Compiled by Laurie Ward.

Fauver Hill Study Club. Compiled by Irene Radcliffe and Eleanor Robinson.

First Congregational Church of La Crosse. Compiled by Charles Haas.

Hillview Health Care Auxiliary. Compiled by Vivian Strong.

Holmen Lutheran Church. Compiled by Pearl Johnson.

Jewish Women's League. Compiled by Carol Ziff and Pam Strauss.

Job's Daughters, Bethel #27 International Order. Compiled by Mary Callaway.

La Crosse Area Quilters. Compiled by Mary Herzog.

La Crosse Area Retired Educators Association. Compiled by Pauline Abel.

La Crosse Community Theatre. Compiled by Sally Cremer, Jo Ann Jenkins, Libby Shirmacher, Julia Steinke Saterbak, and Marilyn Wood.

La Crosse Education Association. Compiled by Barbara Schultz.

La Crosse Shrine Auxiliary for Crippled Children. Compiled by Pauline Abel.

Lutheran Hospital Auxiliary. Compiled by Marilyn McElligott.

North Presbyterian Church of La Crosse. Compiled by Arlene Boyle.

Our Redeemer Lutheran Church of La Crosse. Compiled by Cindy Berg.

Our Savior's Lutheran Church of West Salem. Compiled by Vernetta Romskog.

St. Francis Auxiliary. Compiled by Marian Johnson.

St. John's Lutheran Church of La Crosse. Compiled by Helen Berg.

[St. Joseph the Workman] Cathedral Women's Organization. Compiled by Lilly Lecheler.

Twentieth Century Club. Compiled by Florence Whiting.

Women of Olivet Lutheran Church. Compiled by Neva Ritter.

Women's Political Caucus, La Crosse County Chapter. Compiled by Sharon Ryan.

Reminiscing Sessions

La Crosse Association for Responsible Citizens. Oct. 27, 1994.

La Crosse Family Planning Center/Options in Reproductive Care. Jan. 4, 1995.

Lutheran Hospital - La Crosse Nursing Alumnae. Oct. 26, 1994.

New Horizons. Oct. 31, 1995.

Organization for Campus Women, University of Wisconsin-La Crosse. June 13, 1995.

Secondary Sources

Bryhn, Estella Krohn. *Around the Coulees*. West Salem, Wisconsin: La Crosse County Countryman, 1974.

Bryhn, Estella Krohn. *Early Schools of La Crosse County*. West Salem, Wisconsin: Block Printing, 1985.

Cowan, Ruth Schwartz. *More Work for Mother: The Ironies of Household Technology from the Open Hearth to the Microwave*. New York: Basic Books, Inc., Publishers, 1983.

Davies, Celia, ed. *Rewriting Nursing History*. Totowa, New Jersey: Barnes & Noble Books, 1980.

Dolbier, John and Dolbier, Joan. *From Sawmills to Sunfish: A History of Onalaska, Wisconsin*. Onalaska, Wisconsin: 1985.

Gilkey, George R. *The First Seventy Years: A History of the University of Wisconsin-La Crosse, 1909-1979*. La Crosse, Wisconsin: University of Wisconsin-La Crosse Foundation, 1981.

Haas, Charles E. *Bless the Work of Our Hands: A History of the First Congregational Church of La Crosse, Wisconsin, 1852-1972*. La Crosse, Wisconsin: First Congregational Church, 1984.

Harvey, Brett. *The Fifties: A Women's Oral History*. New York: HarperCollins Publishers, 1993.

Heider, Hazel Rahn. *Along the Waterloo Road*. West Salem, Wisconsin: 1981.

Hessel, Susan T. *Recollections 1909-1973: Campus School, University of Wisconsin-La Crosse*. La Crosse, Wisconsin: The University of Wisconsin-La Crosse Foundation, Inc., 1992.

Hoy, Suellen. *Chasing Dirt: The American Pursuit of Cleanliness*. New York: Oxford University Press, 1995.

Kerber, Linda K. *Women of the Republic: Intellect and Ideology in Revolutionary America*. New York: W.W. Norton & Company, 1986.

Kerber, Linda K. and De Hart, Jane Sherron, eds. *Women's America: Refocusing the Past*. New York: Oxford University Press, 1991.

Kessler-Harris, Alice. *Out To Work: A History of Wage-Earning Women in the United States*. New York: Oxford University Press, 1982.

Kessler-Harris, Alice. *Women Have Always Worked: A Historical Overview*. Old Westbury, New York: The Feminst Press, 1981.

Kindschy, Errol. *Leonard's Dream: A History of West Salem*. West Salem, Wisconsin: 1981.

Kohler, Ruth De Young. *The Story of Wisconsin Women*. Kohler, Wisconsin: The Committee on Wisconsin Women, 1948.

Lagerquist, L. DeAne. *From Our Mothers' Arms: A History of Women in the American Lutheran Church*. Minneapolis: Augsburg Publishing House, 1987.

Ludwig, Sister M. Mileta, FSPA. *A Chapter of Franciscan History, 1849-1949*. New York: Bookman Associates, 1949.

Lurie, Nancy Oestriech. *Mountain Wolf Woman: The Autobiography of a Winnebago Indian*. Ann Arbor, Michigan: University of Michigan Press, 1961.

McBride, Genevieve G. *On Wisconsin Women: Working for Their Rights from Settlement to Suffrage*. Madison, Wisconsin: The University of Wisconsin Press, 1993.

McDonald, Forrest. *Let There Be Light: The Electric Utility Industry in Wisconsin, 1881-1955*. Madison, Wisconsin: The American History Research Center, 1957.

Melosh, Barbara. *The Physician's Hand: Work Culture and Conflict in American Nursing*. Philadelphia: Temple University Press, 1982.

Organization for Campus Women. *Women Who Forged the Way*. University of Wisconsin-La Crosse, 1994. Videocassette.

Reminiscences of Early La Crosse. Liesenfeld Press, 1928.

Rothman, Sheila M. *Woman's Proper Place: A History of Changing Ideals and Practices, 1870 to the Present*. New York: Basic Books, Inc., Publishers, 1978.

Sanford, Albert H. and Hirshheimer, H. J. *A History of La Crosse, Wisconsin, 1841-1900*. La Crosse, Wisconsin: La Crosse County Historical Society, 1951.

Sapiro, Virginia. *Women in American Society, Second Edition*. Mountain View, California: Mayfield Publishing Co., 1990.

Sebold, Sister Theodine, *FSPA. Continuity and Change: The History of Viterbo College, 1890-1980*. La Crosse, Wisconsin: Viterbo College, 1989.

Sims, Stanley L. *La Crosse Lutheran Hospital: A History, 1899-1979*. La Crosse, Wisconsin: Lutheran Hospital Foundation, 1981.

Strasser, Susan. *Never Done: A History of American Housework*. New York: Pantheon Books of Random House, 1982.

Vicinus, Martha. *Independent Women: Work & Community for Single Women*. Chicago: The University of Chicago Press, 1985.

Newspapers, Newsletters, and Directories

Coulee Gazette

La Crosse County Countryman

La Crosse Daily Republican and Leader

La Crosse Tribune

La Crosse Tribune and Leader-Press

Past, Present & Future, La Crosse County Historical Society

West Salem Journal

La Crosse City and County Directories, 1880 to 1990.

Index

Page number in *italics* indicates photo/illustration.
Page number followed by *n* indicates endnote.

The author

Born at mid-century, Margaret Sturm Larson
graduated from the University of Illinois in
1973 with a degree in American history and
literature. She and her husband, Tim, settled
in La Crosse in 1977 where they have raised
two sons, Ben and Sam. She has balanced
family life, friendships, and interests in
education, politics and history with work as a
free-lance editor.